SOUTH MIDDLESEX

A New England Heritage

by Stephen W. Herring

Pictorial Research
by Elizabeth C. Merrylees
"Partners in Progress" by David L. Horn

Produced in cooperation with the
MetroWest Chamber of Commerce

Windsor Publications, Inc.
Northridge, California

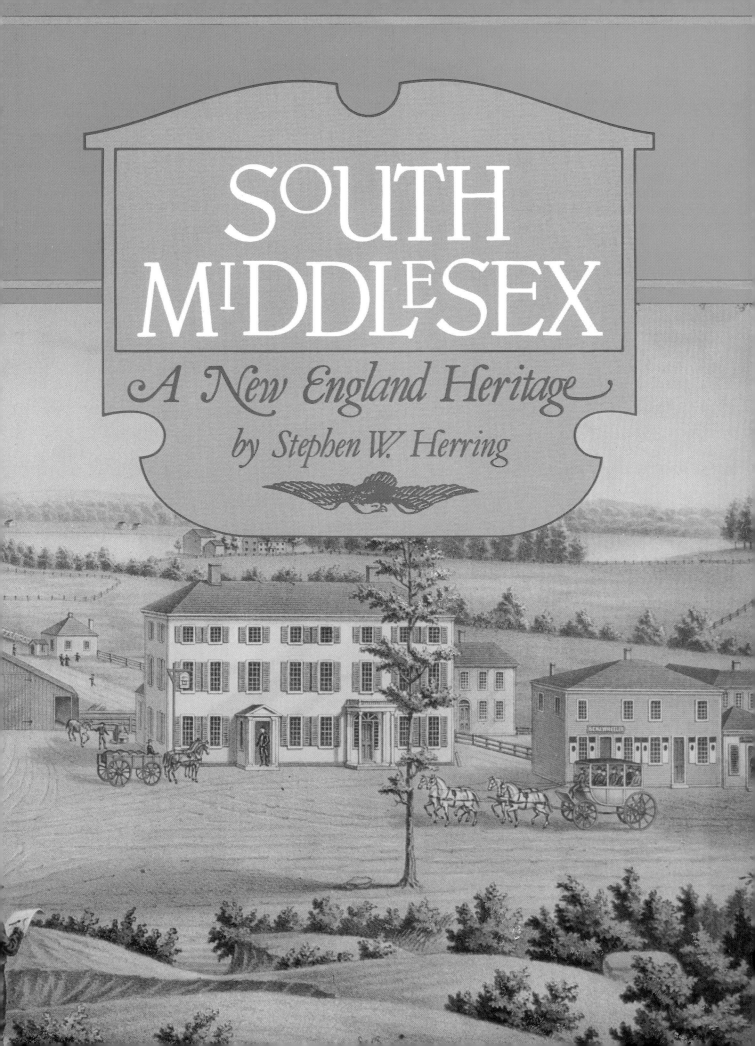

SOUTH MIDDLESEX

A New England Heritage

by Stephen W. Herring

Windsor Publications, Inc.—History Book Division
Publisher: John M. Phillips
Editorial Director: Teri Davis Greenberg
Design Director: Alexander D'Anca

Staff for *South Middlesex: A New England Heritage*
Editors: Lane A. Powell, Karl Stull
Assistant Editors: Laura Cordova, Marilyn Horn
Director, Corporate Biographies: Karen Story
Assistant Director, Corporate Biographies: Phyllis Gray
Editor, Corporate Biographies: Judith Hunter
Production Editor, Corporate Biographies: Una FitzSimons
Layout Artist, Corporate Biographies: Mari Catherine Preimesberger
Editorial Assistants: Kathy M. Brown, Marcie Goldstein, Pamela Juneman, Pat Pittman
Sales Representative, Corporate Biographies: Mary Whelan

Designer: Christina McKibbin

Library of Congress Cataloging-In-Publication Data:

Herring, Stephen, 1943-
    South Middlesex: A New England Heritage.
    Bibliography: p. 244
    Includes index.
    1. Middlesex County (Mass.)—History. 2. Middlesex
County (Mass.)—Description and travel. 3. Middlesex
County (Mass.)—Industries. I. Title.
F72.M7H25 1986   974.4′4   86-22441
ISBN 0-89781-179-8

Pages 6 and 7: The prosperous mill village of Saxonville in 1876 used waterpower from the falls of the Sudbury River to run many mills, and during the Civil War these mills produced blue serge and blankets for the Union Army. Nobscot Mountain looms in the distance. Painted circa 1876 by Dr. Enos Bigelow. Photo by Gregg Shupe. Courtesy, Philip Degozzaldi

Endsheets: The new technology of the textile industry required fewer workers than shoe and straw factories, as this 1843 illustration shows. Tending the looms was an occupation suitable for women and children. From Handbook of Silk, Cotton and Woolen Manufacturers, *1843. Courtesy, Framingham Historical Society*

Contents

*To the guardians of the past—
the historical societies
of these nine New England towns*

Turnpikes were built in straight lines to minimize the distance between major cities like Boston and Worcester. In this old woodcut a stagecoach barrels into the Boston entrance for the forty-mile run to Worcester that would take it through Natick, Framingham, and Southborough. From The Turnpikes of New England, *1919. Courtesy, Framingham Public Library*

INTRODUCTION

There are many forces that hold the nine towns of South Middlesex together as a region, and one of them is a common heritage as a unique piece of New England. Visible reminders of this heritage can be found throughout the area—tall, white church steeples, rambling stone walls, granite direction markers, sturdy homes from the Georgian and Greek Revival periods, and all those odd Indian and British names used for roads, ponds, villages, and the towns themselves. Once in a while the corner of some ancient burying ground can be glimpsed, where old slate markers stand as reminders that many generations before us have called this place home.

The physical traces of earlier generations represent a heritage that spans three and a half centuries and includes the lives of thousands who have lived within the borders of the nine towns that make up the South Middlesex region of Massachusetts. This book is intended for those who wish to delve below the surface to gain a deeper appreciation and fuller enjoyment of the heritage that is such a vital ingredient in the character of this region. It tells the story of South Middlesex on three levels. On its most obvious level, particularly in the first two chapters, this is the story of nine individual New England towns—their origins, incorporation, and development—with emphasis on the unique characteristics that make each town special in its own right. On a second level is the story of how these nine towns gravitated toward each other to become the regional entity that is so familiar today. While there are hints of this in the first chapters, in Chapter 3 the regionalizing process takes shape with the industrial and railroad developments of the nineteenth century. The third and more subtle level of this story is the human heritage of South Middlesex—the heritage of hardy Puritans and resourceful Yankees. Chapters 5 and 6 show how this human heritage has been carried on in the heterogeneous population of the twentieth century.

A book of this scope cannot possibly provide a comprehensive history of all nine towns. It is hoped, however, that the reader will be given enough of the color and flavor of each town to inspire further research among the existing town histories that are listed in the bibliography at the back of this book.

The collection of information and illustrations used in this book would not have been possible without the help and cooperation of historians and historical organizations in all nine towns. We are particularly indebted to Forrest Bradshaw and George D. Max of Sudbury; Ann Schaller, Henri Prunaret, and the late John "Archie" Morris of Natick; Betsy Johnson and Anne Shaughnessy of Sherborn; Ralph and Marjorie Maish of Framingham; Ruth Ward, Rose Leveille, and Jacqueline Bash of Hopkinton; Joanne Hulbert of Holliston; Kay Allen and Jeanne Davis of Southborough; Josephine Goeselt of Wayland; and Cynthia and Bob Winterhalter of Ashland.

1 AGE OF THE FLINTLOCK, BIBLE, AND PLOW (1630-1760)

The history of South Middlesex goes back to the very beginnings of New England—back to the 1620s when the small Plymouth colony proved that it was possible to survive the long New England winters.

When the Pilgrims went exploring beyond the security of Plymouth Plantation, stories of what they found filtered back across the Atlantic, where investors and speculators in England listened eagerly for news of opportunities for profit. There were large, deep bays north of Plymouth that would make excellent harbors. Codfish abounded. From the interior came reports of beaver, timber, and a rich soil. In 1629 a Reverend Higginson wrote back home, "It is a land of divers and sundry sorts all about Massachusetts Bay, and at Charles River is as fat black earth as can be seen anywhere."

The company that was formed in London to exploit the resources of that land was the Massachusetts Bay Company, named after the tribe of Indians that lived around those bays north of Plymouth. King Charles I chartered the company in 1629, and after some preliminary exploration and settlement, the first true flood of immigrants to America began. It was called the Great Migration, spearheaded by John Winthrop aboard the *Arabella*. Winthrop had been appointed governor of a colony that within ten years would number over 20,000.

The Massachusetts Bay Company charter had two provisions that were of importance to the development of South Middlesex. The first was the definition of territorial limits. The northern boundary was set at three miles north of the Merrimack River, and the southern boundary was three miles south of the Charles River. But the western boundary was "the South Sea," or the Pacific Ocean. Thus the potential for Massachusetts was a strip of land fifty miles long and over 3,000 miles wide. This area today reaches through eight states and meets "the South Sea" at the southwest corner of Oregon. To the colonists, this provision of the charter meant that the greatest opportunity for inland growth lay due west. As the area that would become South Middlesex occupied the land from fifteen to thirty miles west of Boston harbor, it

A skull, crossed bones, and an hourglass on a 1713 gravestone in Sherborn show the Puritan obsession with mortality and the day of judgement. Puritanism would remain a strong influence well into the next century. Courtesy, Framingham Historical Society

11

is not surprising that its exploration and settlement would begin within a few years of the landing of Winthrop and the *Arabella*.

The second provision of the charter to affect South Middlesex was its missionary goal to "win and invite the natives of the country to the knowledge and obedience of the only true God and Saviour of mankind." This intent was of such importance that the first seal of the colony featured an Indian speaking the phrase, "Come over and help us."

With the leadership of the colony in the hands of sincere Puritans, missionary work was encouraged and supported, and the most prominent of the early missionaries was the Reverend John Eliot (1604-1690). Eliot's work would lead to the founding of one South Middlesex town (Natick), and would have an important effect on the others.

The Indians actually provided the solution to the immediate problem of avoiding a winter of possible starvation. In 1630 Nipmuc Indians from the Connecticut River valley heard of the plight of the English, and, eager to trade for European goods, carried sacks and bushels of corn 100 miles to Boston. The trail used by those Indians would become known as the Connecticut Path, and it passed through today's South Middlesex towns of Wayland, Framingham, Sherborn, Ashland, Holliston, and Hopkinton. It wound between the Charles River to the south, and a major tributary of the Merrimack River to the

The Massachusetts Bay colonists coexisted peacefully with the native inhabitants of the new land for forty-five years after the colony's founding. But by 1675, Wampanoag Chief Metacomet had become so displeased with the English practice of buying up Indian land, and converting Indians to Christianity, that he reacted by waging a year-long war—here his forces try to roll a cart filled with burning flax into a Sherborn garrison. Courtesy, Betsy Johnson

north (now known as the Concord and Sudbury rivers). The path avoided crossing either river, fording only Cold Spring Brook at a place the Indians called Pout Rock. These rivers and the Connecticut Path were the framework for the exploration and settlement of the South Middlesex towns.

A book published in London in 1634 called *New England Prospect*, by William Wood, extolled the potential of fur trapping along the inland rivers. The book also attracted support for the establishment of trapping stations deep into the interior. These stations became settlements that led to the establishment of the first inland towns of Massachusetts. Two such towns were Concord, incorporated in 1635, and Springfield out on the Connecticut River, organized in 1641.

William Wood also wrote that another reason for exploring the inland was "a straightness of accommodation and want of more meadow." If he wanted more meadow he certainly found it along the Concord and Sudbury rivers. The Indians called this region "Musquitaquid," meaning "great meadow." The tall hay that grew on the wide floodplains of these rivers meant that livestock and an agrarian economy could be supported with a promise of success, although without the quick cash turnaround offered by trade in cod or beaver.

The noted Massachusetts historian, Walter Muir Whitehill, has written, "Massachusetts is better to look at than to try to cultivate," and this applies to South Middlesex as well as to any other part of the state. While the soil of South Middlesex is one of the most fertile in New England, the glaciers that brought it also left each acre peppered with thousands of rocks and heavy stones. Fortunately, the Puritan ethic of patience and hard work fit very well with the lot of the South Middlesex farmer. These farmers had to use oxen rather than horses to clear the land, haul boulders, and pull tree stumps. With typical resourcefulness they used the displaced stones to mark property boundaries, creating the stone walls that remain to this day as a part of the area's heritage.

Once in a while the stones that were turned up by the plow had been blackened by the fire of some ancient Indian dwelling, reminding the farmer that this land had not always been his. The natives of South Middlesex were of the Nipmuc tribe; some early records referred to their territory as Nipmug country. Around 1616 an epidemic decimated the Nipmuc and other tribes of New England, and much of their cultivated land and many of their villages were abandoned. When the first explorers were mapping out the South Middlesex area in the 1630s, there were no Indian villages and only a few scattered Indian families

The first seal of the Massachusetts Bay colony features an Indian speaking the unlikely phrase, "COME OVER AND HELP US." The colony charter provided for bringing Christianity to the natives, a goal that John Eliot and other settlers were closely associated with. Today's Massachusetts state seal still features an Indian, but not the phrase. Courtesy, Massachusetts Historical Society

Above: The first Boston to Worcester train chugged into Unionville (now Ashland) in 1834, met by a cheering crowd and a grand reception attended by Daniel Webster, Governor Levi Lincoln, and hundreds of townspeople. The painting is a WPA mural in the Ashland Post Office, painted about 1940. Photo by Gregg Shupe

Right: The meetinghouse at Rocky Plain in the West Precinct of Sudbury was a plain, unpainted building during the eighteenth century. When a bell was procured, it was housed in a belfry across the road. Courtesy, Goodnow Public Library, Sudbury

Left: In the 1800s, many styles of straw bonnets were made in several South Middlesex towns, and one of these styles is modeled by a "block head" plaster form. The forms were used to shape and mould the bonnets while they were being made. In this case, the form was decorated with a face that is now considered nineteenth-century folk art. Behind the block head is a blue paisley shawl, a favorite lady's wrap in those days. Courtesy, Framingham Historical Society

Right: John Eliot, "Apostle to the Indians," founded the praying Indian town of Natick in 1651. He went on to set up many other Christian Indian villages, including Magunco, now a part of Ashland. He is shown holding a copy of his Indian-language translation of the Bible. Courtesy, Henry E. Huntington Library and Art Gallery, San Marino, California

Below: The Bible sent to Holliston by its namesake, Thomas Hollis, Esq., of London, England, is displayed at the First Congregational Church at Holliston Center. It was rescued after many years of hard use at the town's poor farm. Courtesy, Holliston Historical Society

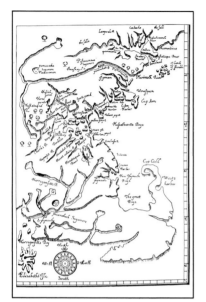

The exaggerated width of the rivers in this 1634 map from William Wood's New England Prospect *indicates the importance of inland waterways to the first settlers. The Sudbury and Charles rivers embrace the area at the far left (marked here by two trees) that would become South Middlesex. Courtesy, Framingham Historical Society*

and individuals. These remaining Indians were recognized as legal owners of the thousands of acres that were opening up to settlement, and settlers were obliged to buy their real estate twice—first from the Bay Colony and then from the local natives.

The transactions with the Indians involved written deeds. Payment was in wampum (strings of polished shells) or some other commodity that the Indians found desirable. English shirt manufacturers, for instance, found a ready market for shirts dyed purple, magenta, or other bright colors that Englishmen would not think of wearing but that could be used to trade to the Indians for large portions of the Indians' homeland.

****

As late as 1638 South Middlesex was still a wilderness, penetrated by explorers and settlers going to the Connecticut River valley. The first party of explorers was led by John Oldham in 1633. A few years later a large party of Cambridge settlers, with 110 head of cattle, was led by the Reverend Thomas Hooker. This was a two-week journey that would result in the founding of Hartford and the colony of Connecticut.

In 1638 the territory between Boston and South Middlesex was occupied by Watertown (1630) and Dedham (1636). In that year the boundaries of these towns plus Concord to the north were fixed. The stage was set for the settlement of South Middlesex.

Sudbury was settled first. It was established as a plantation in 1638 and as the nineteenth township of the Massachusetts colony in September 1639. Some of the first settlers, like John Stone, migrated from Watertown. Others came out to Sudbury almost directly from the boat. Peter Noyes and John Bent, for example, landed in April 1638 on the *Confidence*. They were granted land in Sudbury plantation where they would become, one year later, the founders of a New England town.

To avoid any confusion between the Sudbury of 1639 and the Sudbury of today, it should be pointed out that all references to Sudbury up to the year 1780 include both Sudbury and Wayland. Even more confusing is the fact that the original settlement of Sudbury is within the bounds of today's town of Wayland. The Sudbury of today is actually a westward expansion from the original settlement that retained the original name when the two towns split up.

The method by which lands were laid out in Sudbury as compared with the medieval traditions of various regions of England is a fascinating study made by Sumner Chilton Powell and published in his

Pulitzer Prize-winning book, *Puritan Village*.

The industrious and enterprising Sudbury Puritans had a mill before they had a meetinghouse. It was a gristmill, built by the appropriately named Thomas Cakebread in 1639. The meetinghouse was not completed until 1643. It was built by John Rutter who received three acres of land for his trouble. This meetinghouse had no steeple or bell, and of course no heat. Drums were used to summon the faithful to services, and to keep their feet warm they used their dogs, if they could keep them quiet. The site of the first meetinghouse is now marked by a stone in the ancient North Cemetery just a half mile north of Wayland Center.

In 1654 a history of New England now known as *Johnson's Wonder Working Providence* was published in London. It describes Sudbury and its minister, the Reverend Edmund Brown, mainly in the context of the great meadows that were the primary natural feature of the town. The Reverend Brown is described as one "whose labor in the doctrine of Jesus Christ hath hitherto abounded, wading through this wilderness work with much cheerfulness of spirit." The author then breaks into verse as he extolls:

Both night and day Brown ceaseth not to watch
  Christ's little flock, in pastures fresh them feed;

The worrying wolves shall not thy weak lambs catch;
  Well dost thou mind in wilderness their breed.

The name of Sudbury came from the town in Suffolk, England where the Reverend Brown preached before coming to the New World.

The year that the Sudbury meetinghouse was built, 1643, was also

Above: John Stone, the first settler of Framingham, negotiated the purchase of several acres in the Saxonville area with local Nipmuc Indians in 1656. The deal was closed when this deed was signed in the presence of Indian Superintendent Daniel Gookin. The land included the falls of the Sudbury River, where Stone built a gristmill. Courtesy, Framingham Historical Society

Above left: The Reverend Thomas Hooker and his followers, after a falling out with Massachusetts powers, migrated along the Connecticut Path in 1636 to find a new start. They found their new home at Hartford where the new colony of Connecticut was established. The person traveling "first class" in this woodcut was Mrs. Susan Hooker. Courtesy, American Antiquarian Society

17

The seal of the town of Sudbury features the monument dedicated to Captain Samuel Wadsworth and his men who died defending the town from the Indian invasion of King Philip in 1676. The monument was not erected until 1852. Courtesy, Town of Sudbury

the year that Middlesex County was created, along with Suffolk and Essex counties. Cambridge was designated the "shire town" or county seat of Middlesex County. The fortunes of Cambridge's Harvard College (1636) were to be intermingled with the development of the South Middlesex towns for the next 100 years. Two of the proprietors of Sudbury were Henry Dunster, first president of Harvard, and Herbert Pelham, first treasurer of Harvard.

In the western Sudbury lands, over the river, there lived an Indian named Cato who sold his land to "the planters of Sudbury" for £5. Cato converted to Christianity and took the name Goodman. Today Goodman's Hill is a familiar Sudbury landmark.

Sudbury had been a town for twelve years before the second South Middlesex town, Natick, was founded. While most South Middlesex towns originated from the westward flow of English settlers, this was not the case with Natick. Natick would be the first of John Eliot's praying Indian towns.

John Eliot had been ordained in the Church of England, but he was attracted to the Puritan paradise of Massachusetts. He landed in 1631 and was ordained as the minister of the Roxbury church. By 1641 he began fulfilling the provision of the charter to bring the native "heathens" around to the true faith. He learned their language and preached to them in their own tongue. Around Boston he found Indians willing to be organized into a new "tribe." Many of these were Indians who had displaced themselves from their own land by selling it for glass beads and colored shirts. Also, a disorganization had occurred among the Nipmucs upon the death of a "squaw sachem" (a female chief). They broke up into several bands, and Eliot was able to attract many while others came under the influence of the Wampanoags to the south.

At first Eliot tried to gather his Christian Indians into a community at Nonatum (Newton), but this was too close to English settlements. Looking west beyond the settled territory, Eliot found an ideal spot for a fresh start on the banks of the Charles River. In 1651, with funding from a London society for "Propagating the Gospel Among the Indians of New England," and with the moral charge of the Massachusetts Bay Charter backing him, Eliot approached the Great and General Court of the colony. The court, with the cheerful consent of Dedham, gave Eliot 2,000 acres around the Charles River and provided for the organization of a special town governed locally by the Indians, although actually a ward of the General Court. The town was closely controlled and scrutinized by the political and religious authorities of the colony. The Indians called their town Natick, the name used by the Speens and

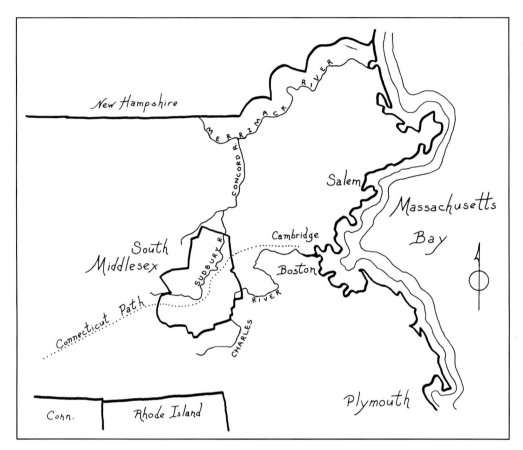

Above: When Middlesex County was formed in 1643, its county seat or "shire town" was set at Cambridge, home of Harvard College. This seal was not adopted until 1905. Courtesy, Framingham Historical Society

Left: The settlement of South Middlesex, outlined on this map of eastern Massachusetts, was influenced by the presence of the Sudbury and Charles rivers and the Connecticut Path, the exploration routes of the 1630s. The vast meadows surrounding the Sudbury River attracted the earliest settlers, who founded Sudbury Plantation in 1638. Courtesy, Framingham Historical Society

Below: John Rogers, a nineteenth-century sculptor famous for his historic works, completed this model of John Eliot preaching to the Indians as a prototype for a public monument that was never built. Courtesy, John A. Morris

Natick's unusual town seal is more square than round, and features the decorative borders of the Eliot Bible as its outline. Natick's special heritage as an Indian town is depicted, and 1651 is claimed as the founding date, even though full status as an "English" town was not achieved until 1781. Courtesy, Town of Natick

other local Nipmucs meaning "place of hills." Eliot was their spiritual leader, and for their political leader they chose one of their own—appropriately named Waban, or "wind."

As other "praying towns" were established it became necessary to appoint a superintendent of Indians for the colony. This was Daniel Gookin (1612-1687), a man of military background who would reach the rank of major general. One recent Massachusetts history calls Gookin the "primary factotum and real estate agent of the Bay Colony fathers."

Gookin was very interested in the Indians, and he kept logs and notes on the Indian towns. This is his description of Natick:

This town consisteth of three long streets: two on the north side of the river; and one on the south; with house lots to every family. There is a handsome large fort, of a round figure, palisaded with trees; and a foot bridge over the river, in form of an arch, the foundations of which is secured with stones. There is also one large house built after the English manner. The lower room is a large hall, which serves for a meeting house on the Lord's day and a school house on the week days.

By 1658 Eliot felt the need for more land to isolate his Natick Indians from the encroaching settlements of Sudbury to the north and Dedham to the south. Again Eliot approached the General Court. But this time he asked for 4,000 acres and this time Dedham was not so cheerful about it. After years of negotiation Eliot got his land, and Dedham was compensated with a grant of 8,000 acres in the Connecticut River valley. The Dedham grant would be incorporated as the Town of Deerfield, a town that would have a long history of Indian attacks and massacres. Eliot's extra 4,000 acres included parts of the future town of Framingham. The geography of South Middlesex would have been quite different had the Natick Indians not sold off large parcels of that land to white settlers such as Samuel Gookin, son of Daniel, and Samuel How of Sudbury.

It took ten years for Eliot to convince the Puritan Bay Colony fathers that the Indians of Natick could actually organize a Puritan church. After the Indians had undergone extensive training and examination, they were allowed to "gather" a church in 1660. The next year Eliot introduced the New Testament, which he had translated into the Indians' language. He would follow this up three years later with a translation of the Old Testament.

The Indian Bible was a translation of English into a basically phonetic language using the English alphabet. The words were often long and awkward. The longest word in Eliot's Bible takes thirty-four letters and means "Kneeling down to him" (Mark I:40). The Reverend Cotton Mather, the leading Puritan clergyman of the colony and biographer of Eliot, teased him about these words, claiming that they must have been growing ever since the fall of the tower of Babel.

Natick was the model Indian town. The church was to be a sort of seminary for Indian preachers in the other towns. The town government followed the lines of established English towns. They had Indian selectmen and constables and followed the forms of English legal procedure, preferably in the English language. The difficulty the Indians had in adapting to these standards is clearly and humorously illustrated in this Natick arrest warrant:

You, you big constable, quick you catch um Jeremiah Offscow, strong you hold um, safe you bring um afore me.

Thomas Waban, Justice Peace

The other praying towns were as far away as Tewksbury and Uxbridge, and at its high point in 1674 the total Christian Indian population of Massachusetts was 3,600. The seventh of these towns was gathered back within the borders of South Middlesex. This is commonly known today as Magunco (there are many variations on this spelling), which is the easiest to pronounce of the various Indian names associated with it. The Nipmuc natives called it Quansiqomog, and the Christian Indians gave it the name Wagwonkkommonk ("place of great trees"). Although it has passed through the jurisdiction of Sherborn, Natick, and Hopkinton over its long history, Magunco is today on the west side of the town of Ashland.

A church was never formed at Magunco, but the enterprising Indians did make cedar shingles to sell to the English settlers. Eliot wrote that he thought the Indians made better shingles than the whites. The town did not last more than one generation, but several of the Indians were buried there. When the Central Turnpike (Route 135) was put through in the 1820s, some Magunco graves were found only three feet under the surface.

****

The establishment of Natick forced English settlement to expand south, skirting around and beyond Natick where Millis and Milford would evolve. This flow would reenter the South Middlesex area at Boggestow, where Sherborn would be founded.

Nicolas Wood and Thomas Holbrook were the first to build houses at Boggestow. North of Boggestow—the land that is now Sherborn Center—belonged to John Hull (1624-1683), a Boston merchant, goldsmith, and colonial mintmaster. This land was simply an asset owned

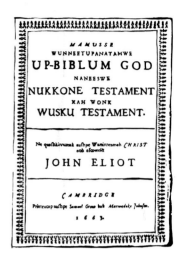

John Eliot's vision of converting the native population of Massachusetts to Christianity required a Bible in the Indian language. Eliot's Indian Bible was the result of a prodigious task that merged the Algonquin dialect with the English alphabet. Eliot also produced an Indian grammar and dictionary. Courtesy, Natick Historical Society

In 1974, on its 300th anniversary, Sherborn adopted the Pine Tree Shilling as the main feature of its town seal. This shilling was one of the coins made by colonial mintmaster John Hull, first owner of much of the land that would become Sherborn. Courtesy, Town of Sherborn

by Hull, who would never settle in Sherborn.

As mintmaster, John Hull produced the first coinage of the New World outside the Spanish empire. From 1652 to 1682 he made threepence, sixpence, and shilling coins minted with designs representing the willow, oak, and pine tree. When the colony was desperate for a medium of exchange, these coins were ordered by the General Court without the sanction of Parliament. Cleverly, the General Court kept the date on all coins at 1652 so that it would appear that they were minted during the confusion of Cromwell's rule. After all, it was John Hull who said that these Bay Colony fathers were "no babes nor windyheaded men."

Hull was no fool himself. At one time, for every twenty shillings that he coined he was allowed to keep one shilling and threepence. In 1974 the Town of Sherborn honored Hull by adopting the design of the pine tree shilling for its town seal.

The Boggestow people had to cross the Charles River to attend services and town meetings at Medfield, but frequent flooding often made this hazardous or impossible. By 1674 the settlement was large enough to justify township status. The name of the town was first spelled "Sherborne." Later, "Sherburn" had become the general spelling. Finally, in 1852 the spelling was officially set at "Sherborn." Confusion over this simple name was compounded in 1687 when one of the large islands off Cape Cod was incorporated as Sharborn, later also known as Sherburn. This ambiguity was cleared up in 1795 when the island's name was changed to Nantucket.

In 1674 the incorporators of Sherborn were unaware that within a year their town, as well as all of South Middlesex, would be engulfed in a terrible Indian war. Their plans to set up the usual town institutions were interrupted, and it became more important to build garrison houses than to build a meetinghouse. Also, some adjustment of boundaries with Natick was sought, as Magunco fell within Sherborn, and it seemed appropriate that it instead be associated with the Indian town. But this too was postponed.

The trouble started with the Wampanoag tribe that had been so hospitable to the Plymouth Pilgrims in 1620. Under Chief Massasoit a benevolent and peaceful relationship existed between the Wampanoags and the English for forty years. Upon the death of Massasoit, leadership of the tribe fell into the hands of his son, Metacomet. As was the custom with Indians of strange sounding names, Metacomet was given an English name, Philip. When he learned that the head man of all the English was called King, Metacomet styled himself "King Philip, chief of the Wampanoags."

Above: Blood was shed in several South Middlesex towns during the terrible Indian uprising of 1675-1676 known as King Philip's War. This map shows the major attacks and confrontations that occurred within modern-day town boundaries. Also shown are the two praying Indian villages that were evacuated to Deer Island in Boston Harbor during the war. Courtesy, Framingham Historical Society

Left: King Philip was the Anglicized name taken by Wampanoag Chief Metacomet, who attempted to rid Massachusetts of the white man in the uprising of 1675-1676. Courtesy, American Antiquarian Society

Right: The massacre of Sherborn's Eames family in 1676 during King Philip's War is visualized in an engraving by a late-nineteenth-century artist. Thomas Eames was away from home getting supplies when his wife and several children were killed and his house and barn destroyed. This site is now part of Framingham. From History of Middlesex County, 1880. Courtesy, Framingham Public Library

King Philip did not like seeing his fellow Indians, who had little comprehension of the idea of land as private property, sell off their birthright for trinkets. He was also displeased with the large number of his kind that were accepting this strange and alien Christian faith. In 1675 Philip realized that the only way to save the Indian land and culture was to exterminate this infestation of English before it was too late, and he almost succeeded.

The first battles involved Plymouth Colony, but Philip was driven out of Plymouth. From there he headed north, gathering Nipmucs to his cause. In western Massachusetts his forces attacked such towns as Deerfield, Northfield, and Springfield—massacring many inhabitants. Philip's army worked its way east, leaving a trail of death and destruction, heading for South Middlesex.

By the late fall of 1675 the colonial authorities were becoming nervous about the large communities of Christian Indians. They feared that the Indians could turn against them at any time. In a safety measure comparable to the confinement of Japanese-Americans in concentration camps during World War II, most of Eliot's Indians were rounded up and exiled to Deer Island in Boston harbor. Deprived of basic necessities, these Indians were left to suffer through the winter. They would leave many of their number buried there.

In February 1676, on a bridge just south of Sherborn, residents found an ominous note posted by King Philip. Along with a vow to wage war for twenty-one years, the note stated "The Indians lose nothing but their lives. You must lose your fair houses and cattle."

In the same month, an outlying farm of the Sherborn community was attacked by local Nipmucs (under the spell of Philip's exhortations), and some Magunco praying Indians (bitter about the Deer Island internment and missing stores of Magunco corn). The farm belonged to Thomas Eames, who had gone into Boston to procure ammunition and seek replacement for the soldiers that had guarded his house the previous summer. During this time his wife and several small children were left on the farm without protection. When the attack occurred Mrs. Eames defended herself with boiling soap and kitchen utensils, but was killed along with five of the children. The other children were carried into captivity. The Eames' land was in the southern part of today's Framingham, on Mount Wayte. For this reason the Eames Massacre is important to the history of both Framingham and Sherborn.

In May, the Fairbanks-Bullard garrison house of Sherborn was attacked. The Indians rolled a cart filled with burning flax down a hill to crash it into the fort and set it ablaze. But as the story goes, the cart got stuck on a rock, and the Indians that tried to dislodge it were easily picked off by the defenders in the fort.

The most severe fighting of King Philip's War in South Middlesex took place in Sudbury. In February the main force of Philip's army slaughtered fifty in Lancaster, taking the minister's wife into captivity. In March the Indians destroyed Marlborough. A contingent of twenty Sudbury men staged a hit-and-run raid on the Indians encamped near the ruins of Marlborough. Fourteen Indians were killed, including at least one who had taken part in the Eames Massacre. King Philip withdrew from the area but returned in April to seek his revenge.

On April 21, 1676, King Philip attacked Sudbury with full force. Townspeople fled to the safety of their garrison houses. It was at Sudbury that the colonists would make their stand and turn the tide against the chief. From the west came Captain Samuel Wadsworth of Milton and his company, which had been dispatched to Marlborough. Although it was too late to save that town, several men from the Marlborough garrison joined Wadsworth's pursuit of the Indians into Sudbury. From the north a company of twelve from Concord fought the Indians at the bridge in the river meadow. Many of the Concord company were killed, the rest were captured or retreated. Advancing from Watertown in the east came Captain Hugh Mason, later reinforced with a company of praying Indians from Charlestown. Mason succeeded in pushing about 200 Indians back to the west side of the river. Unfortunately, the English forces from the east could not penetrate the steep west side of Sudbury in time to save Captain Wadsworth, whose company had been ambushed near Green Hill. Wadsworth and twenty-eight of his men fell in hand-to-hand combat. The memory of Wadsworth and his men is highly honored in Sudbury. At their graves in South Sudbury stands a tall obelisk erected in 1852, and this monument is the main feature on the Sudbury town seal.

The line had been drawn at Sudbury, and Philip would go no farther. Other battles followed, but the movement soon fell apart. In August King Philip was assassinated by one of his own people, and the war came to an end. When it was all over the English counted 600 dead and another 200 captured. Fifty towns had been abandoned or

Samuel Sewall, a Bay Colony judge who presided at several witchcraft trials, owned land within the bounds of today's Sherborn, Holliston, and Ashland. In 1685 he attended the installation of Sherborn's first minister, Daniel Gookin. Courtesy, Framingham Historical Society

destroyed, and damages were estimated at over £100,000.

The English communities recovered, but the lasting damage of the war was on the praying Indian towns. When the Christian Indians were returned from Deer Island, many were disenchanted with the white man and returned to their more natural way of life. Only four of the fourteen Indian towns survived the war. Natick was one of them but Magunco was not, although some Magunco Indians joined the Natick community.

Magunco was still a piece of Indian real estate, however, and the plan to have it transferred from Sherborn to Natick went forward and was accomplished in 1679. The net effect of this land deal was to move the Town of Sherborn about a mile and a half to the east. Sherborn gave up 4,000 acres, including Magunco, on the west. On the east Sherborn received 4,000 acres from Natick, which included Peter Hill, Brush Hill, and Dirty Meadow. This land also included the farm of Daniel Morse, who was relieved to find himself put within the bounds of an English town without having to move a stick of furniture.

After 1676 Natick began a long decline, with alcohol an increasing problem among the Indians. Of this affliction Eliot said, "A great apostasy defied us." Eliot died in 1690 and an able successor to his pulpit was Daniel Takawambait, but the decline could not be reversed. By 1698 only ten church members remained, and in 1716, when Takawambait died, the church was dissolved. It would be another sixty-five years before white settlers could control enough property to organize the town on their own.

After 1676 Sherborn moved on to the business of township. Thomas Sawin, another appropriately named miller, constructed the first Sherborn mill, a sawmill. The product of this mill was used to build a meetinghouse in 1680, but it took another five years to settle a minister. Sawin would later be asked by the Natick Indians to build a gristmill for them. He did this and was given land within Natick, becoming the first accepted white inhabitant of that town. The gristmill was built in the part of Natick that is now the Broadmoor Audubon Sanctuary.

At this point the presence of two important Bay Colony personalities, Samuel Sewall and Thomas Danforth, began to weigh in the affairs of the developing South Middlesex area.

Samuel Sewall (1652-1730) was a Harvard graduate, a printer, and a public official. He would gain lasting fame as a judge who presided over the Salem witchcraft trials of 1692. He married the daughter of John Hull and therefore inherited Hull's Sherborn grant. It is said that Sewall's dowry consisted of his bride's weight in Hull's pine tree shillings. In any case, we know that the dowry amounted to about £500 sterling, and calculations indicate that such an amount in shillings could equal the weight of a young lady.

We are fortunate that Sewall kept a meticulous diary. On Thursday, March 26, 1685, Sewall records that he went out to Sherborn to attend the ordination of their first minister—another son of the Indian superintendent, also named Daniel Gookin. (This Gookin, like his father, was a friend to the Indians, and he often worked with Eliot, preaching to them. The memory of the Reverend Gookin was so important to Sherbornites in 1873 that they seriously considered changing the name of the Congregational church to the Gookin Evangelical Society.) Sewall's diary also records a trip to Sherborn in 1703 when he spent several days overseeing the platting of his lands that reached west into the center of today's Holliston.

Sewall's good friend was Thomas Danforth (1622-1699), an older and wiser magistrate who was not taken in by the witchcraft madness as Sewall was. Danforth was for many years deputy governor of the colony, and he had served as treasurer for Harvard College and Middlesex County. For his services to the colony, he began accumulating grants of land in 1660. Added to these grants were purchases of his own, so that by the time of his death he had amassed over 16,000 acres in South Middlesex, mostly in today's Framingham.

Danforth referred to his land as Framingham Plantation, using the name of his native town in Suffolk, England. Other references to this land call it "Mr. Danforth's Farms." It became apparent that a town could be made by combining the Sudbury out-dwellers, the settlers of "Sherborn Row" to the northwest of Sherborn, and Danforth's Farms. But settlers would have to move onto the Danforth land to tie the area together. Danforth began leasing land to the Buckminsters in 1693, but they did not move in for another ten years. The families that did move in, in 1693, came from a completely unexpected source.

Witchcraft was not new to New England in 1692. There had been isolated incidents, trials, and a few hangings. But there had been nothing to compare with the events of Salem Village and the surrounding towns of Essex County where the hysterics of several girls, and some women too, caused the deaths of twenty people.

One family was particularly victimized. The daughters of William Town of Topsfield had married and settled around Salem Village (now the Town of Danvers). These three women had lived full and peaceful lives, having children and grandchildren, when the finger of accusation was pointed at them. All three sisters were tried and convicted on the "spectral evidence" of the accusers' hallucinations.

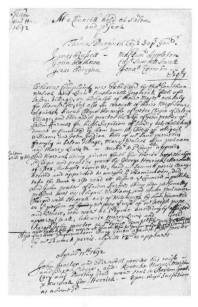

Thomas Danforth and Samuel Sewall were members of a prestigious panel of examiners who determined that Sarah Clayes, among others, should be tried for witchcraft, according to this 1692 document. The handwriting may be that of the Reverend Samuel Parris, who often sat as a recorder for the judges. Courtesy, Essex Institute

Adapted in 1900, the seal of Framingham recalls the town's beginning as Danforth's Farms. A common misconception regarding this design is that the building over the legend is in some way related to Danforth's Farms, but it is actually May Hall, part of Framingham State College. Courtesy, Town of Framingham

The two older sisters, Rebecca Nurse and Mary Easty, did not escape the fate of Gallows Hill. But the younger sister, Sarah Clayes (sometimes spelled Cloise or, later, Cloyes), did escape. The circumstances of her escape and her whereabouts as a fugitive are shrouded in mystery. In the spring of 1693, after the persecutions had stopped, Sarah and her family built a house on part of Danforth's Farms, twenty-five miles southwest of Salem Village. The role that Thomas Danforth may have had in the drama of Sarah Clayes' escape and relocation is open to speculation. We only have the clue of Sewall's remark that Danforth did much to put an end to "the troubles under which the country groaned in 1692."

The homestead of Peter and Sarah Clayes on Cowasock Brook, only two miles west of the fateful Eames homestead, was the nucleus of a colony of Salem emigrants. In addition to the Clayes' own large family, some of Rebecca Nurse's children and their families moved in. In all, about fifteen families created a district that became known as Salem End.

Petitions for township for Framingham Plantation started in 1693, but the Salem End families were not sufficiently organized to contribute to them at that time. The fact that Danforth had his own plan and timetable for the incorporation of a model town may also have contributed to the failure of the early petitions.

Then Thomas Danforth died in 1699. Danforth's old friend Samuel Sewall attended the funeral, and through Sewall's diary we are permitted a glimpse of the proceedings. Rings, gloves, and scarfs were distributed to mourners according to rank. Of Sewall's role in the affair he writes, "I helped lift the Corps into the Tomb, carrying the feet." To which he immediately adds, "Had cake and cheese at the house."

The petition for Framingham township submitted in early June 1700, bearing among others the signature of Peter Clayes, was accepted. Homage was paid to Thomas Danforth's contribution when, in 1900, the legend "Danforth Farms" was put on the town seal. Had he been less modest, the town may very well have been named Danforth.

There is an ironic footnote to the trials and tribulations of the Salem End families. The witchcraft trouble had started in the home of the Salem Village minister, the Reverend Samuel Parris, whose daughter and niece came under the influence of his slave Tituba and her voodoo stories. When the trouble passed, Parris was discredited and dismissed. He left Salem Village and wound up as a schoolmaster in, of all places, Sudbury. One can only wonder what the Clayes, Nurse, and Town families of Framingham thought of this specter from their painful past coming so close to their new home. Samuel Parris' house still stands as the Noyes-Parris House, south of Wayland Center.

As for the Sudbury out-dwellers and the people of Sherborn Row, their parent towns were not going to let go of these taxpayers without a fight. Sudbury was willing to let the out-dwellers go for compensation in the form of 2,141 acres to the south. These acres were settled by white families known as the Natick Farmers, who did not clearly belong to either town. This southern part of Sudbury is now known as Cochituate, a village of Wayland.

Sherborn was not so willing to release the inhabitants of Sherborn Row. A long court battle consumed nine years, during which time the fifteen families in question continued paying taxes to Sherborn. Finally Sherborn gave up its claim in consideration of a grant of 4,000 acres of land farther west. Sherborn Row is now downtown Framingham. The grant to Sherborn, called New Sherborn, was settled by many Sherborn emigrants. New Sherborn later became the Town of Douglas.

The town seal of Hopkinton features a scene depicting the first meetinghouse and the house of the Reverend Roger Price, the Anglican minister who established a country retreat in Hopkinton for those who chose the Church of England over the Puritan church. Courtesy, Town of Hopkinton

****

The dramatic nature of life at the end of the seventeenth century was due not only to the presence of "witches" but also of pirates. People in the inland towns felt secure from the raiding and plundering of pirates along the coast, but they were eager to believe that pirates penetrated the interior to secrete their treasure. Two stories concerning pirate gold in South Middlesex persist, both involving Captain Kidd.

One legend says that a chest of Kidd's treasure was buried on the shores of Learned Pond in Framingham, at a place where a tree had fallen into the water. A superstition evolved from this story that the chest would rise to near the water's surface from time to time. The lucky soul to spy it could then have it if he were quick enough to place a key or some other piece of metal on the lid. A poem written in 1895 by Clara Trask, a Framingham writer and poet, called "The Legend of Learned Pond," relates that the last man to see the chest was Nathaniel Pratt. It says that Pratt was so frightened by the sight that he did not have a chance to get out his jackknife to lay on the lid before the chest disappeared into the mud forever. The poem closes with a warning of a curse on this treasure:

Now, listening hearers, warning take, and lovers
*   pray be shy*
Of Learned's pond, when evening shades steal
*   down the darkening sky,—*
For Captain Kidd, who "sailed and sailed, and
*   spied three ships from Spain,"*

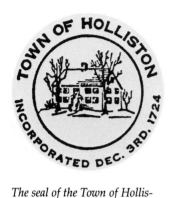

The seal of the Town of Holliston shows the Timothy Leland house, where the first town meetings were held in 1724. Holliston had petitioned to become a precinct of Sherborn when the General Court made it a town instead, and assigned the name of Holliston to honor Harvard benefactor Thomas Hollis of London, England. Courtesy, Town of Holliston

*Is watching still his treasures hid on land, and on
    the main,
And if you broke the magic spell laid on this
    chest of gold,
The pirate's ghost might drag you down in
    Learned's waters cold.*

A story from Sherborn may have more basis in fact than the Legend of Learned Pond. Down behind Scudder's Hill in a rough wooded area called The Goomer, William Bull, a mate of Captain Kidd, is said to have buried two saddlebags of gold in 1704. Records show that this land was actually owned by a William Bull at that time.

****

During the first quarter of the eighteenth century, the influence of Harvard College on the evolution of South Middlesex was at its height when Hopkinton and Holliston came into being.

In 1715 Holliston was simply the western part of Sherborn, and beyond it was Natick's abandoned Magunco real estate. Beyond that lay only wilderness with two or three brave settlers. Incredibly, within a few months the Indians would have a buyer for their 9,200 Magunco acres, and this plus another 2,000 acres (containing the unwary brave settlers) would be incorporated as the Town of Hopkinton.

The moving force behind the sudden materialization of Hopkinton was a group called the Trustees for the Charity of Edward Hopkins. Edward Hopkins (1600-1657) had been governor of the colony of Connecticut, and afterwards he returned to his native England, where he died. His will included a bequest to support the training of ministers in New England. The training of ministers was the function of colleges at that time, and an English court, perhaps arbitrarily, declared Harvard as the beneficiary, although by that time Yale College had been founded in Hopkins' own colony of Connecticut.

It was the job of the trustees to invest Hopkins' bequest to provide a regular income for Harvard. They did this by following the medieval practice of purchasing a large tract of land to be rented to tenant farmers. The General Court pushed through the incorporation of a virtually empty township. The only remaining task was to get people to live there to provide the rent—and income for Harvard.

With all the low-cost private property available, the idea of Old World farm tenancy did not find many takers, even at one penny an acre. In 1718 the president of Harvard wrote to some Framingham farmers to interest them in working the Hopkinton land. These farmers responded with a long list of the advantages of working your own land rather than someone else's, and politely declined the invitation.

The embarrassment of a town with no officers, no meetinghouse, and no minister lasted until 1724. Up until then some population had trickled in from adjacent towns. In 1719 eighteen Scotch-Irish families, who came almost directly from the docks of Boston, settled in Hopkinton. Among this group was Joseph Young, ancestor of Mormon leader Brigham Young.

To encourage the small population to organize a real town, the Hopkins trustees provided £100 to build a meetinghouse and 100 acres to support a minister. The first town meeting was in 1724 at the home of John How. At the outset, the little town could not agree on a site for their meetinghouse. Three sites were proposed and the final selection had to be by lot. The meetinghouse was completed in 1725 on a high hill in the center of the town, not far from the spot where Boston Marathoners of a later century would start their 26.8 mile run.

The year Hopkinton began holding town meetings, in 1724, was also the year in which the western part of Sherborn was incorporated as Holliston. Sherborn stretched twelve miles from east to west, and it is not surprising that the "dwellers on ye West side of Dopping Brook" should want their own meetinghouse, "for the sake of Future Peace and Good Neighborhood." But the population of 150 was not ready for the full responsibilities of township. They only wanted to be a precinct. East and west precincts had been established a few years earlier in Sudbury, a town divided by the wide and often flooded Sudbury River. Sudbury did not become two towns in 1720, and certainly no one would expect that Sherborn, divided only by Dopping Brook, would become two towns in 1724.

But once again Harvard College changed the course of South Middlesex history. The unwitting petitioners for a west Sherborn precinct submitted their request at about the same time that a London merchant, Thomas Hollis, Esquire, made a generous donation to the college. The General Court, seeking to show its appreciation, seized upon the Sherbornites' petition and amended it for full township, arbitrarily assigning the name of Holliston. The hapless settlers on the west side of Dopping Brook suddenly found themselves with a town to organize—a town named after someone they had never heard of!

Understandably, it took Holliston a few years to get going as a town. Its first town meetings were held in the home of Timothy Leland. This historic house was unfortunately lost in a fire in 1946, but it has been preserved on the town's seal. In 1727 Samuel Sewall, in the last years of his life, contributed eleven acres of his holdings toward

Southborough broke away from Marlborough in 1717, ten years after Westborough had split off. When the bit of land called Fiddle Neck was added to the southern edge of the town, a permanent link to the other towns of South Middlesex was created. Courtesy, Town of Southborough

Captain Joseph Ware was one of the victims of the epidemic that swept Sherborn and Holliston in 1753 and 1754. His tombstone records the fact that in Sherborn this pestilence was known as the Memorable Mortality. Courtesy, Betsy Johnson

retaining a minister, and the Reverend James Stone was hired the next year. The meetinghouse was finished in 1731, financed by a tax that allowed up to half to be paid in labor. Sherborn, Holliston's parent town, provided the congregation with a pewter tankard for use in communion services. A large pulpit Bible was sent from London by Thomas Hollis, the town's namesake.

The land in the center of Holliston was once owned by Lieutenant Henry Adams, who was killed in King Philip's attack on Medfield. Adams himself did not live in Holliston, but it is said that his son, Jasper Adams, did have a homestead there, making him the first settler of Holliston. The presumed site of this homestead, where they say Jasper sent smoke signals to his father in Medfield, is marked by a long boulder called Jasper's Rock.

Another subdivision around this time came from a parent town outside the bounds of South Middlesex but closely related to the area's history. Marlborough had been incorporated in 1660 by several Sudbury settlers who had pushed beyond the limits of the western grants that comprise today's Sudbury. Marlborough fanned out for miles in all directions, and it was inevitable that this area would be made into several smaller towns.

First to incorporate was Westborough (1717), then Southborough (1727); these were the western and southern parts of the original Marlborough. In 1766 the northern part of Westborough broke off as Northborough, although it was still west of Marlborough. The northern part of Marlborough did not separate until 1866, and it was called Hudson.

Of these towns, only Southborough falls into the South Middlesex group—despite its natural regional ties to Marlborough and (after 1731) its inclusion in Worcester County. Southborough would be drawn into the web of industrial and commercial activity that characterized South Middlesex after the Revolutionary War. A major contribution to the future of Southborough came as a minor real estate adjustment made at the time of its incorporation. Framingham owned Fiddle Neck, a narrow appendage of land reaching almost three miles from its southwest corner. When Southborough was incorporated it seemed natural to include Fiddle Neck in the new town, where it would simply fill out its southern border down to the Sudbury River. The river, of course, meant waterpower, and Fiddle Neck's river frontage would give Southborough two of its most important industrial villages of the nineteenth century—Cordaville and Southville.

With the 1727 incorporation of Southborough, there would be no further towns formed in South Middlesex until the Revolutionary War.

Meanwhile, the eighteenth century in New England was not as quiet as one might think. The people still worried about Indians, especially during the sporadic French and Indian conflicts. The trail of the Connecticut Path beyond Framingham was lost early in the eighteenth century, since its route passed through hostile Indian villages. Of greater danger than the Indians were the various illnesses and epidemics that moved through from time to time. In 1714 an epidemic in Natick killed forty Indians and helped loosen the Indian hold on that town.

The epidemic that most seriously affected the white towns occurred in the winter of 1753-1754. It took as many as thirty lives in Sherborn and devastated Holliston, where fifty-three of their population of 400 died, including the minister's wife. Holliston called it the Great Sickness, while Sherborn, with a flair for the romantic, called it the Memorable Mortality.

Puritan observers at the time, aware that the citizens of Holliston were regularly taking each other to court, considered this disease a judgement on them for their "litigious spirit." No mention was made as to what Sherborn's sin may have been. Unfortunately, the Great Sickness cooled Holliston's "litigious spirit" only temporarily. The town retained its reputation for litigation through the eighteenth and nineteenth centuries. At one time during the 1850s every citizen in Holliston was subpoenaed to appear in court.

A smallpox epidemic in 1792-1793 swept through a wider area. There were pesthouses and smallpox cemeteries in Sudbury, Framingham, Holliston, and Hopkinton.

To keep the people's minds from the Indians, diseases, and the other hardships of eighteenth-century life, there were plenty of issues to make the traditional New England town meeting an arena of loud controversy. The most popular of these issues involved meetinghouses, ministers, and support for the poor.

In Framingham it was decided that a new meetinghouse was needed in 1725, but it took them ten years to agree on a site. At one point when all seemed settled, lumber was gathered at the designated site only to be taken by a powerful minority family to build a barn. They paid for the lumber only when the meetinghouse was built at a place suitable to them.

The issue of church doctrine had a major role in the early history of Hopkinton. The eighteen Scotch-Irish families that helped establish the town leaned toward a Presbyterian form of worship, while the others followed the more orthodox Congregational line. This tension led to the emigration of many of the Scotch-Irish farther west. They settled at Blanford where more trouble must have been caused, for the record shows that they unsuccessfully tried to change the name of that town to Glasgow.

Perhaps from spite, or at least as a parting shot, the Scotch-Irish sold their land not to settlers of the accepted faith, but to a minister of the Church of England! The Reverend Roger Price (1692-1762) was rector of King's Chapel in Boston. He purchased 850 Hopkinton acres in 1735 as a country retreat for Anglicans. In a reversal of the roles played by Puritans and the Church of England a century before, Price claimed that this land would be "a sanctuary for persecuted Churchmen who are drove from other places."

Of the Anglicans that joined the Reverend Price, the most prominent was Sir Henry Frankland (1716-1768), who built an imposing mansion on land that covered much of the old Magunco praying town. The house had three floors, Italian marble fireplaces, and required sixteen slaves to maintain in the style that Sir Henry was accustomed to. Frankland was collector of the Port of Boston and a King's Chapel vestryman. One of the reasons for his taking refuge in Hopkinton was the fact that he was living with a woman beneath his station, a woman he had never married. This woman was Agnes Surriage, and Frankland had discovered her scrubbing floors at an inn in Marblehead. The story of Sir Henry and Agnes is one of the great romantic tales of old New England. Sir Henry took Agnes with him on a visit to England in 1754 where they received the same cold shoulder that drove him from Boston to Hopkinton. On a side trip to Portugal, Sir Henry was riding through the streets of Lisbon in an open carriage when the infamous earthquake of 1755 struck, toppling buildings all around him. The street opened up, swallowing Frankland and his carriage, and burying him under dust and rubble. Miraculously, Agnes was able to track him down and rescue him from certain suffocation. Out of gratitude and humility, Frankland married Agnes, and the Marblehead scrubwoman became Lady Frankland, baroness of Thirsk.

Great romances had little to do with the reality of day-to-day life, when money was tight, and extracting money from towns was never easy. Even the ministers had a hard time. Framingham's first minister, the Reverend John Swift, frequently addressed letters to town meetings requesting salary owed him. In Holliston, the Reverend Joshua Prentiss, in keeping with the spirit of litigation in that town, sued the town for £426 in back pay. The most eloquent case for a better salary for ministers was put by the Reverend Nathaniel Howe of Hopkinton in one of his sermons:

In 1770, as the American Revolution approached, life in the South Middlesex towns was still very primitive. With a population of about 7,000 spread over 150 square miles, there was a good deal of wilderness and unexplored area remaining. From 100 Years Progress, 1874. Courtesy, Framingham Historical Society

Born down with the fatigue of manual labor, pressed into the woods in the winter, to the plough in the spring, and into the meadow in the summer, to support my family comfortably, and fulfill my promises, I felt the business of the ministry was greatly neglected;—that it was impossible for me to do what ought to be done in my profession, unless the people did more toward my support.

If the towns were stingy toward their own ministers, one can imagine their attitude toward support for the poor. Welfare was strictly a town responsibility in the eighteenth century, and most towns had a workhouse or poor farm, usually managed by a town board called the Overseers of the Poor. Sudbury's workhouse was set up around 1751, "that Idle and Disorderly People may be properly employed." Framingham had a workhouse on the town common as early as 1735.

A favorite tactic was to claim that a pauper belonged to another town, and the only expense incurred was to pay someone to haul the pauper to the border of the other town. The poor were often shuttled back and forth between towns that would not acknowledge them. In one case the individual involved wrote to the selectmen of Holliston, "I beg that you meet with the Selectmen of Medway and decide whose poor I am." Once accepted by a town, the fortunate pauper had the privilege of working the treadmill in the workhouse or toiling on the poor farm.

In the 1760s the petty issues of meetinghouses, ministers, and supporting the poor were swept aside as a major confrontation with England brewed, a confrontation that would change the history of the world as well as the history of South Middlesex.

2 AGE OF THE YANKEE TINKER, TRADER, AND FARMER (1760-1830)

New Englanders had always cherished their autonomy within the British Empire. Back in 1676 Governor Leverett said, "The laws made by our King and Parliament obligeth them in nothing but what consists with the Interests of New England." This feeling was put to the test in 1689 when the autocratic Governor Edmond Andros was ejected from power, and in the 1770s it would be tried again.

The first recorded actions of the South Middlesex towns involved the Stamp Acts, usually boycotting goods imported from England. Holliston referred to these goods as "superfluities from abroad." Hopkinton actually listed proscribed items, including snuff, mustard, clocks, and glue.

When Boston was occupied by British troops, a secret Committee of Correspondence set up lines of communication between the city and the outlying towns. The South Middlesex towns quickly set up their own committees and joined this subversive network.

In 1770 the shocking news of the Boston Massacre spread to the countryside. As the people of South Middlesex scanned the list of victims one name stood out—Crispus Attucks. Attucks was an old Nipmuc name, and Crispus Attucks was a mixed breed of Indian and Negro who was born near the Framingham-Natick line. He had been owned as a slave by Deacon William Brown in Framingham. Attucks ran away in 1750 and went to sea. Deacon Brown put an ad in the *Boston Gazette*, but there was no trace of him until his name appeared on the list of those killed when the redcoats fired into the Boston mob. Some historians claim that Crispus Attucks was the first man to fall for the cause of American Independence.

Through the Committees of Correspondence the towns were encouraged to arm themselves and enlarge their militia companies, or start new "minuteman" companies to be ready to march on a minute's notice. South Middlesex town records show the purchase of cannon,

The Asa Sanger house in Sherborn was built in the early 1700s. When it was re-shingled in June 1775, the men on the roof claimed they could hear the rumble of cannon from the Battle of Bunker Hill, twenty miles away. This picture, taken about 1880, shows the house when it was about one hundred fifty years old. Courtesy, Sherborn Historical Society

Crispus Attucks is the central figure in this rare engraving of the Boston Massacre. Attucks, part Indian and part black, was a slave in the Brown family of Framingham who ran away to sea in 1750, only to resurface in 1770 as a casualty in the Boston Massacre. Courtesy, Framingham Public Library

powder, bullets, and flints. South Middlesex itself was a source of military armaments. Three Sherborn families, the Holbrooks, Lelands, and Pratts, made flintlock muskets and musket balls. Saltpeter for making gunpowder also came from Sherborn. Out at Fiddle Neck, Andrew Newton had an iron forge where it is said he made cannon and cannonballs.

The British sent out spies to learn the location of munitions and to get an idea of the strength of the provincial militia. One pair of spies, disguised as surveyors "in brown clothes and reddish handkerchiefs around our necks," dined at Framingham's Buckminster Tavern. There they had a good view of the minutemen drilling on the village green. In their detailed written report to General Gage the spies admitted that they "did not feel very easy at seeing such a number so very near us." They must have felt even less easy when the minutemen came over to the tavern for refreshment when they had completed their drilling. But after some time the minutemen left for their homes, "full of pot-valor."

The presence of spies in the area probably prompted some companies to drill in secret. A veteran of the Sudbury minutemen remembered "drilling at night on cold barn floors."

The inevitable confrontation finally came in April 1775. The spies had gotten word to General Gage of a large store of munitions at Concord, just north of Sudbury. They did not know that these supplies had been secretly distributed among other towns, including Sudbury.

An expedition of British regulars was sent out during the very early hours of April 19. The colonists had their own spies, and news of the expedition was signaled from the tower of Boston's Old North

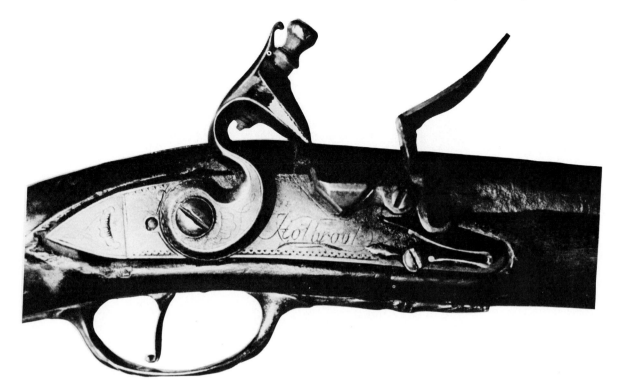

Above: One Sherborn family that made muskets for the patriots was the Holbrooks, whose name appears on the flintlock of this later fowling piece. The Holbrooks later became the dominant apple cider producers in a town filled with cider mills. Courtesy, F. Klay Collection

Left: The Lelands were another of the gun-making families of Sherborn at the time of the Revolutionary War. A Leland ancestor had been a member of the court of Henry VIII, but his descendants made arms to fight the soldiers of George III. Courtesy, F. Klay Collection

Church. Paul Revere and others spread the news, in the words of the poem by Henry Wadsworth Longfellow, "to every Middlesex town and village."

At this time South Middlesex consisted of seven towns. Each one had some form of minuteman company, including Natick where the white settlers had all but pushed out the original Indian owners. The Natick company had eighteen men, while Sudbury, the largest town in Middlesex County at that time (it still included all of Wayland), had 302 men organized under six companies.

Participation in the fighting on the day of "the shot heard 'round the world" (From Ralph Waldo Emerson's hymn) depended on time and geography. The minutemen of South Middlesex were just getting into their leather breeches and priming their flintlocks when the first shots rang out from Lexington green at about 5:00 A.M. Many were on the roads, cutting across meadows and jumping stone walls when the volleys were exchanged at Concord's North Bridge.

The glory of the day remained for those troops who could engage the enemy on their return to Boston. Even in this endeavor only the men from the closest towns saw action—Sudbury, Framingham, and

Facing page, top: A list of casualties printed shortly after the Battle of Lexington and Concord includes names from Sudbury and Framingham. Asabel Reed and Deacon Josiah Haynes of Sudbury were killed, and among the wounded were Daniel Hemenway of Framingham, and Joshua Haynes of Sudbury (not listed here). Courtesy, John Carter Brown Library, Brown University

Facing page, bottom: The cannon from Fort Ticonderoga that surprised the British and forced them out of Boston were hauled across the length of Massachusetts during the winter of 1775-1776. The "cannon train" drawn by oxen moved slowly under the stern eye of Henry Knox, later a general on Washington's staff. Their route crossed several South Middlesex towns. Courtesy, Framingham Historical Society

Natick. Asabel Reed and the elderly Deacon Josiah Haynes of Sudbury were killed. Joshua Haynes of Sudbury was wounded as was Daniel Hemenway of Framingham. The companies of all the South Middlesex towns pursued the British as far as Cambridge. (The wounded Daniel Hemenway was put in a field hospital where some British troops were also brought. One British officer, in his zeal to harass the enemy at every opportunity, persisted in shaking Hemenway's cot with his foot. The officer stopped only when Hemenway promised to pin him to the floor with a bayonet if he touched his cot again.) The day of the Battle of Lexington and Concord ended with the British bottled up in Boston.

A few months later the redcoats broke out at Charlestown (then a part of Middlesex County), and the Battle of Bunker Hill followed. South Middlesex soldiers who missed their chance at Lexington and Concord got plenty of bloody action at Bunker Hill. Peter Salem, a former Framingham slave given his freedom so that he could serve in the army, is credited with firing the shot that killed British Major Pitcairn. Back in Sherborn, men shingling a roof claimed they could hear the cannon of Bunker Hill twenty miles away.

In 1775 the Revolution was primarily Massachusetts' war, even though Virginia's General George Washington had been put at the head of the army at Cambridge. During the winter of 1775-1776 a strategic plan was carried out that would push the war to the other colonies. Fort Ticonderoga in New York had been seized from the British. The plan was to bring the fort's large arsenal of cannon across the length of Massachusetts and set them up on the heights around Boston, where the threat of bombardment would force the redcoats out. The task of bringing these guns to Boston was given to General

Henry Knox.

The route of the "Knox Cannon Train" was a secret that is not clearly known to this day, although the route did pass through today's Sudbury, Framingham, and Wayland. Framingham seems to have been a holding area where cannon and oxen were hidden in various barns while the foundations were being prepared to receive the guns. It is known that John Adams came out to Framingham on an inspection trip, staying at Buckminster's Tavern.

The plan worked, and the British left Boston only to reappear at New York. Once the war became a continental struggle, the possibility of American independence increased. In the early months of 1776 South Middlesex towns such as Holliston and Hopkinton were passing resolutions encouraging independence. In February Hopkinton stopped using the phrase "in His Majesty's Name" in its town warrants. Fortunately, in July of that year the Second Continental Congress cooperated and declared the thirteen colonies to be the independent and United States of America.

Although the war moved south, hundreds of South Middlesex men served and there were many casualties. Holliston had eight men at Valley Forge during the brutal winter of 1777-1778, and three did not survive. One of Framingham's minuteman commanders, Captain Micajah Gleason, was killed at White Plains. Also at White Plains, two Sherborn men, Jonathan Holbrook and Joseph Ware, were advancing on enemy artillery when each man lost an arm as a cannon ball roared between them. Framingham may also claim its minister as a casualty of

this war. The Reverend Matthew Bridge answered Washington's call to serve as chaplain at Cambridge, only to die shortly afterwards of a camp fever.

In addition to the heavy financial burdens of war, the South Middlesex towns had to deal with loyalists, or Tories, in their midst. In Holliston, twenty were identified as Tories, and bonds of £100 were put on them until 1781. These twenty were not fully freed of their stigma until they submitted written recantations and apologies to the town.

Nathaniel Brinley, a man of wealth and a suspected loyalist, had estates in both Boston and Framingham. He was arrested in Boston once the British had evacuated and was banished to Framingham, where he was kept under tight house arrest and a £600 bond for many months.

Prominent among the officers serving from South Middlesex was General John Nixon of Sudbury. He married Micajah Gleason's widow and helped her run Gleason's Tavern in Framingham after the war. Nixon's brother Thomas rose to the rank of colonel. Thomas' son, Thomas Nixon, Jr., started the war as a fifer and came out a captain. His fifer's music book still exists, and in it can be found the popular tune "Yankee Doodle." The term Yankee, introduced during the war through this ditty, would come to characterize a new nation. In South Middlesex the end of the Revolutionary War meant the end of the era of the Puritan and the beginning of the age of the Yankee.

****

In the closing years of the Revolutionary War important changes occurred in the status of two South Middlesex towns. Sudbury became two separate towns, and Natick gave up its special status as an Indian town to be incorporated with full township rights and responsibilities.

Sudbury had been divided into precincts in 1722, just after the village of Cochituate was annexed to make up for the loss of the out-dwellers to Framingham. According to one petition, this division was needed because, "by reason of the flood of water . . . we are forced to seek our spiritual good with the peril of our lives." The precinct on the east side of the river was sometimes known as Pine Plain, and the precinct on the west side as Rocky Plain, especially the high area where the west meetinghouse was built.

The annexation of Cochituate pulled the geographic center of the east precinct to the south. It was planned to move the old meeting-house a half mile down to a new village site by putting it on sleds in the winter, but this was abandoned and a new meetinghouse was completed in 1726 at today's Wayland Center.

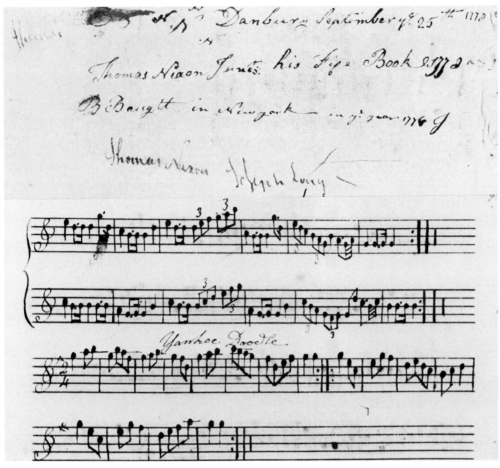

Thomas Nixon, Jr., of Sudbury and Framingham, was a fifer at the Revolutionary War's start because he was too young to be a soldier. His fifer music book contains many tunes, including the brief Yankee Doodle. Also shown here is the inside front cover of the book, with Nixon's signature. Courtesy, Framingham Historical Society

By 1780 the population of the west precinct exceeded the east by about two to one, and the east-siders were unhappy with the tax burden (most of the poor lived on the west side). With the expense and inflation of the Revolutionary War, the financial burden was very heavy. As the east precinct was the one that wanted the separation, they had to come up with a new name despite the fact that the east side was the original Town of Sudbury. They chose to be known as East Sudbury, and the west side retained the name of Sudbury. (The confusion that this created was resolved in 1835 when East Sudbury took the name of Wayland.) With the creation of East Sudbury, the number of towns in South Middlesex came to eight.

Natick has been counted as one of the South Middlesex towns since 1651, but it was not a full township in the legal sense until 1781. From the time of King Philip's War to the Revolutionary War, the Indian population of Natick slowly eroded. In 1721 they had their first white minister, and 1734 saw the first white man to hold a town office. By 1745 the white population was strong enough to make a move to relocate the meetinghouse in South Natick from the corner of town to a more central site. A section of Needham (surrounded on three sides by

Sudbury was divided into two towns in 1780. The settlers in the eastern part initiated the separation, and had to take the new name of East Sudbury even though theirs was the older part of the original Sudbury. To avoid confusion, East Sudbury was renamed Wayland in 1835. Courtesy, Town of Wayland

Natick) called Needham Leg or Hog End was annexed to increase the white population. But the General Court felt a loyalty to the old Indian town and rejected the petition to relocate the meetinghouse.

Interestingly, the struggle between whites and Indians was not based on town sectionalism or segregation. The dwellings of whites and Indians were intermingled throughout the town, even at South Natick where John Eliot first organized his praying town. When the white population finally organized their town in 1781, the General Court's attachment to its Indian heritage is seen in its refusal to allow the town to take a new name. The petition had asked for the town to be named Eliot. Today Natick is the only South Middlesex town with an Indian name.

A few years later, in 1787, Natick joined with Sherborn, Holliston, and Hopkinton in a bid to secede from Middlesex County. These four towns made up the southern half of South Middlesex. Their remoteness from the county seat at Cambridge, and even the district court at Concord, prompted them to try to become a county unto themselves. The other Middlesex towns objected, and the petition was denied with the comment that a proliferation of government and its expense is a thing to be avoided.

The memory of British abuses had caused a suspicion of too much government, but it was becoming obvious in 1787 that there was not enough government as far as the new United States was concerned. The government under the Articles of Confederation was weak, and states were beginning to deal with each other as foreign countries. A Massachusetts crisis—Shays' Rebellion—illustrated the need for a stronger central government.

****

Daniel Shays (1747-1825) was born in Hopkinton into one of the Anglican families of the Reverend Price's community. Shays was baptized in the Church of England, but he followed a military career on the side of the colonies. He was an ensign at Bunker Hill, and was promoted to captain. After the war he lived in western Massachusetts where taxes and inflation were creating a serious economic crisis. Hundreds of discontented farmers had taken to arms. Under the leadership of Daniel Shays, they marched on the courthouses that were the source of the hated taxes and foreclosures.

Many South Middlesex militia contingents were sent out to quell the disturbances. John Ware of Sherborn was among them. Ware entered a tavern near Brookfield, not knowing it was in the hands of Shays' rebels. He was taken prisoner and put in an upper room. From this room Ware managed to signal a passing company of cavalry which immediately surrounded the tavern, bringing about his release.

The rebellion was stopped, Shays was later pardoned, and he lived out his life in New York. But the specter of rebellion remained. A country without a strong national government to create a national army if needed disturbed the retired General George Washington. The general decided to attend the Constitutional Convention in Philadelphia, and his support helped bring about the Constitution of the United States that has endured to this day.

As the first president under the new Constitution, Washington toured the country. Traveling on the Hartford Road (Route 16), he passed through Holliston, Sherborn, and Natick on his way from Boston. He is said to have stopped at Littlefield Tavern in Holliston and Sanger Tavern in Sherborn. Somewhere in Holliston a pewter tankard is treasured as having been used by the Father of Our Country, while in Sherborn a cup and saucer are also thus venerated.

This was not Washington's first journey through South Middlesex. In 1775, when he took command of the army at Cambridge, he came through Sudbury on the Boston Post Road (Route 20), and he may have stopped at the Red Horse Tavern. The Red Horse was later made famous by Longfellow when his *Tales of a Wayside Inn* was published, containing, as the landlord's tale, "The Midnight Ride of Paul Revere." Today the inn is still in operation as Longfellow's Wayside Inn.

In the last decade of the eighteenth century the new federal government, with its policy of neutrality, encouraged domestic manufacturing. Patents were offered to protect inventions. Eli Whitney, a native of neighboring Westborough, was one of the first Yankee inventors to take advantage of this for his cotton gin. Also, imprisonment for debt was abolished, opening the door for credit and finance, to the horror of many an old Puritan.

But it was the old Puritan virtues of discipline and hard work combined with new Yankee ingenuity and business sense that would propel New England to the forefront of American industry. Because of its location at the heart of New England, South Middlesex was well suited to participate in this new Industrial Revolution.

It started on a small scale, in the old forges and mills of the eighteenth century. By 1796 Holliston had a scythe factory and Sherborn was making pitchforks. Also in Sherborn, the Dowse family was tanning leather, so important to the later shoe industry. This leather was also used in the manufacture of whips and bookbindings. In 1800 Mary Rice began braiding straw by hand in Framingham. She fashioned the braid into the hats and bonnets that were becoming so popular. This cottage industry spread to other South Middlesex towns and was supplemented with similar products such as willow baskets.

South Middlesex entered the nineteenth century with Framingham as the largest town, having a population of 1,625. Sudbury's dominance had been lost when East Sudbury broke away, but Sudbury was still large enough to be second in population to Framingham in 1800 with 1,372 people. The smallest of the eight towns was Natick with only 694. Little did anyone then realize that forces were at work which would put Natick at the top of the list. Within fifty years Natick would have a population greater than all of South Middlesex in 1800.

The new century found South Middlesex still a predominantly agricultural region, and agriculture would remain in some form throughout the century. In fact, a rural quality has been retained in parts of all South Middlesex towns throughout the twentieth century, particularly Sherborn and Southborough. But for those looking to make a profit in the early 1800s, South Middlesex offered many advantages and opportunities.

During the eighteenth century there was no major market town or center in South Middlesex. All the towns were within a day's ride of the great market and seaport of Boston, and this was sufficient for the small-scale farmers and millers of that time. But men with larger plans saw the need for better transportation. Until railroads came on the scene in the 1830s, the most promising schemes involved turnpikes and canals.

Isaiah Thomas (1749-1831), who had gotten into trouble running a patriotic press in British-occupied Boston, moved to Worcester where he continued publishing his newspaper, *The Massachusetts Spy*. Thomas recognized the great possibilities that were opening up as the new nation looked west, especially after the Louisiana Purchase of 1803. He knew that Worcester, standing between Boston and the West, could benefit from the country's westward expansion, and he became one of the driving forces behind the Boston-Worcester Turnpike. The turnpike opened for business at its four tollhouses in 1806, and much of its route passed through Natick, Framingham, and Southborough.

The Boston-Worcester Turnpike (Route 9), the older Boston Post Road (Route 20) through East Sudbury and Sudbury, and the Hartford Road (Route 16) through Natick, Sherborn, and Holliston put all the South Middlesex towns except Hopkinton on major east-west arteries from Boston. In 1820 Hopkinton was included when another commercial road, the Central Turnpike (Route 135), was opened a few miles south of the Boston-Worcester Turnpike.

The turnpikes tended to follow straight lines rather than wander from village to village as the older roads did, encouraging the development of new villages along their routes. For the Boston-Worcester Turnpike the new villages were Felchville in Natick, Framingham Center in Framingham, and Fayville in Southborough. This road was used by the celebrated Marquis de Lafayette in 1815, and the village of Fayville was honored when Lafayette, an old friend of Washington's, stopped there for refreshment.

The most obvious business opportunities presented by the highways were taverns, livery stables, and stagecoach lines. By 1830 Natick had a tavern on all three of its major highways. At Framingham Center, the halfway point between Boston and Worcester, up to seventeen stagecoaches would stop each day. A familiar sound in that village was the coach driver's horn, announcing his arrival.

The tavern and hotel at Framingham Center was run by Abner Wheeler, who also ran a general store. Abner and his brothers, Benjamin and Eliphalet, were typical of the enterprising Yankees who were taking advantage of the new economic opportunities. They had recently moved down from Lincoln where they had been carpenters. In addition to a tavern and two stores, these brothers were involved with the organization of a cotton mill and a woolen mill in the village of Framingham known as Saxonville.

Most stagecoaches of this time were taking passengers through South Middlesex on their way to such places as Boston, Fitchburg, Worcester, Springfield, Albany, Hartford, or New York City. But there was one place in South Middlesex that was bringing people in from these places. This was the Hopkinton Mineral Springs. The springs were discovered in 1816 just south of today's Lake Whitehall. In the true spirit of Yankee enterprise, the springs were quickly developed into a popular resort. For many years this spa was visited by the wealthy and powerful who were seeking to benefit from the health-giving waters. A contemporary tour book of Massachusetts claimed that these waters (containing carbonic acid, carbonate of lime, and iron) were "salubrious and making a trip to Hopkinton springs both pleasant and fashionable."

The time of stagecoaches and taverns was also a time of highwaymen. One such character who operated around South Middlesex was Michael Martin, alias Captain Lightfoot. Martin's career of highway robbery came to an end when he recognized himself in a wanted poster in a Holliston tavern in 1821. He panicked and stole someone's horse in his rush to get away. The owner of the horse tracked him down and was surprised to learn that this was no mere horsethief, but the infamous Captain Lightfoot himself. As with Captain

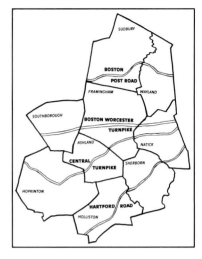

The main roads from Boston to the west all passed through South Middlesex. As the post roads of the eighteenth century were supplemented with the turnpikes of the early nineteenth century, the importance of South Middlesex to commerce and industry grew and was recognized by the new breed of Yankee businessmen. Courtesy, Framingham Historical Society

Right: Boston, within a day's ride of South Middlesex, offered a cornucopia of useful and exotic goods from all over the world, as shown in these columns from an 1806 Boston Gazette. Yankee businessmen saw the turnpikes, canals, and later the railroads as a money-making method of bringing these goods to new markets. Courtesy, Framingham Historical Society

Below: New highways such as the Boston-Worcester turnpike were private ventures, raising capital by selling shares. At one end of this 1807 stock certificate is a small engraving showing the road, a tollhouse, and the pike that was turned to allow travelers to pass after the toll was paid. Courtesy, American Antiquarian Society

Flour and Naval Stores,

At No. 48, Long wharf,

TWELVE hundred barrels Wilmington Tar, Pitch, and Turpentine—50 barrels Baltimore fine Flour—5 hhds best retailing Sugar—40 bbls of kiln died Meal, kegs manufactured Tobacco.

Wanted on Freight,

A VESSEL of about one hundred tons, to go to a southern port
September 8

Salt Wine and Lemons.

ONE thousand hhds Salt—200 quarter casks of Sherry Wine, of an excellent quality, and 50 boxes Lemons—imported in the ship Samson, Isaac Atkins, matter from Cadiz, and for sale by

NATH'L GOODWIN No. 5, Long Wharf.

For Sale, Freight or Charter.

The above ship SAMSON, burthen 237 tons, 4 years old—she is tight, strong and burthensome, and may be ready to receive a cargo on board in a fortnight. sept. 8

Fresh Flour.

LANDING this day, and for sale, at No. 5, Butlers-Row——Superfine and fine Baltimore FLOUR. *In Store*—10,000 lbs Island Cocoa ; 8 tons Brazilletto Wood ; 60 boxes China, 49 ps each ; 4 boxes Bengal Indigo entitled to debenture ; 13 bbls Corn Meal ; 300 lbs Carolina Indigo ; 50 boxes Spanish Cigars ; 50 do Philadelphia and New-York Starch ; Cambooses and Stoves.

Wanted, a VESSEL, about 100 tons burthen which can have a full freight to Baltimore....Apply as above Sept. 4

Ammidon & Boyle,

No. 13, Central-wharf, *Have for sale,*

EIGHT thousand pieces blue Yellow Nankins, 400 boxes marble and white Soap, 250 wt. first quality Nutmegs, few cases Silks, entitled to debenture, Hyson Tea, Ravens Duck, English Porter, Pig Lead, old Cognac Brandy, and few boxes Sugar. Sept 8.

ly for sale, American Hats. Sept. 8

Elegant 6-4 Shawls.

6-4 Crimson, Scarlet and Orange color'd twilled Silk SHAWLS. Likewise, superfine Queen Cloths, of the most fashionable colours for Ladies Habits. *Also* an extensive assortment of EUROPEAN GOODS, suitable for the approaching season, for sale, at No. 56, CORNHILL, opposite the Old State House. Sept 8

Ruggles & Hunt,

No. 6, *Marlboro'-street*, *Have for sale,*

THREE trunks Morocco Roan and Kid Skins, of various colours, the Roans principally Red—few casks London Porter and Berton Ale, of good quality—100 kegs Durham Mustard, of prime quality—7 casks Copperas. Sept 4

Samuel Stuart,

HAS taken Store, No. 24, CORNHILL, where he is opening a general assortment of ENGLISH GOODS, received per the late arrivals from Liverpool, together with an assortment of INDIA GOODS—Italian Crapes—sewing Silk—elegant silk Shawls, &c. sept. 8

India Cottons.

FOR SALE, at No. 69, *Long-Wharf*—40 bales India Cottons, consisting of Beerboom Gurrahs—Lucknow Sannahs—Salgazie—Checks—Cutlers—blue gilla Hhkfs. and white Hhkfs. with borders—all entitled to debenture. Sept. 8

Carpets and Carpetings.

JOHN BALLARD, Jr. & CO. have received by the SALLY, from Liverpool, a great variety of CARPETS and CARPETING, of the latest and most fashionable Patterns, which they offer for sale, at No. 32, *Marlboro'-street*, by wholesale and retail. Sept. 7.

Elegant Marble Ornaments,

Just received, at LEVERETT'S *Furniture*

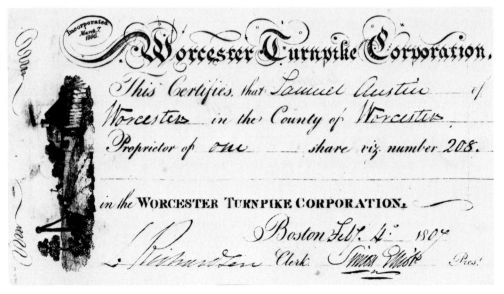

Incorporated March 7, 1806. **Worcester Turnpike Corporation.**

This Certifies, that Samuel Austin of Worcester in the County of Worcester Proprietor of one share viz number 208.

in the WORCESTER TURNPIKE CORPORATION.

Boston Feb'y 4th 1807.

Clerk. Pres.

Kidd, legends of the existence of Mike Martin's buried loot persisted for many generations.

Another colorful figure from this time was Richard Potter (1783-1835), considered America's first native-born magician. Potter was born at Hopkinton's Frankland Manor, the son of Dinah, one of the Frankland slaves, and an unknown white father. Some accounts of Richard Potter speculate as to the identity of his father, and one states that Sir Henry Frankland himself was responsible even though Frankland had been dead for fifteen years when Potter was born.

Richard Potter was a traveling magician or conjurer, but instead of rabbits, he would pull doughnuts out of a hat, after appearing to fry them in the hat. He was also a ventriloquist, and he could throw a squeal into the mouth of a roast pig at an inn table where he was not welcome because of his mulatto color. Potter accumulated some wealth and settled in Andover, New Hampshire, in an area that now bears the name Potter Place. A novel, based on the adventures of Richard Potter and called *Conjuror's Journal,* by Frances Shine of Framingham, was published in 1978.

While stagecoaches plied the roads and turnpikes of South Middlesex, the new breed of manufacturer and merchant was frustrated with the coach's inability to handle large and heavy loads. It was cheaper for a Boston merchant to send a large shipment across the

Above: Fayville welcomed the Marquis de Lafayette as an honored guest during his 1815 journey through New England. The village probably looked much as it did in this 1850s photograph. In the foreground is the small railroad station for the Agricultural Branch Rail Road from Framingham. Courtesy, Southborough Historical Society

Left: Stagecoach service on the turnpikes and other roads of New England was enhanced with the development of the Concord coach. This coach, later used extensively in the American West, made the long, dusty rides more comfortable. From 100 Years Progress, 1874. Courtesy, Framingham Historical Society

Atlantic to Liverpool than to have it hauled the forty miles inland to Worcester. Although this problem would eventually be solved by the railroad, in the 1820s the most promising solution seemed to be canals.

In 1828 the Blackstone River was converted into a navigable canal, connecting Worcester with the seaport of Providence, Rhode Island. Providence was soon connected with New York City via Robert Fulton's new steamboats. This strengthened the commercial importance of Worcester, and consequently the link to Boston through South Middlesex. South Middlesex almost became directly involved with the New England canal system when a canal was proposed to connect Norwich, Connecticut, with the Charles River in South Natick. But canal building was a time-consuming and expensive process requiring long stretches of stone embankment and dozens of water locks along the way. And the resulting barge service was only as fast as the man and horse at the end of the tow rope could walk.

There was also the Middlesex Canal, connecting Boston with the Merrimack River near Lowell. This canal did not come through South Middlesex, but it did have a negative impact when, in 1828, a dam at North Billerica was rebuilt where the canal crossed the Concord River. The new dam backed up the river waters all the way down to the Sudbury River, flooding Sudbury's rich meadowlands. This put an end to the era of meadow hay as a major natural resource for Sudbury and East Sudbury. The flooding, however, made the river plains more suitable for cranberries.

****

The South Middlesex cottage industries were not too concerned with heavy shipping, for their products tended to be lightweight and their production would not amount to more than one cartload in a week. One of these industries, however, would grow out of all proportion to the others once the railroad came through—the manufacturing of shoes. This industry began in South Middlesex in 1793 when Ariel Bragg of Holliston took twenty-two pairs of shoes he had made to Providence and came back with eight dollars profit in his pocket.

Up to this time shoes were made as a sideline by farmers who called themselves "cordwainers." With new markets opening up, many of these shoemakers went into business full time, hiring others and performing their work in small shops called "ten footers." An important improvement in the method of making shoes was developed in 1820 by Joseph Walker of Hopkinton. He perfected the use of small wooden pegs to attach soles to the "uppers," doing away with laborious stitching.

Left: The new method of pegging, rather than stitching, shoe soles to uppers improved productivity, but the process was time-consuming and arduous when done by hand. The pegging method was developed by Joseph Walker of Hopkinton in 1820. From 100 Years Progress, 1874. Courtesy, Framingham Historical Society

Below: The beginnings of the textile industry in South Middlesex are seen in this 1816 ad printed in the Massachusetts Spy and Worcester Gazette. Wool carding machines combed and straightened the fibers for spinning into cloth. Courtesy, Framingham Historical Society

Wool Carding.

JAMES RICE informs his friends and the publick, that he has put his Machines in excellent order for Carding Wool, and tends them himfelf. His Carding Machine is covered with new Cards, and his Picking Machine is entirely new.——Alfo, he has a Machine for Spinning Wool. He flatters himfelf that he fhall not fail of giving fatisfaction to all thofe who may favour him with their cuftom. ☞ It is particularly recommended to Cuftomers to fort their Wool well, before they bring it to the Factory.

Southborough, July 9, 1816.

The mill was often the focal point of the small villages that sprang up throughout New England in the early years of the nineteenth century. Mills were at the heart of South Sudbury, Saxonville, Unionville, and Cordaville in the South Middlesex towns. From Great Industries of New England, *1872. Courtesy, Framingham Historical Society*

In Natick, which was to become the predominant shoe town of South Middlesex, Asa Felch started operations in 1827. In Southborough it was the Newton family. Another early entrepreneur was Captain Enoch Kidder of Sudbury, who built a shoe shop in South Sudbury in 1814. Kidder (1777-1865) had been trained as a tanner. His shop also contained a grocery where villagers would smoke and gossip the evenings away. A patriotic gentleman, Kidder kept two flintlock muskets hanging in his store along with a picture of the Battle of Bunker Hill.

The shoe shops, mills, taverns, livery stables, and dozens of other small enterprises tended to cluster where smaller roads intersected the highways or bridged the mill streams. These clusters became the many villages that were to be more important in everyday life than the towns themselves. Harriet Beecher Stowe, who spent a good deal of time in Natick (the native town of her husband, Calvin Stowe), wrote of New England at this time as "a sort of half Hebrew theocracy, half ultra-democratic republic of little villages."

The villages that evolved in the early nineteenth century established a social and economic network that prevailed for over 100 years. When local newspapers came along they would print news by village, not by town. South Middlesex during this time was not a group of

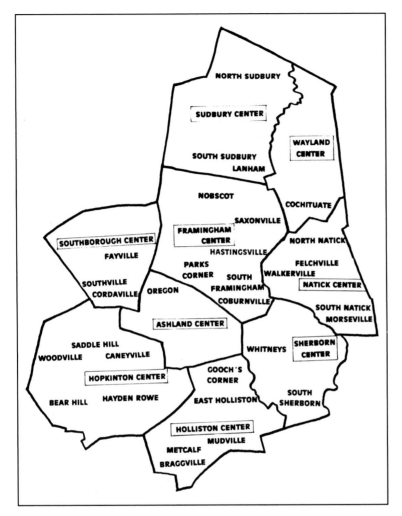

NORTH SUDBURY

SUDBURY CENTER

WAYLAND CENTER

SOUTH SUDBURY
LANHAM

NOBSCOT

COCHITUATE

SAXONVILLE

SOUTHBOROUGH CENTER

FRAMINGHAM CENTER

NORTH NATICK

FAYVILLE

HASTINGSVILLE

PARKS CORNER

FELCHVILLE
WALKERVILLE

SOUTHVILLE
CORDAVILLE

OREGON

SOUTH FRAMINGHAM

NATICK CENTER

COBURNVILLE

SOUTH NATICK
MORSEVILLE

ASHLAND CENTER

SADDLE HILL

WHITNEYS

SHERBORN CENTER

WOODVILLE

CANEYVILLE

HOPKINTON CENTER

GOOCH'S CORNER

BEAR HILL

HAYDEN ROWE

EAST HOLLISTON

SOUTH SHERBORN

HOLLISTON CENTER

MUDVILLE

METCALF

BRAGGVILLE

As commerce and industry grew in the nineteenth century, South Middlesex organized itself into dozens of small villages. Some of these villages remain as familiar town districts, while others are long forgotten. One village, Unionville, became a new town in 1846—the town of Ashland. Courtesy, Framingham Historical Society

eight towns but of about two dozen villages with names like Felchville, Saxonville, Woodville, Braggville, Park's Corner, and Hayden Rowe.

One of the customs of that time was to use signboards at intersections to point out the directions to the various villages, often giving the number of miles. We are fortunate that in one town these guide signs have been preserved for us, in stone. In 1876 Sudbury decided to replace its wooden guide boards with one-ton granite markers. Painted arrows and sometimes pointing fingers guide the traveler to nearby villages and towns, and some stones add historical reminders of the sites of King Philip's War and the route taken by the minutemen to Lexington and Concord. Today there are forty-two such markers in Sudbury, maintained by a town officer called the stone warden.

Though a town might contain several villages, only the central village would have the meetinghouse where both town and church meetings were held. Yet in the time between the Revolutionary War and the official separation of church and state in Massachusetts in 1833,

Abner Wheeler, one of the most successful and enterprising Yankees of Framingham in the early nineteenth century, was a proprietor of the Boston-Worcester Turnpike and Saxonville Mills. He also had a store and ran the hotel at Framingham Center when stagecoaches were the only way to travel. Courtesy, Framingham Historical Society

the idea that one could choose a religion other than that of the established church was taking hold.

Religious diversity had almost become a custom in Hopkinton by the end of the eighteenth century. In addition to the Scotch-Irish Presbyterians and the Anglicans that played a part in its history, Hopkinton had accommodated Baptists, Anabaptists, and one Quaker. They had a Methodist church in Hayden Rowe by 1810, and later many relatives of Brigham Young would follow him to the Mormon Zion in Utah.

The Methodist and Baptist churches were the first major alternatives to the established Congregational church in South Middlesex. Two of the earliest Methodist societies in New England were formed in the 1790s—in Framingham, and in Holliston, where services were held in a barn.

Baptist preaching in Framingham can be traced back as far as 1757. In 1772 Ebenezer Marshall opened the upper room of his tavern at Park's Corner for Baptist services. An important person in Framingham's history was the Reverend Charles Train (1783-1849), who was ordained a Baptist minister in 1811. He served in many town offices, and as a state representative and state senator as well. His son, Charles R. Train (1817-1885), was a U.S. representative, Middlesex County district attorney, and Massachusetts attorney general. In the third generation, Arthur Train (1875-1945) gained national attention as a writer and author of the popular Mr. Tutt stories that appeared regularly in the *Saturday Evening Post*. In 1931 Arthur Train wrote of his New England heritage in a book called *Puritan's Progress*.

The new wealth coming into South Middlesex and the division of labor used in the new manufacturing ventures created a Yankee middle class that would grow and dominate during the balance of the nineteenth century. From this middle class would come a profusion of cultural and social organizations that would flourish in later Victorian times. In the early part of the century these organizations began as missionary aid and charity societies. One such organization was the Female Benevolent Society of Framingham, founded in 1814 to afford aid to the indigent and to disseminate religious information. The unusual feature of this society was its provision for paying dues in straw braid. To join, one had to pay seventy-five cents, or thirty yards of straw braid. Annual dues were thirty-seven cents or fifteen yards of braid.

In 1816 a Female Reading and Benevolent Society was formed in Sherborn. And in 1822 the Female Society of Framingham and Vicinity for Promoting Christianity Among the Jews was founded with annual dues of fifty-two cents.

Typical activities of these early societies were captured in the diary of a Mrs. Webster of Hopkinton, shown in the following extracts:

June 11 We have a new organization in the Missionary Society. The ladies appear to take hold of it with interest.

Saturday, 15th. Met the "Children's Mite Society" at 2. Fifty-seven children present. They brought contributions to the amount of $2.30.

April 7 The Ladies' Missionary Society met here this afternoon.

March 10 The young ladies of our Sunday School have recently formed a benevolent society to meet semi-monthly, and braid straw, and appropriate the avails of their work to getting clothing for destitute children, that they may attend the Sabbath school.

These early "female" organizations would evolve into the powerful antislavery, temperance, and women's rights movements of the nineteenth and twentieth centuries.

The men were more attracted to fraternal organizations. One of the earliest in South Middlesex was the Middlesex Lodge of Free and Accepted Masons, instituted in 1795. The ceremony was conducted by Paul Revere, Grand Master of the Grand Massachusetts Lodge, at the home of Esquire Jonathan Maynard, first master of the new lodge in Framingham.

Jonathan Maynard (1752-1835), according to legend, owed his life to his Masonic affiliation. During the Revolutionary War Maynard was captured near West Point in upstate New York by Mohawk Indian allies of the British. The Indian chief was Joseph Brant, who had been educated among the English and had actually become a Mason himself. Maynard, as the story goes, was about to be burned at the stake when he made the Masonic sign of distress. Brant recognized the signal and released his brother Mason unharmed.

The Middlesex Lodge was joined later by other Masonic lodges, plus Knights of Pythias, Knights Templar, Odd Fellows, and many others. But this social evolution of the Yankee middle class would not occur until many more lawyers, bankers, doctors, merchants, and other professionals and businessmen made their appearance. The real growth of this middle class did not begin until railroads brought new business, new labor, and a new age.

Top: The Reverend Charles Train, Framingham's Baptist minister, was also a teacher, preceptor of the Framingham Academy, state representative, and orator. One of his sons became attorney general of Massachusetts. Courtesy, Framingham Historical Society

Above: Jonathan Maynard was Framingham's first postmaster, and the first master of the Middlesex Lodge of Masons. As a justice of the peace for many years, he was often known as Squire Maynard. A school and street in Framingham were named in his honor. Courtesy, Framingham Historical Society

3 AGE OF STEAM, SWEAT, AND BLOOD (1830-1865)

The transition from Puritan to Yankee control of South Middlesex was completed around 1830 when the grip of the old Puritan church was broken by the legal separation of church and state. Although Massachusetts did not make the separation official until 1833, the towns were divesting church property to newly created and independent parishes as early as 1820. After almost two hundred years, town warrants would no longer contain questions relating to ministers' salaries and church buildings.

The old Puritan church was further weakened as other denominations drew off members. Methodist and Baptist churches continued to grow. Immigrants from Britain and Europe brought traditions of worship from their homelands and started Episcopal, Presbyterian, Lutheran, and Roman Catholic churches. Intellectual stirrings within America, particularly in the Boston area, spawned new churches, such as the Universalist and the Unitarian.

The ministers and deacons of the old church did not take this challenge lying down. They regrouped and reorganized. The Andover Theological Seminary became the intellectual headquarters of a revitalized church that at first used the name Evangelical, then became generally known as Congregational. While avoiding the term "Puritan," this denomination kept its ties to the early days of New England by giving its churches such names as Pilgrim, Plymouth, and Mayflower. In South Middlesex there is a Plymouth church in Framingham, and Pilgrim churches in Sherborn and Southborough.

In many South Middlesex towns the Congregational churches were forced to vacate the buildings and property that had been used by the Puritans for generations. In each parish the number of full church members (those who had accepted the covenant) was usually a minority. The parish majorities were inclined to a more liberal doctrine, and the new Unitarian view seemed the most generally acceptable. The Unitarians took over the existing church property in Framingham, Sudbury, Wayland, Sherborn, and Southborough, usually taking the name First Parish. Congregationalists held forth in Natick, Holliston, and Hopkinton. In Holliston the Unitarians were organized for a period

The railroad would spark a transformation in South Middlesex social and economic life as it supplanted the turnpike and the stagecoach as the preferred mode of transportation. The first trains through South Middlesex looked more like lines of stagecoaches. The locomotive in this 1835 illustration is similar to the six-ton "Yankee"--the first used on the Boston and Worcester line. It burned wood, and the engineer stood in the open without protection. From 100 Years Progress, *1874. Courtesy, Framingham Historical Society*

as the Third Parish. In Southborough the Unitarian hold was short-lived. By the 1850s the dwindling Unitarian organization returned the church and its property to the growing Pilgrim Congregational church.

The phenomenon of popularity that the Unitarians enjoyed in the 1830s, and which contributed to the "great schism" in the church, did not reach far beyond eastern Massachusetts. This led some pundits to make the irreverent claim that the Unitarians believed in "the fatherhood of God, the brotherhood of man, and the neighborhood of Boston."

In those towns where the Unitarians were successful, actual church membership was small and there was difficulty maintaining the buildings. A new, smaller church was built in Framingham. In Sudbury the Unitarian Reverend Linus Shaw could not live on his minister's salary, so he ran a candy factory near his home. While the factory is long gone, children continue to be intrigued by the name given to the street it was on—Candy Hill Road.

One of the ministers who studied at the Andover Theological Seminary was the Reverend Francis Wayland (1796-1865), who later became a leading figure in the Baptist Church and president of Brown University in Rhode Island. Although the Reverend Wayland was never a minister in any South Middlesex town, he was honored by East Sudbury in 1835 when that town changed its name to Wayland.

Francis Wayland was admired by and a friend of East Sudbury lawyer and judge Edward Mellen (1802-1875), a Brown University graduate. (Judge Mellen's small white lawyer's office still stands at Wayland Center.) A gift from Francis Wayland in 1849 helped create the Wayland public library.

Wayland was one of the towns with a parish that elected to go with the Unitarians. Thus Wayland's handsome 1815 Christopher Wren-style edifice with its Paul Revere bell became a Unitarian church, while the Congregationalists (calling themselves Trinitarians) built a new church a few yards down the road. One of the Unitarian ministers of Wayland, the Reverend Edmund H. Sears, was also a literary editor, poet, and somewhat of a mystic. In 1849 he wrote a poem that began, "It Came Upon the Midnight Clear." The poem was later set to music and has become one of the most popular of Christmas hymns.

****

At the same time that the religious life of South Middlesex was being transformed by the separation of church and state and the Unitarian movement, another force was taking shape that would

Above: The Reverend Francis Wayland, after whom the town of Wayland was named, was also closely associated with Rhode Island as president of Brown University in Providence. Courtesy, Brown University Library

Above left: This circa 1840 wood-cut shows Framingham Center's village green framed by the two churches created by the Unitarian schism of ten years before. The orthodox Trinitarian church is on the left, and the Unitarian First Parish is on the right. In the center is the town hall, and at the right in the distance, partly hidden by the First Parish Church, is Framingham Academy, recently founded as a college preparatory school. Courtesy, Framingham Historical Society

transform its social and economic life as well.

In the early 1830s three railroads reached Lowell, Worcester, and Providence simultaneously like spokes from the hub of Boston. The route to Worcester passed through Natick Center and two villages in the southern part of Framingham (Clark's Corner and Park's Corner). It then swung south, crossed the river near Shepherd's paper mill and passed through a village in the east part of Hopkinton called Unionville. From there it traveled along the edge of Fiddle Neck through Southborough.

The original plan for the Boston and Worcester Railroad called for the track to pass through Framingham Center. But the Wheeler brothers and others with interests in the turnpike and stagecoach lines opposed the plan, and the track was laid two miles farther south. There is a story that the directors of the new railroad visited the villages along the route to determine the best locations for stations. In Framingham they had to choose between Clark's Corner and Park's Corner. It is said that they chose Clark's Corner because the meal served by Captain Clark was superior to the meal provided at Park's Corner. While this makes for a good story, it is much more likely that the nearness of Farm Pond as a water supply for the many thirsty locomotives that would pass through every day was of greater importance in the decision. Once the choice was made, Clark's Corner was destined to become the thriving industrial and commercial center known as South Framingham, and later as downtown Framingham.

The Wheeler brothers had no way of knowing that the ability of this new invention to whisk passengers and freight in and out of Boston and to the West would cause the turnpike companies to fail and the stagecoach lines to wither. Natick's historian Oliver Bacon, who

Wayland's Edward Mellen by about 1844 was already a lawyer, library benefactor, and chief justice of the Court of Common Pleas. It was probably his admiration for the Reverend Francis Wayland that prompted him to suggest Wayland as a new name for the town when it was called East Sudbury. Courtesy, Wayland Historical Society

lived through the transition from turnpikes to railroads, expressed his feelings in a poem that begins:

The old turnpike is a pike no more,
Wide open stands the gate.
We have made us a road for our horse to stride,
Which we ride at a flying rate.

Construction of the railroad reached South Middlesex in 1834 and was completed to Worcester in 1835. New banks were formed to finance new businesses. Among the new businesses were hotels designed to cater to the railroad trade. One of the first of these railroad hotels was built by Captain John Stone (1779-1858) in Unionville. The opening of the railroad as far as Unionville must have been considered some form of milestone, as there was a big celebration attended by 300 townspeople and such dignitaries as Daniel Webster and Governor Levi Lincoln. After the arrival of the train and the speeches there was a "collation" (probably a buffet lunch) at Stone's Hotel.

Captain John Stone of Unionville was a descendant of the John Stone who was one of the first proprietors of Sudbury and the first settler of Framingham. Captain Stone ran his hotel for only a few years. After that, for most of the nineteenth century it was known as Scott's Hotel. Following a long period of private use during the twentieth century it was reopened as John Stone's Inn, a popular restaurant complete with a ghost said to be that of old Captain John Stone himself.

The railroad did not bring overnight success and prosperity to South Middlesex. As the proprietors of the Massachusetts Bay Company had realized two centuries before, great resources cannot be turned into great profits without plenty of people. This problem was solved when, in the 1840s and 1850s, a new wave of European immigrants found jobs and opportunity in the towns along the routes of the railroad. The towns that especially benefited from this influx were those involved with shoe and boot manufacturing—Holliston, Hopkinton, and Natick. During this period the population of Natick actually quadrupled, and by 1865 Natick could boast eighty-five shoe shops and factories, mainly at Natick Center and Felchville.

Most of the immigrants at that time were Irish, driven from their homeland by land evictions and a terrible potato blight. It is estimated that by 1875 over 200,000 Irish had arrived at Boston seeking jobs and homes. Many thousands of these found their way to South Middlesex, where employment was found on the farms, in the shoe shops, and in the growing number of textile mills. In 1846 a branch railroad was

BOSTON AND WORCESTER RAIL ROAD.

THE Passenger Cars will continue to run daily from the Depot near Washington street, to Newton, at 6 and 10 o'clock, A.M. and at 3½ o'clock, P. M. and

Returning, leave Newton at 7 and a quarter past 11, A.M. and a quarter before 5, P.M.

Tickets for the passage either way may be had at the Ticket Office, No. 617, Washington street ; price 37½ cents each ; and for the return passage, of the Master of the Cars Newton.

By order of the President and Directors.
a 29   epistf   F. A. WILLIAMS, Clerk.

Above: Every Christmas, the hymn "It Came Upon the Midnight Clear" is sung at the Unitarian First Parish Church of Wayland because it was written, as a poem, by their mid-nineteenth-century minister, the Reverend Edmund H. Sears. Courtesy, Wayland Historical Society

Left: The introduction of the Boston and Worcester Rail Road in 1835 brought tremendous changes to the quiet, rural towns. Hotels, factories, and new homes were being built even before the first train came through. Courtesy, Framingham Historical Society

constructed from Natick Center to Saxonville in Framingham, where a substantial Irish community developed. Here the parish of Saint George was established.

By 1847 another branch railroad, planned to run from Framingham to Milford, was built as far as Holliston. To push the railroad beyond Holliston Center required the construction of a tunnel and a stone-arched bridge, and these projects brought many Irish laborers to Holliston. The Irish settled in a district near Holliston Center to be known as Mudville.

In addition to the Irish, many Germans were among the immigrants of the 1840s and 1850s. A neighborhood of Germans in the shoemaking village of Cochituate in Wayland was called German Hill. (German Hill Road remained as a reminder of that village until World War I, when anti-German sentiment brought about a change of name to Pemberton Road.)

****

It was during the 1840s and 1850s that the villages of Fiddle Neck in Southborough came into being. To the west of Fiddle Neck lay Southville, a shoe- and boot-making center. To the east, Milton H. Sanford built factories where he manufactured wool blankets. The village that grew around these factories may well have been called Sanfordville, but Milton Sanford preferred to honor his wife, Cordelia,

The Framingham Hotel was located on the turnpike at Framingham Center, but in 1835—a year after the railroad's introduction—the hotel had to offer stagecoach service to the new railroad depot at South Framingham two miles away. This hotel remained in business until about 1930. Courtesy, Framingham Historical Society

FRAMINGHAM HOTEL,

BY R. P. ANGIER. THE SUB-scriber, returns his thanks to his friends and the Public, for their former *patronage* and would inform them that he is " *at home,*" and will be happy to wait on them to *every thing kept in a good Public-House.*

He has made arrangements to have CAR-RIAGES in readiness at the **DEPOT**, of the Boston and Worcester Rail-Road, in *Framingham*, to convey persons to the Village and Saxonville, Daily. Fare to the Village 25 cents, to Saxonville, 50 cents.

He can accommodate *a few* BOARDERS, with private rooms, per day or week.

At his *LIVERY STABLE, Horses* and *Carriages*, at reasonable rate, can be had at *command.*

R. P. ANGIER.

Framingham, May 9, '35.   tf   2

by having the village called Cordaville.

A few miles down the Sudbury River from Fiddle Neck were the mills of Unionville. One of these mills, which produced cotton cloth, was run by the Middlesex Union Factory Company. The manager of this mill was James Jackson (1795-1864), an ardent Whig and supporter of Henry Clay. Jackson was one of the first of the leading men of Unionville to see the need for a new town. Unionville, as a village of Hopkinton, was remote from the town center, and it enjoyed a new independence provided by the railroad. On the other hand, Unionville was hemmed in by Framingham to the north and Holliston to the east, which limited its future expansion.

Jackson's first attempt to form a new town was in 1837. His

petition crumbled under the opposition of all three existing towns and many local residents. By 1846 the political and legal issues among the towns were worked out, and a larger proportion of residents signed a new petition. An act of incorporation for a new town was passed and went into effect on March 16, 1846. James Jackson's idol, Henry Clay—the man who ran for president four times and who said he would rather be right than president—provided the inspiration for the new town's name. Clay lived on a large estate in Kentucky called Ashland. In honor of the great Whig, the new town took the name Ashland as its own. Ashland encompassed the village of Unionville plus thousands of acres from surrounding Hopkinton, Holliston, and Framingham. It was the ninth and last of the South Middlesex towns to be incorporated.

When Ashland came into being, some property of the older towns suddenly came within the boundaries of the new town. Holliston's poor farm, for example, found itself in east Ashland, but Holliston was content to leave it there. Ten years later Ashland put its own poor farm in the same neighborhood as Holliston's.

While Holliston was happy to leave its poor farm in Ashland, some Hopkinton residents were not as pleased about losing their fire engine. The hand tub was originally purchased by Hopkinton but was included in the settlement with the new town. Some Hopkintonites took it upon themselves, however, to reappropriate the fire engine in the middle of the night. It was later returned under a court order. Ashland eventually purchased another pumper and named it "Magunko", after the old praying Indian village that fell within its boundaries.

The incorporation of Ashland took hundreds of residents away

Extending the Framingham and Milford Railroad beyond Holliston in 1847 required special feats of civil engineering such as the construction of this railroad bridge in southern Holliston. This work brought many of the newly arrived Irish from Boston to settle in Holliston. Courtesy, Holliston Historical Society

63

The last of the nine South Middlesex towns to be incorporated was Ashland, carved from Hopkinton, Holliston, and Framingham in 1846. The name was inspired by Henry Clay's Kentucky estate, also called Ashland. Courtesy, Town of Ashland

from Hopkinton, along with the only railroad that had entered Hopkinton up to that time. In spite of this, Hopkinton's population doubled between 1840 and 1860. By the 1850s Hopkinton was employing about 1,000 people in the shoe and boot industry, doing over one million dollars' worth of business each year. Hopkinton would hold onto its position as second largest of the South Middlesex towns into the 1860s.

The shoe industry grew rapidly in South Middlesex through the increased labor supply brought by immigration, by the specialization of tasks, and through the development of machines to help perform the work. Steam power was then introduced to run the machines and increase production. This caused the shoemakers to move from their small shops to increasingly larger wooden factories. Another industry that moved from the cottage to the factory during this period was straw braid and bonnet manufacturing. As a cottage industry, the straw was worked mainly by women, and this was continued in the straw factories. In Framingham in 1855 straw braid and bonnet factories employed 300 women and only fifteen men.

While shoe and straw factories were multiplying in the 1840s, the waterpowered mills experienced their first setback at the hands of a powerful and ever more thirsty city of Boston. The small ponds in the Boston area were failing to meet the growing demand for fresh water, and engineers were sent out to find suitable bodies of water in the countryside. In 1846 a chain of lakes called Long Pond, connecting Wayland, Framingham, and Natick, was selected and taken over by law. The outlet of the lake was dammed up, knocking out the waterpower for three carpet mills owned by William A. Knight (1792-1870) in Framingham. Knight had been building up the mills since his poorer days in 1830, when his wife had fished for their supper by lowering a hook from their living quarters above the mill into the running waters of the brook below. Knight was given $150,000 to compensate for the loss of his mills, but 132 mill hands found themselves out of work.

The promoters of the new water supply wanted to give some romance to the enterprise. So they had the name of the lake changed from Long Pond to Lake Cochituate, using an old local Indian name. In 1848 Cochituate water was introduced into Boston with great fanfare, including the publication of a new song, "The Grand Cochituate Quick Step."

As the economy of South Middlesex grew and immigrants supplied farm and factory labor, the old Yankee stock became more middle-class in their ways. They built new homes, schools, churches, and town halls resembling classical Greek temples. The main road through Holliston Center was lined with large and impressive homes displaying the wealth of the owners and managers of the shoe and straw factories. Even some shoe factories of the period sported pillared Greek porticos.

Academies were formed for the higher education of the children. There was the Holliston Academy, the Hopkinton Academy, the Framingham Academy, the Sherborn Academy, and in Sudbury, the Wadsworth Academy. For culture, there were lyceums for guest lecturers and debating societies. In the 1850s libraries cropped up in almost every town when the state allowed local taxes to be used for public libraries. It was Wayland's state representative, the Reverend John Burt Wight, who introduced the legislation that made public libraries possible in Massachusetts. (One of the earliest public library buildings in South Middlesex still in use as a library is the small, octagonal Goodnow Public Library in Sudbury, built in 1862. This building has been fully enclosed within later additions and is now known as the Octagon Room.) Other state legislation in the 1850s provided for public high schools. As these high schools were formed they often absorbed the existing academies.

The importance of providing trained and qualified teachers for the public schools of Massachusetts was recognized by the state in 1839, when it began creating a system of "normal schools." These teachers' colleges offered a two-year course of instruction for women to prepare them to teach in any school system in the state. The first of these normal schools was established at Lexington. The need to expand forced this school to move first to West Newton in 1844, then to Framingham in 1853. The move to Framingham was encouraged by offers of land and building funds from the town and local citizens.

The State Normal School at Framingham (today's Framingham State College) found its permanent home in Framingham Center at the top of a steep hill called Bare Hill. A century and a half before, sentinels had stood on this hill watching for Indians while Sunday services were being held in the meetinghouse below. After 1853 the hill became known as Normal Hill.

While the new industries and institutions were getting all the attention, farming was still the bedrock of South Middlesex life. In 1840 agricultural pursuits employed 715 adult male workers in Framingham, while 463 men were involved in manufacturing. Sixteen received Revolutionary War pensions as a means of support, fifteen were doctors or lawyers, three were in the navigation trade, and six were judged insane or idiotic.

William A. Knight, seen here circa 1840 in a carte de visite *photograph, owned several mills on Cochituate Brook in Framingham. In the mid-1840s his mills were closed when the City of Boston took over Lake Cochituate as a source of fresh water. Courtesy, Framingham Historical Society*

Above: The specialized tasks of shoe factory workers are illustrated on this 1862 Hopkinton Bank note, reflecting the importance of that industry locally in the nineteenth century. Courtesy, Hopkinton Public Library

Right: The new technology of the textile industry required fewer workers than shoe and straw factories, as this 1843 illustration shows. Tending the looms was an occupation suitable for women and children. From Handbook of Silk, Cotton and Woolen Manufacturers, 1843. Courtesy, Framingham Historical Society

The farmers were also moving with the times. They kept up with the latest equipment and methods by reading such regional publications as *The Massachusetts Ploughman*, and by organizing into such groups as the Middlesex South Agricultural Society (founded in 1854) and the Grange.

The Massachusetts Ploughman was edited by William Buckminster (1784-1865) of Framingham, a descendant of the Buckminsters who leased most of Danforth's Farms. At first William Buckminster practiced law, but it was said that his temper got the better of him in the courtroom. He found his niche in the field of agricultural improvements. In addition to his work on the *Ploughman*, Buckminster invented a corn planter in 1839, and he was the first president of the Middlesex South Agricultural Society. Another early president of the agricultural society was Elias Grout (1816-1894), a gentleman farmer and teacher from Ashland who traveled through the antebellum South to buy cotton for Yankee mills.

The classical Greek style is strongly represented in Wayland's old town hall, built in 1841. Nevertheless, the building has served many purposes: this 1900 view shows it as Lovell's Market, and after that it was for many years known as Collins Market. Courtesy, Wayland Historical Society

****

On the political side, in the 1830s and 1840s the Yankee middle class of South Middlesex leaned toward the Whig party. Many local leaders, such as James Jackson of Ashland and Enoch Kidder of Sudbury, were active in Whig politics. The most remarkable of all Whig leaders in South Middlesex was Henry Wilson (1812-1875) of Natick,

Above: Women in 1894 had few career options open to them, but teaching was one of them. These students at the State Normal School at Framingham listen attentively as they prepare to become schoolteachers. Courtesy, Framingham Historical Society

Right: The short-lived Wadsworth Academy in Sudbury, opened in 1857, had been in operation for only a few years when the Greek-temple-like building burned down. From History of Sudbury, 1889. *Courtesy, Goodnow Public Library, Sudbury*

Far right: The will of John Goodnow provided funds to build this small, octagonal library in South Sudbury. The building is now one room within a much enlarged structure, still serving as the Goodnow Public Library. From History of Sudbury, 1889. *Courtesy, Goodnow Public Library, Sudbury*

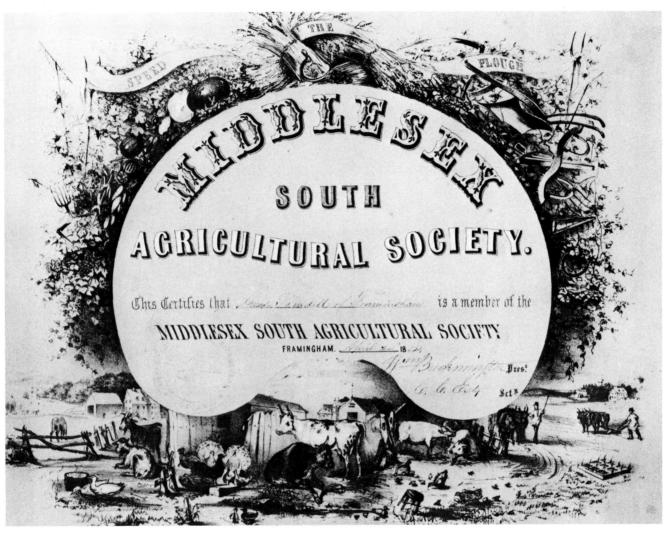

whose political career would take him to the United States Senate and the office of Vice President of the United States.

Henry Wilson's political drive was propelled by strong antislavery feelings that may have been rooted in his own experience as an indentured farm laborer. He was born in Farmington, New Hampshire, and given the name Jeremiah Jones Colbath. In 1833, when his indentured servitude was satisfied, he changed his name and walked one hundred miles to Natick to seek his fortune in the new shoe industry. By learning the trade from the bottom up and extending his education at various academies, Wilson was soon running his own shoe factory, employing up to 109 workers. The tiny shop where Henry Wilson began his shoemaking career can still be seen in West Natick. In 1840 the same spirit of Whig hoopla that elected William Henry Harrison president with the slogan, "Tippicanoe and Tyler Too," got Henry Wilson elected to the Massachusetts legislature with the nickname Natick Cobbler.

One of the first truly regional organizations of South Middlesex was the Middlesex South Agricultural Society, formed in 1854. For many years its annual cattle fair was held at what is now Bowditch Field on Union Avenue in Framingham, and for years the second day of this cattle show was a school holiday in Framingham public schools. Courtesy, Framingham Historical Society

Henry Wilson of Natick, circa 1856, just after "the Natick Cobbler" had switched from the Whig to the Republican party. Wilson had just become a United States senator and would later serve as vice president under President Ulysses Grant. From History of Natick, 1856. *Courtesy, Framingham Historical Society*

In 1848 Massachusetts Whigs were offended when the national Whig party nominated General Zachary Taylor, a slave owner from Louisiana, for the presidency. At this turn of events, Henry Wilson was one of many Whigs who deserted the party for the Free Soil party, a forerunner of the Republican party. In an attempt to unify the party, Whig leaders sent a popular Illinois "stump speaker" and Whig congressman on a speaking tour of Massachusetts. Abraham Lincoln spoke in Worcester and probably passed through South Middlesex on his way to his next engagement in New Bedford. But both Abraham Lincoln and Henry Wilson would wind up in the Republican party. Wilson was already a U.S. senator when Lincoln failed to attain that office after his famous debates with Senator Stephen A. Douglas. Under President Lincoln, Wilson was chairman of the Senate Military Committee, a position of great responsibility during the Civil War. After the war, Wilson was one of the congressmen who led the move to remove President Andrew Johnson by impeachment.

In 1872, when he had spent eighteen years in the Senate, Wilson was called upon to replace the affable Schuyler "Smiler" Colfax in the vice presidential slot of the Republican ticket headed by Ulysses S. Grant. Vice President Colfax had been tainted by the corruptions and scandals of Grant's first term. Grant and Wilson easily defeated the Democratic ticket, headed by New York publisher Horace Greeley. Vice President Wilson's term was cut short when he suffered a stroke in 1875. The Natick cobbler died in Washington on November 22 of that year. He is buried at Dell Park Cemetery in Natick. Henry Wilson's house still stands on West Central Street, in the Henry Wilson Historic District of Natick.

In South Middlesex during the 1850s, Henry Wilson's voice was not alone in the mounting outcry against slavery. The pleasant female benevolent societies of earlier years and the lyceum debating groups evolved into rather militant antislavery organizations. One of the earliest of these organizations was founded in 1836 by Edward Walcott (1810-1876) of Natick.

It is presumed that Walcott, who had made a fortune in the shoe business, was also involved in the illegal smuggling of slaves from the South to Canada, known as the Underground Railroad. Slaves were concealed on Walcott's property, then hidden under a load of produce to be hauled to the next "station" on the route to freedom. From Natick the next stop was in Sudbury, at the barn of Israel How Brown. This barn was not far from the shoe shop where Enoch Kidder was holding antislavery meetings and working to establish the Republican party in Sudbury. From Sudbury, Israel Brown transported the slaves, hidden in the false bottom of a wagon, to the next stop in Lancaster.

When Edward Walcott's house was torn down in 1930, its place in the history of the Underground Railroad was further confirmed with the discovery of a forgotten tunnel underneath. Many other houses and buildings in South Middlesex have reputed connections with the Underground Railroad. These include John Stone's Inn in Ashland, where a secret basement room was found during recent renovations.

Another influential abolitionist in South Middlesex was Lydia Marie Child (1802-1880), who had moved to Wayland in 1852 to care for her aged father. Lydia Child was a well established writer and poet, best remembered for her "Thanksgiving poem" that starts, "Over the river and through the woods to Grandfather's house we go." She spent most of her life engaged in antislavery activities and other liberal causes. And she found Wayland a pleasant retreat from the clamor of New York and Boston, where she often traveled in her work.

A friend of Child's was William Lloyd Garrison, perhaps the most famous of all abolitionists. He was publisher of *The Liberator*, a radical antislavery newspaper in Boston. The most dramatic and outrageous act in Garrison's long career was his public burning of a copy of the U.S. Constitution. He denounced the Constitution for its recognition of the institution of slavery. It is not generally known that the occasion Garrison selected for his act of defiance that shocked the nation was an antislavery rally in Framingham. The rally was held on July 4, 1854, at Harmony Grove, a pleasure park with a large natural amphitheater near the shores of Farm Pond. Today the site of Harmony Grove is marked with a plaque bearing the words: ANTISLAVERY ROSTRUM.

While abolitionist feelings were strongly expressed in South Middlesex, these feelings did not necessarily represent the majority. On one occasion abolitionist Henry C. Wright wrote a fiery antislavery statement called the Natick Resolution, because he happened to be visiting in Natick at the time. A mass meeting was soon held to disassociate the town from the statement. Southborough's Moses Sawin resigned from the church when the membership declined to "testify against the sin of slavery." Daniel S. Whitney, a Southborough evangelist and abolitionist, was once accosted with the accusation, "Mr. Whitney, you have nigger on the brain!"

The abolitionist movement was one of many forces that culminated at the end of the 1850s in the Civil War. During the four years of that terrible conflict over 2,500 men from the nine South Middlesex towns saw service in either the army or navy. This represented over 10 percent of the entire population of the region. Of those who served, over 200 died of wounds or disease. At least two South Middlesex men

Edward Walcott made his fortune in shoe manufacturing in Natick, and then turned his attention to the anti-slavery movement. As a participant in the Underground Railroad during the 1850s, he harbored runaway slaves in his house before they were secretly transported to the next "station" in Sudbury, the barn of Israel How Brown, and then to Lancaster. From History of Natick, 1856. Courtesy, Framingham Historical Society

Above: Couples and families enjoyed afternoons at Harmony Grove, a commercial pleasure park opened on the shores of Farm Pond at South Framingham in the 1850s. Harmony Grove was also the site of antislavery and temperance rallies. In the 1890s Harmony Grove became a railroad yard and housing development.

Right: The program for the Washington's birthday service at Plymouth Church in Framingham in 1862 included singing Julia Ward Howe's "Battle Hymn of the Republic." This occasion is presumed to be the first public singing of this famous Civil War tune. Courtesy, Framingham Historical Society

The 130th Anniversary

OF THE

Birth-day of Washington,

AS COMMEMORATED AT

FRAMINGHAM,

SATURDAY EVENING, FEB. 22, 1862.

PROCLAMATION BY THE PRESIDENT.

National observance of Birth-day of Geo. Washington.

WASHINGTON, Feb. 19. By the President of the United States A Proclamation.

It is recommended to the people of the United States, that they assemble in their customary places of meeting for public solemnities on the 22d day of February instant, and celebrate the anniversary of the birth of the Father of his country, by causing to be read to them his immortal Farewell Address.

Given under my hand, and the seal of the United States.

ABRAHAM LINCOLN.

By the President—WM. H. SEWARD, Secretary of State.

Clergymen taking part in the Exercises.

Rev. J. C. BODWELL.
" J. A. GOODHUE.
" B. G. NORTHROP.
" J. H. PETTENGILL.
" S. D. ROBBINS.

S. B. WILDE, Printer, Framingham Centre.

VOLUNTARY.

SINGING—Italian Hymn.
PRAYER. By Rev. J. A. Goodhue.
SINGING. WASHINGTON.

To Thee, beneath whose eye,
Each circling century
Obedient rolls,
Our nation, in its prime,
Looked with a faith sublime,
And trusted in—" the time
That tried men's souls."

Nor was our Fathers' trust,
Thou Mighty One and Just,
Then put to shame;
" Up to the hills " for light,
Looked they in perils night,
And from you guardian light,
Deliverance came.

Then, like an angel form,
Sent down to still the storm,
Stood WASHINGTON!
Clouds broke and rolled away;
Foes fled in pale dismay;
Wreathed were his brows with bay,
When war was done!

God of our sires and sons,
Let other Washingtons
Our country bless;
And, like the brave and wise,
Of by-gone centuries,
So now that true greatness lies
In Righteousness.

Reading of Washington's Farewell Address.
By Mr. George N. Bigelow.

SINGING— Hail Columbia.

ADDRESSES.

Reading of Holmes' Poem—" Voyage of the good ship Union."
By Mr. Francis Jaques.

" BATTLE HYMN OF THE REPUBLIC."

MINE eyes have seen the glory of the coming of the Lord :
He is trampling out the vintage where the grapes of wrath are stored :
He has loosed the fateful lightning of His terrible swift sword :
His truth is marching on.

I have seen Him in the watch-fires of a hundred circling camps,
They have builded Him an altar in the evening dews and damps;
I can read His righteous sentence by the dim and flaring lamps:
His day is marching on.

He has sounded forth the trumpet that shall never call retreat;
He is sifting out the hearts of men before His judgment-seat:
Oh, be swift, my soul, to answer Him! be jubilant, my feet!
Our God is marching on.

In the beauty of the lilies Christ was born across the sea,
With a glory in his bosom that transfigures you and me:
As he died to make men holy, let us die to make men free,
While God is marching on.

Addresses.   Singing—Star Spangled Banner.
Singing—Old Hundred.   BENEDICTION.

died at the infamous Confederate prison camp at Andersonville, Georgia: Thomas Taber of Sherborn and Curtis Smith of Sudbury.

It is said that the women of Holliston often went right to the field hospitals and camps in the South to retrieve their wounded or sick men. In Framingham women organized themselves into the Ladies' Sanitary Commission to prepare boxes of food and other necessities for the wounded and sick. When Julia Ward Howe's poem, "The Battle Hymn of the Republic," was published in 1862, it was first publicly sung at the Framingham Plymouth Church at a Washington's birthday service.

It was during the Civil War that Henry Wadsworth Longfellow's *Tales of a Wayside Inn* was published, bringing lasting fame to Sudbury's Red Horse Tavern and rousing the patriotism of a nation at war with its stirring "Midnight Ride of Paul Revere."

For all its tragedy, the Civil War did bring business to South Middlesex. The Saxonville Mills of Framingham turned out thousands of yards of blue kersey cloth for Union uniforms. Both Saxonville and Cordaville were major suppliers of army blankets for the troops and their horses.

As the Civil War came to an end, soldiers returned from the battlefields and went back into the factories. New markets opened up in the West, and the Yankee middle class was ready to enter a new phase of Victorian prosperity.

Abolitionist, poet, and writer Lydia M. Child lived in this house in Wayland from 1852 to 1880. She is best known for her poem "Over the River and Through the Woods." Courtesy, Wayland Historical Society

4 AGE OF BUSTLES AND BASEBALLS (1865-1900)

After the Civil War, while the attention of the nation was drawn to the West and the expansion of the railroad across the continent, plenty of railroad construction was going on back in New England. In 1865 a branch connecting South Framingham with Northborough was extended to Fitchburg. Two years later the old Boston and Worcester Railroad linked up with other lines to the west and became the Boston and Albany. Around 1870 new lines from South Framingham reached the great textile city of Lowell to the northeast and Mansfield to the southeast, connecting with lines to Taunton and New Bedford.

South Framingham had become a railroad hub with lines going off in six directions, a fact that was represented in the town seal adopted in 1900 showing railroad tracks as the spokes of a wagon wheel. By 1885 there were one hundred trains stopping at South Framingham every day. In 1871 the Hopkinton Railroad linked the Boston and Albany line at Ashland with Hopkinton Center, then went farther south to Milford and Providence.

As the railroads were branching out, so was Boston's demand for fresh water. In 1875 the waters of the Sudbury River and Framingham's Farm Pond were taken over by the state, and work began on a three-year project to construct large reservoirs along the Sudbury River in Framingham and Ashland. The state took 851 acres of farm and meadowland for this purpose.

Ashland industry was particularly hard hit by the land seizure. Cutler's Mills was one of several businesses forced to relocate or close down. A major new industry planned for Ashland was a factory that would bleach, dye, and print patterns on cloth for the big Jordan Marsh department store in Boston. Several expensive stone buildings had already been erected when it was learned that the Sudbury River, as a water supply, could not be used for the disposal of the dyes and bleaches. So the operation never began.

Stonecutting and masonry skills were required for the building of reservoirs and stone railroad bridges. Laborers were drawn from many of the Italian families that were arriving at Boston, as southern and eastern Europe joined the great exodus to America. Today the

Downtown Hopkinton in 1890 offered pleasant shopping, as seen in this idealized Victorian view from a pamphlet promoting local business. However, before the era of paved streets, the downtown area was frequently choked with dust or mired in mud. Courtesy, Framingham Historical Society

Right: Railroad expansion began in earnest after the Civil War, and the Framingham & Lowell Railroad Company—opened in 1871—connected the Framingham railroad center with the mill town of Lowell. Dignitaries from Rhode Island, Connecticut, and other locations in Massachusetts attended the spike-driving ceremony. Courtesy, Framingham Historical Society

Far right: A map on the reverse side of the invitation to the Framingham & Lowell Railroad spike-driving ceremony in 1871 showed the importance of Framingham as a railroad center. It had connections to Canada, Maine, Vermont, New Hampshire, Rhode Island, Connecticut, and New York. Courtesy, Framingham Historical Society

Framingham and Lowell
RAILROAD COMPANY,
SPIKE DRIVING AND OPENING.

Sir :

You are invited to be present at the driving of the last spike, and attend the formal opening of this Road, which will take place

TUESDAY, AUGUST 22d, 1871.

PROGRAMME !

A special train will leave South Framingham at 8.00 A. M. passing over the New Road and arriving at Lowell at 9.15 A. M. Returning over the New Road, leaving Lowell at 10 A. M. arriving at South Framingham at 11 A. M., thence to Providence, and from there to Stonington arriving about 2.00 P. M.

By invitation from the Stonington Steamboat Co. the party will make a trip upon the waters of the Sound, in one of the elegant new Boats of the Line. Returning to Stonington at 4.00 P. M. where a collation will be served at the Wadawanuck House, after which the party will return to Boston and Fitchburg by special train.

This Circular will pass the bearer over all the connecting roads for the purpose of attending the Opening.

Trains to connect with the above special train

Will leave Boston from Boston and Albany Depot at 7 A. M. Providence at 6.15 A. M., Fitchburg at 5.30 A. M., Taunton at 6.30 A. M., Stonington at 2 A. M., Worcester at 7 A. M. New York via Stonington Boat at 5 P. M. on the 21st, New York via Providence and New York Steamboat Line at 5 P. M. of the 21st.

Note.—Parties unable to leave Boston at 7 A. M. can join the excursion at Lowell, at 9.15, or at South Framingham at 11, or at West Concord at 8.30 A. M.

COMMITTEE OF ARRANGEMENTS.

E. P. CARPENTER,   H. A BLOOD,   GEO. A. TORREY,
S. H. HOWE,   GEO. E. TOWNE,   D. S. BABCOCK,
A. A. FOLSOM.

BOSTON CLINTON FITCHBURG AND MANSFIELD FRAMINGHAM LOWELL RAILROADS, AND CONNECTIONS.

reservoirs, with their stately Victorian stone gatehouses, provide some of the best scenic views in South Middlesex.

A small, hardly noticeable railroad turnout from the Saxonville Branch Railroad put the village of Cochituate on the rail system in 1874, bringing labor and business to the expanding shoe factories of James Madison Bent and other enterprising Yankees. Among the new laborers coming to Cochituate were large numbers from Nova Scotia and Quebec. It is said that the only friction among immigrants in Cochituate was between these two groups of Canadians. As Cochituate grew to exceed the population of Wayland Center, political friction developed. The division was so deep that the residents could not get together to plan a celebration of the town's centennial in 1880. In 1881 a petition was circulated to make Cochituate a separate town, but it was not successful.

To the outside world, the residents of Cochituate, regardless of their ethnic background, were known as Broganites, a name derived from the brogan—a rough work and farm shoe that was the major product of the Cochituate factories. But many of the shoe workers actually lived in nearby Natick and Saxonville. By the late 1850s, Natick had become the largest South Middlesex town, and would hold on to that distinction almost to the end of the century. In 1887 Natick seriously considered becoming a city. Immigration helped Natick keep ahead of the other towns as Russians and Poles supplemented the traditional inflow of Irish and Germans. As late as 1895 the Natick population was 20 percent foreign born, and half of those were Irish.

Above: In 1847 Natick Center and the village of Saxonville were joined by the Saxonville Branch Rail Road. This photograph was taken circa 1880 near the spot where the Saxonville Village apartments stand today. Courtesy, Framingham Historical Society

Facing page, bottom: In the 1870s Boston's demand for fresh water was satisfied with the construction of a system of reservoirs and aquaducts reaching as far as Ashland and Framingham. Stately gatehouses and bridges were built with labor from southern and eastern Europe. Courtesy, Framingham Historical Society

Above: In Holliston in the 1880s factories sprung up for every need. In East Holliston stood a comb factory, at right, that later became a nail factory run by Zephaniah Talbot. To its left is the Wilder Pump Shop, which is still there today. Courtesy, Holliston Historical Society

Above, right: By the 1880s almost all South Middlesex towns were involved in the shoe- and boot-making industry. This map shows the location of shoe and boot factories as of 1884, and illustrates why Natick and Holliston were considered the leading "shoe towns" of the period. Today there is hardly a trace of that industry that dominated the region's economy a century ago. Courtesy, Framingham Historical Society

Natick was the leading shoe town of South Middlesex, employing over 1,500 workers in the shoe trade in 1880.

Shoe production increased in other South Middlesex towns as well. By 1874 Holliston's annual production was worth one million dollars. Hopkinton was making 3,000 pairs per day by 1890.

The booming business along the route of the Boston and Albany and its branches encouraged some investors to build a second east-west railroad through South Middlesex. The Massachusetts Central Railroad opened in 1880, passing through Wayland Center and South Sudbury near the route of the old Boston Post Road. But no boom followed. The single track of the Massachusetts Central could not compete with the two-way traffic and network of interconnections offered by the Boston and Albany. In a few years the company had to reorganize. Later it was absorbed by the Boston and Maine system. Its route through South Middlesex is now abandoned. This line's primary service to the community was for commuting passengers to Boston (fifty cents in 1880) and hauling farm produce. In 1882 Wayland was sending 1,900 cans of milk to Boston per week. Wayland and Sudbury were also exporting meadow hay, manure (sold by the cord), potatoes, and apples.

Apples brought Sherborn as close as it would ever get to boasting a major industry. Sherborn's many apple orchards, producing such varieties as the Russet and the Porter (the latter developed by Sherborn's eighteenth-century minister, the Reverend Samuel Porter), gave rise to the apple cider business. There were up to twenty cider mills operating in Sherborn. The biggest was the Holbrook Mill, considered in 1893 to be the largest in the world, producing 40,000 barrels of cider per year. The local area could not meet the demand for apples at the Holbrook Mill, so carloads were brought in from as far away as Virginia.

Sherborn was situated on one of the north-south railroad lines that came into being after the Civil War. In 1882 these lines became the northern division of the Old Colony Railroad. With South Framingham as the nerve center for this division, the company built the Old Colony Hotel near the depot to accommodate its crews and passengers. The hotel still stands in downtown Framingham as a reminder of a railroad company that has long gone from sight.

Another hotel near the depot was the South Framingham Hotel

Left: Erected Circa 1880, these buildings of J. Holbrook & Sons were advertised as the "Largest Cider Mill in the World." The Holbrook mill had opened in 1853 in Sherborn in a much smaller building. The trains seen here on special sidetracks were from the Framingham and Mansfield Railroad. Holbrook shipped his "champaign cider" all over the country as well as to Europe. Courtesy, Sherborn Historical Society

Below: The South Framingham Hotel, originally built for the stagecoach traffic of the old Central Turnpike in the 1820s, was conveniently located near the railroad depot. But its nearness to the tracks and its attached livery stable probably created uncomfortable conditions for many of its guests. Courtesy, Framingham Historical Society

Above: Leonard Morse was a Natick businessman who made his fortune in real estate. His name would have been forgotten had his wife not left a bequest in 1889 to establish Leonard Morse Hospital, now a regional health care facility. Courtesy, Framingham Historical Society

run by Simeon Twitchell (1827-1879). This was one of the old turnpike hotels, built for the Central Turnpike about 1820. Twitchell kept a menagerie of goats and other barnyard animals. Their odors blended with those from the attached livery stable to create a unique atmosphere that his summer guests could not have appreciated. The hotel had a restaurant, and Twitchell also had the food concession at Harmony Grove and the railroad station. For five cents you could buy one of his extra large raised doughnuts that was particularly popular among travelers at the depot looking for a quick meal on the run. The reputation of this doughnut spread far and wide and it became known as the Famous Framingham Doughnut. Unlike the Old Colony Hotel, the South Framingham Hotel did not survive the nineteenth century. It was torn down in 1894 and replaced by a coal facility.

For all its benefits, the railroad brought its share of problems. From the hundreds of boxcars that moved through South Middlesex every day came members of a new nomadic class of society called tramps. These wandering beggars put a demand on the welfare resources of the towns that would have horrified the Overseers of the Poor of the previous century. Sherborn recorded 672 tramps lodged and fed in 1876, and the town report for that year bemoaned that tramps were "coming in on us like an army of locusts, threatening to devour all our substance." In 1872 the position of Tramp Officer was created by Ashland. During the 1870s the news got around that Wayland provided full hot meals to indigents, and that town was swamped with tramps until 1879 when the meals were reduced to crackers and water.

Right: The town of Sherborn, lacking a physician, invited Dr. Albert H. Blanchard to settle there and become the town doctor. He accepted, and here Blanchard poses with his horse and carriage circa 1875. Courtesy, Joseph Blanchard

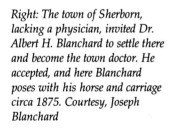

Other problems brought about by the railroads were the ghastly accidents that occurred with regularity along the line. Deaths and dismemberments were graphically described in the local papers. The accidents led to the founding, in the 1890s, of one of the earliest South Middlesex hospitals, the Framingham Hospital. Located not far from the tracks of South Framingham, this hospital later merged with the Union Avenue Hospital to become the Framingham Union Hospital. In 1899 another hospital was begun in Natick from a bequest honoring businessman Leonard Morse. Today Framingham Union and Leonard Morse hospitals are the two major health care facilities for South Middlesex and beyond.

Hospitals were one of several charitable undertakings of the Victorian middle class that also included the Widows and Orphans Benevolent Society (1859) in Sherborn, and the Home for Aged Men and Women (1886) in Framingham. But charitable works could not fill the void left when the great crusade to abolish slavery ended with the Civil War. A new crusade was found in the war against alcohol.

Temperance activity in South Middlesex had been going on quietly since the early nineteenth century. One of the earliest organized efforts was Holliston's Society for the Promotion of Temperance, founded in 1827. Well before that some individual families maintained a standard of abstinence, while New England rum and West Indian flip flowed freely at most social and official gatherings. One family that chose to abstain was the Temple family of Framingham, a family that produced several ministers and teachers. When Thomas Temple died in 1773, an outspoken local citizen was surprised to find no spirits offered at the wake. He also noticed how well the family concealed their grief and remarked as he was leaving, "Queer funeral—no toddy! no tears."

Sherborn has been one of the most dry of all the South Middlesex towns. Some say that this tradition goes back to 1822 when Galim Bullard invited his neighbors to help him erect a new boundary stone at the Framingham border. Bullard provided a hogshead of rum and an unlimited supply of hard cider to show his hospitality. The result was a "celebration" that developed into a near riot, sending women and children into the woods for protection.

In the 1870s the temperance movement gained strength and momentum. It became organized on the national level with such groups as the Women's Christian Temperance Union. But as a women's issue, political clout was missing as long as women were not allowed to vote. The goal of the temperance groups was to influence the men who did vote. Temperance meetings were common, and large rallies were

EVENING ENTERTAINMENT.

There will be given in the

Town Hall, Framingham,

WEDNESDAY, DEC. 4, '89,

In connection with the Fair
in aid of the

HOME FOR AGED MEN AND WOMEN,

An Evening Entertainment, commencing at 7.30 P.M., when there will be presented a Drama,

"AN AUTOGRAPH LETTER,"

And Kinder Symphony

"SLEIGH RIDE,"

By Local Talent.

Tickets with Reserved Seats, 35 Cents, can be obtained on and after Wednesday, Nov. 27, at E. F. Kendall's store, Framingham, and at W. W. Haynes', South Framingham.

DOORS OPEN AT 7 O'CLOCK.

GENERAL ADMISSION, · 25 CENTS.

Before the days of government subsidy, money for a Home for Aged Men and Women was raised through an evening of entertainment at the Town Hall of Framingham. All the entertainers were "Local Talent," and even the children (" Kinder") participated. Courtesy, Framingham Historical Society

Right: A young man slays the serpent of alcoholism on the masthead of a pledge form, a common tool of the temperance movement. The treasurer of the society, John H. Temple, came from a family with a long history of abstinence. Courtesy, Framingham Historical Society

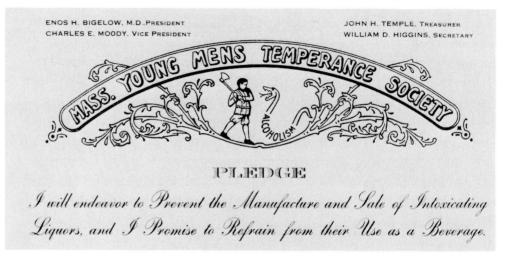

Above: To rehabilitate the women inmates at the Sherborn Reform-atory (seen her circa 1880), the prison trained them in garden-ing, rug and quilt making, and food canning. Their products were exhibited at agricultural fairs. Today the prison is known as MCI-Framingham. Courtesy, Framingham Historical Society

Right: A summer day on Heard's Pond in Wayland, circa 1880, with Sudbury and Nobscot Mountain in the distance. A white parasol protects the lady's complexion, and the horse-woman is, of course, riding sidesaddle. Photo by Alfred Wayland Cutting. Courtesy, Wayland Historical Society

held at Harmony Grove where abolitionists once ruled the day.

For many of the towns the opportunity to vote on the alcohol issue came once a year with the licensing question: "Should the sale of alcoholic beverages in this town be licensed for the coming year?" In the smaller towns there was a clear and continuous "no." In the larger towns with substantial foreign-born populations, the vote alternated from year to year. During dry years, however, it was often easy to find a drink. Keiley's saloon in Holliston remained open with or without a license, as did the many kitchen bars in Mudville and certain drugstores in Natick where somthing called a "Cochituate cocktail" was dispensed.

In addition to charity and temperance, Victorian society was interested in reform. The best example of this in South Middlesex was shown in the growing concern for women who had been convicted of crimes and were subjected to abuses in the general prison system. The need to correct this condition was brought up by the Reverend Edmund Dowse (1813-1905) of Sherborn, who would serve a phenomenal sixty-seven years as pastor. The Reverend Dowse used his election to the state senate in 1869 to push his cause. The legislation that resulted led to the establishment of a women's prison in, of all places, Sherborn. The Sherborn Reformatory Prison for Women, a large red brick building of appropriate Victorian severity, opened in 1877. One of its early superintendents was Clara Barton, founder of the American Red Cross. And among its inmates were two female members of the infamous Dalton Gang from out in the wild West.

A change in town boundaries in 1924 put the women's prison in Framingham. Today it is known as MCI-Framingham (Massachusetts Correctional Institution). It remains a facility for women. (There was a brief experiment with a coed inmate population in the 1970s and 1980s.) Despite its century-old towers and gables and serious overcrowding, MCI-Framingham is still considered a "country club" among the prisons in the Massachusetts system.

The private wealth that was accumulating in South Middlesex often benefited the towns through the generosity of public-spirited citizens. In many cases the gifts and bequests resulted in private names on public institutions, including high schools such as the Peters High School in Southborough (Henry H. Peters) and Sawin Academy in Sherborn (Martha Sawin), and libraries such as the Fay Library in Southborough (Colonel Francis B. Fay), Morse Institute in Natick (Mary Ann Morse), and Goodnow Library in Sudbury (John Goodnow).

Private citizens were also establishing private schools. Among the most successful of these have been the St. Mark's (1865) and Fay (1866)

The infamous "W Stone" boundary marker was erected in 1822 on the Sherborn-Framingham line. The drunkeness caused by the rum and hard cider served by Galim Bullard when the stone was erected is said to have forwarded the cause of temperance in Sherborn for over a century. The "W" refers to an ancient land grant to Richard Wayte. Courtesy, Sherborn Historical Society

Fashionable young ladies at the Walnut Hill School in Natick enjoy a golf match on a grassy hillside, circa 1900. Founded in 1893 as a college preparatory school, it is located about three miles from Wellesley College. Courtesy, Walnut Hill School, Natick

schools in Southborough founded by the Burnett family, and Walnut Hill School (1893) in Natick founded by Florence Bigelow and Charlotte Conant.

At the head of Southborough's Burnett family was Joseph Burnett (1819-1894). Burnett was a native of Southborough, but his fortune and claim to fame originated on "Tremont Row" in Boston, where he had set up shop as a druggist and where he tinkered with fragrances and flavorings. In 1845 Burnett developed a vanilla extract that soon became a standard cooking ingredient in every American kitchen. Back in Southborough Burnett established "Deerfoot," a country estate encompassing over 500 acres. In addition to St. Mark's School, Joseph Burnett was the founder of St. Mark's Episcopal parish, and he began the diverse and extensive dairy and farming business known as Deerfoot Farm, one of Southborough's major employers well into the twentieth century.

****

It was during the last half of the nineteenth century that the nine towns of South Middlesex began to emerge as a unified region. The railroad tied them together. Horse-drawn streetcars extended the rail network to the villages and neighborhoods, delivering the final blow to the old stagecoaches that had survived by offering shuttle service between the depots and the old turnpike hotels.

The Middlesex South Agricultural Society was regional, and its annual cattle fair at Framingham brought together farmer and non-farmer alike. This fair was so important that students were given one of the few school holidays of that time so that they could attend.

Other regional gathering places included Harmony Grove and Sherborn's Clovernook Grove, where picnic and boating facilities were available. During summers, the New England Chautauqua Assembly at Mount Wayte in Framingham drew people from near and far. Crowds from many towns around Framingham would gather at the Musterfield for the militia encampments where dress parades were held for the governor.

Purchased by the state in 1873, the Musterfield consisted of 115 acres of Pratt's Plain, east of Framingham Center. The Musterfield would later be used as a staging area for sending troops to the battlefields of the Spanish-American War, World War I, and World War II. Over the years the state gave this campground several official names, such as Camp Long, Camp Dewey, and Camp Framingham. But it was always known locally as the Musterfield. Today the governor of Massachusetts will come to the former Musterfield only in the case of a state emergency. The old Musterfield now contains the Civil Defense headquarters for the state with underground facilities for state government in the event Boston has to be evacuated.

A sense of regional unity was encouraged by the local weekly newspapers that started coming on the scene in the 1850s. While these newspapers identified with their towns, they always included columns for news in neighboring towns and villages. The *Tribune*s of Framingham, Ashland, Sherborn, Southborough, and Sudbury were actually local editions of the same paper, all published by Charles J. McPherson.

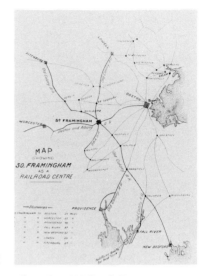

Above: In 1889 South Framingham advertised itself as a railroad center to attract new business and industry. The rail network reached beyond South Middlesex and tied together much of eastern Massachusetts and Rhode Island. Courtesy, Framingham Historical Society

Left: People wait at the ticket office of the Chautauqua campgrounds in South Framingham. Customers who entered were promised "FREEDOM BY THE TRUTH" as proclaimed over the archway. Courtesy, Framingham Historical Society

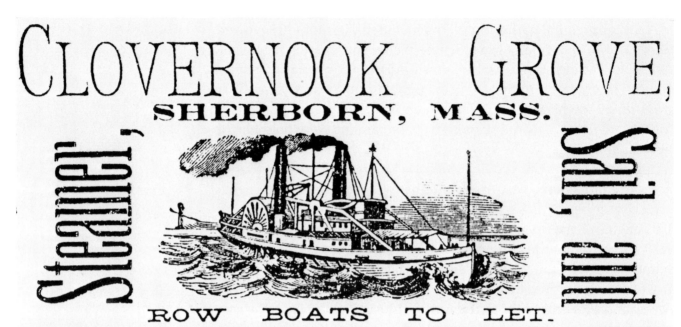

Above: Sherborn's popular Clovernook Grove brought recreation close to home, with a dining hall, picnic sites, and various boating activities. Transportation was provided from the South Sherborn station of the Old Colony Railroad. This advertisement appeared in 1885 in the Framingham Tribune. Courtesy, Framingham Historical Society

Right: The Chautauqua meetings at Mount Wayte in South Framingham brought people from all over New England for two weeks of social activities and education. Families rented rooms in cottages such as this or pitched tents in the area, and had access to dining halls and laundry facilities. Courtesy, Framingham Historical Society

A. W. EAMES,
—PROPRIETOR—
EAMES ❧ MARKET.

Choice Meats of all kinds. Vegetables, Canned Goods, &c.

Our Stock is always complete and of best quality. All orders promptly filled. Goods delivered free.

Summer Street, Ashland, Mass.

Charles McPherson (1856-1929) would later establish the first successful daily newspaper in South Middlesex—the *Framingham Evening News* (1897), forerunner of today's *Middlesex News*, which covers all of South Middlesex plus many towns beyond.

One of the things that made local newspapers feasible was advertising revenue from the many mercantile establishments that opened up in the larger villages and near the depots. These stores were often housed in business "blocks"—large wooden structures with two or three floors. The upper floors contained halls and meeting rooms used by the societies, lodges, and other social organizations that appeared in every town. This business and social buzz of activity introduced an urban flavor into many of the "Main Street" areas. It also brought about a new service that the Puritan forefathers would never have imagined—streetlights.

An advertisement for Eames Market in Ashland, featured in the 1886 Ashland Directory, shows a great difference between old-time grocery stores and the supermarkets of today. Oh, for the days of "Goods delivered free!" Courtesy, Ashland Historical Society

Above: The popularity of Second Empire architecture with its mansard roof design is seen in Holliston's Andrews Block, home to Charles F. Thayer, apothecary, in the 1870s. The masonic symbol in the roof tiles indicates that the upper floor probably contained a Masonic hall. Courtesy, Holliston Historical Society

Right: The Walcott Block in Natick, shown here circa 1880, included a hotel upstairs, businesses on the first floor, and an octagonal cupola on the roof. The building was two blocks from the Natick railroad station and faced the town common. Courtesy, John A. Morris

Ice harvesting, as these 1874 sketches indicate, was not for the thin-skinned. Workers first had to clear away the snow, mark the ice, and saw off large blocks. The blocks were then floated to the icehouse and packed away. From One Hundred Years Progress, *1874. Courtesy, Framingham Historical Society*

Streetlights first appeared in the 1860s as oil lamps mounted in large glass enclosures. In the 1880s electric streetlights were introduced and in some places they were allowed to burn until after midnight, unless, of course, there was plenty of moonlight.

It would be many years before the electricity brought to the streets in the 1880s would be used for such sophisticated applications as refrigeration. Until then the only way to preserve perishables was with "cakes" of ice. Many enterprising Yankees saw the ponds of South Middlesex as an excellent source. During the long winters, ice harvesting and storing was a thriving business, employing many idle farmhands. The nearby railroad lines also made ice shipping practical and profitable. Some of this ice would make its way as far as South America during that hemisphere's summer while New England was frozen in winter.

During summer in New England, baseball was one of the most

Right: Harrison Harwood of Natick was a Middlesex County commissioner from 1872 to 1882. He is best remembered in Natick as the founder of the Harwood Baseball factory, a major producer of baseballs for over 100 years. Courtesy, Framingham Historical Society

Far right: "H. Harwood & Sons, Base Balls" marks the building in Natick Center where baseballs were once manufactured. This photograph was made circa 1900, and although baseballs are no longer made there, the building still stands. Courtesy, John A. Morris

Below: Farm Pond in Sherborn froze in winter to a depth of fifteen to twenty inches, and by January or February ice could be cut and stored in ice houses. Double-wood walls with saw-dust filling would keep ice frozen until the next fall or later. This circa 1895 ice wagon—marked "Farm Lake"—delivered ice to customers. Photo by Edgar Smith. Courtesy, Sherborn Historical Society

popular activities for the young men of South Middlesex. In Cochituate one factory owner generously let workers out early on Saturdays in the summer to play. Baseball clubs were organized on the village level, and "matches" were arranged that often crossed town lines, promoting the feeling of regional sports. A score book that has survived from the 1860s gives the details of games between such teams as the Saxonville Stars, Framingham Monitors, Ashland Heroes, Natick Mystics, and South Framingham Eagles. There was also a team in Natick called the Picked Nine.

Natick was involved with making baseballs as well as playing the game. Harrison Harwood started the business in 1858, using scrap leather from the shoe shops. It took an apprentice many years to develop the skill to hand stitch Harwood's top-quality League Ball. In 1890 Harwood offered a line of baseballs that ranged in price from five cents to a dollar and a quarter.

A bit of baseball culture can also be traced back to South Middlesex. In 1888 journalist Ernest Lawrence Thayer remembered an old Worcester schoolmate named Casey, who came from a village called Mudville. Thayer was probably unaware that Mudville was a village of Holliston when he wrote his poem, "Casey at the Bat," which became a classic expression of America's love for the game. The famous poem closes with the stanza:

Oh, somewhere in this favored land the sun is shining bright,
The band is playing somewhere, and somewhere hearts are light;
And somewhere men are laughing, and somewhere children shout,

Above: W.D. Wilmot, when not atop his 1880s high wheeler, could be found behind the counter at Fred Horne's drugstore in Framingham Center. Courtesy, Framingham Historical Society

Left: Ed and Flo Barnard (Adriel and Flora) stand in front of the Eagle Bicycle Cafe in Southborough, on Boston Road between the Onthank and Brewer farms. This cafe was popular among bicycle enthusiasts in the late 1890s. Courtesy, Southborough Historical Society

Horace Phipps, Livery, Hack, Feed and Sale Stable; First-class teams; Prices Reasonable; Main Street, Hopkinton, Mass.—The man who carries on a first-class livery, hack, feed

Brown. The Maine, and th las. Mass. Tl

Above: Although bicycles were popular in the 1880s and 1890s, the horse and wagon was still king of the road. Livery stables did a thriving business, and any man who wished to get around town had to be skilled with the reins. Courtesy, Framingham Historical Society

Left: In South Natick on a snowy day, the men of the Natick Fire Department pause on their steamer in front of the Old Natick Inn, circa 1880. After the devastating fire of 1874, Natick was eager to keep up with the latest in firefighting equipment. Courtesy, John A. Morris

But there is no joy in Mudville: Mighty Casey has struck out.

Another craze of this time was bicycling, which introduced the era of personal transportation. Starting in the 1870s, bicycles were used extensively for sport as well as transportation. Their use increased in the 1880s, when the high-wheel "ordinary" bicycles were replaced by the "safety" model that had two wheels of equal size. In 1881 Elmer Bent of Cochituate was a local cycling champion. W.D. Wilmot gave exhibitions in costume on his high-wheeler when he was not working at Fred Horne's drugstore in Framingham Center. Framingham's enthusiasm for the bicycle was unusually high. In 1892 almost 600 residents were registered cyclists. Bicycle races were held at Wayside Park, on the trolley line between South Framingham and Saxonville. In South Framingham during the 1890s, the Hickory Wheel Company actually manufactured bicycles for a few years.

The general popularity of bicycles was just a small part of a civilization that included temperance rallies, horse-drawn streetcars, gas lighting, stereoscopic photographs, ladies in bustles, and gentlemen wearing straw hat "skimmers" in the summer and felt bowlers the rest of the year. Although this civilization flourished in the prosperity of the local shoe and straw goods factories, it was destined to die out with them.

****

In 1855 Oliver Bacon looked at the rate of growth in Natick and projected that in the distant year of 1905 Natick would be a city with a population of 182,000. But the actual 1905 population of Natick was only about 10,000, and none of the South Middlesex towns have ever

The Morse & Knowles building in Hopkinton lay in ruins after the fire of 1900. The Park House Hotel appears at right. This fire was the "last straw" for many Hopkinton businessmen, who went to other towns and cities to rebuild their factories. Courtesy, Ye Olde Hopkinton Village Corporation

Right: After the Hopkinton fire of August 26, 1889, the Coburn Boot Company had little left except walls and a smokestack. The company would relocate in Framingham, where the village of Coburnville developed. Courtesy, Hopkinton Historical Commission

When this photograph was taken circa 1915, this building in Cochituate had become the Grange Hall, but it had been built in 1888 as the Knights of Labor Hall when labor unions were first being organized. Courtesy, Wayland Historical Society

officially become cities. By the end of the nineteenth century the growth of all the South Middlesex towns except Framingham had ground to a halt. The shoe and straw towns of Ashland, Holliston, and Hopkinton actually lost population, with Hopkinton dropping almost half its population between 1880 and 1900.

Fires, depressions, labor activity, and changes in the shoe and straw goods industries brought about a reorganization of wealth and population in South Middlesex. This reorganization was the final step in establishing South Framingham as the dominant center and magnet for a regional network first laid out with the railroad construction of the 1860s and 1870s.

The large, boxy wooden factories and business blocks were easy prey to fire. In 1874 Natick Center was almost entirely wiped out by a winter conflagration that consumed thirty-seven buildings worth half a million dollars. Harwood's baseball factory was one of the few surviving buildings. The next year a great fire took twenty-two buildings in Holliston Center, including the Winthrop House, one of the railroad hotels of 1835. The year after that Hopkinton experienced the first of four disastrous fires that would drive out all major manufacturing interests by the end of the century. A prominent insurance man of this period once made the comment that there were three places he would never sell fire insurance, "Hopkinton, Holliston, and Hell!"

In 1892 the shoe factories of Cochituate were nearly wiped out by fire even though they had put in a waterworks and started a fire department after seeing what had happened in Natick. The industrial sections of Southborough were effectively destroyed by fire in 1898.

While fires could be fought, there was little that businessmen could do about the regular cycles of depression that would hit every five to ten years. In 1884 there was a "brogan depression" that forced the factories of Cochituate and Natick to diversify into other styles of shoes in order to survive. Bad business conditions in 1891 closed the

Above: Michael Simpson (1809-1884) owned the Saxonville Mills, later known as the Roxbury Carpet Company. A benevolent industrialist, Simpson built houses for his workers and landscaped the area for their enjoyment. Courtesy, Framingham Historical Society

Left: The park that mill owner Michael Simpson created in the 1800s on the banks of the Sudbury River in Saxonville was still beautiful when this photograph was taken circa 1900. Courtesy, Framingham Historical Society

The Wm. Claflin, Coburn & Company shoe factory became the nucleus of a new village called Coburnville. The company relocated to Framingham after being burned out in Hopkinton. This building later became the R.H. Long shoe factory but was torn down in 1965. Courtesy, Framingham Historical Society

promising Para Rubber Company in South Framingham, makers of rubber boots, shoes, and other products. These depressions also added members to the army of tramps that beleaguered the South Middlesex towns, forcing Sherborn to build a "tramp house and lock-up" in 1894.

To add to the burdens of the factory owners and managers, workers were beginning to agitate for better wages and working conditions. One of the earliest labor actions of South Middlesex occurred in 1860 when about 500 Natick shoe workers whose wages had been cut staged an unsuccessful strike. The factory owners had no problem finding replacements for the strikers, who either returned to work at the lower wages or left town.

The lesson that the workers learned in 1860 was that success depended on organization. But the opportunity to organize would have to wait until the dark days of the depression of 1873 and the railroad strikes in the Midwest were past. In 1879 the previously secretive, Philadelphia-based Knights of Labor was opened up to all workers, and by 1882 a chapter was established in Natick. A Knights of Labor hall was built in Cochituate in 1888. Natick and Cochituate workers who manufactured wooden shoe forms called "lasts" organized the Natick Lasters Union in 1883. A stitchers union followed in 1889.

The labor movement was not widespread in South Middlesex before the twentieth century. One reason for this was the relatively

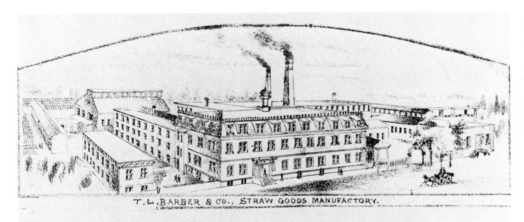

T.L.BARBER & CO., STRAW GOODS MANUFACTORY.

Barber's Straw Goods Factory in South Framingham is pictured in this 1898 lithograph. The building still stands today—the outside has been restored, and the inside has been renovated for commercial use. Courtesy, Framingham Historical Society

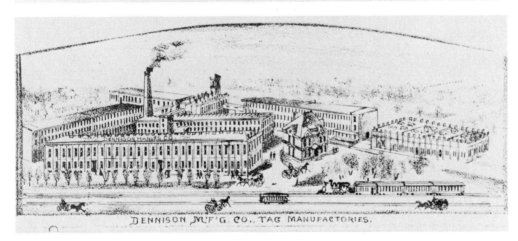

DENNISON M'F'G CO., TAG MANUFACTORIES.

This 1898 lithograph depicts the Dennison Manufacturing Company one year after it had moved into these South Framingham buildings. The buildings still stand, with some additions and changes, and are still used by Dennison. Courtesy, Framingham Historical Society

liberal attitude of some of the local industrialists. James Madison Bent (1812-1888), the Cochituate shoe factory owner who let his men play baseball on Saturday afternoons, was well-liked and respected. It was said of him that he could relax a tense situation with "facetious but courteous remarks."

Another benevolent industrialist was Michael H. Simpson (1809-1884), who owned the Saxonville mills. Simpson built high quality "tenements" for his workers that are still in use today as homes and apartments. He also landscaped the area around the mill and along the river with scenic drives and ponds with rustic bridges, for the enjoyment of his employees and their families.

But during the 1890s the growing power of workers and the annoyance of having to rebuild from ashes every few years forced many South Middlesex capitalists to rethink their strategy. Shoemaking interests moved to cities such as Boston and Brockton where there were larger, more efficient, brick and stone factories, or to the South where labor was not as powerful. Holliston built new factories by town subscription but had little success finding new industries.

The straw bonnet and hat business suffered from a change in

G.F. MacDonald's Horse Shoer and Carriage shop, circa 1880, stood at the corner of Southville Road and River Street in Southborough. The posters on the doors and walls advertise horse auctions, cures for spavin, and the Adam Forepaugh and Sells Circus. Courtesy, Southborough Historical Society

fashion. The glamorous "Gibson girl" of the 1890s did not wear straw bonnets.

Shoe and straw businesses that survived in South Middlesex tended to gravitate toward the regional center in South Framingham. The Claflin Coburn Company fled the fires of Hopkinton to build in southwest Framingham near the Boston and Albany railroad line, where a village called Coburnville appeared. The Barber straw factory, only one block from the South Framingham depot, was in operation into the twentieth century.

As the nineteenth century came to a close, Framingham surpassed Natick as the largest South Middlesex town. This was due in part to the efforts of a vigorous Framingham Board of Trade. Under the leadership of such men as Charles McPherson, the board of trade sought out new industry to keep the factories of South Framingham filled and busy. The board's major coup was the 1897 deal that brought the various plants of Dennison Manufacturing into one consolidated base at South Framingham, in the large brick complex abandoned by Para Rubber. Dennison was a well-established manufacturer of jewelry boxes, tags, crepe paper, and sealing wax; the firm brought immediate and lasting strength to the local economy.

Framingham, Natick, and Ashland—situated on the still vital east-west rail thoroughfare—would be able to hang on to or replace their industries. But Holliston, Hopkinton, and the villages of Southville, Cordaville, and Cochituate would not. Instead they would revert to the rural tranquility found in Sudbury, Sherborn, and the northern parts of Southborough and Wayland, where agriculture was still king.

Beginning in 1879 Sudbury had been quietly expanding its agricultural capacity with the extensive use of greenhouses. At first these greenhouses were used to grow food crops such as cucumbers, lettuce, and tomatoes. But after 1899 the town would earn a reputation for its hothouse pink carnations.

By 1890 Southborough's agricultural activity involved up to 179 farms primarily producing fruit and dairy products. But during the decade, it became the next victim in the ongoing saga of Boston's demand for fresh water. Reaching farther west, the engineers from Boston conceived of one of the most ambitious civil engineering feats to that date. They built a seventy-foot dam in Southborough, which collected water covering 1,200 acres in a basin called the Sudbury Reservoir. The project included building another major dam to create the Wachusett Reservoir in Clinton to the north, and constructing miles of masonry aqueduct running through Framingham and Wayland on the way to Boston. A few small waterpowered mills in Fayville—the last vestiges of Southborough manufacturing—were closed when the reservoir project inundated Stoney Brook.

Today the reservoir, aqueduct, and protected watershed land has placed 23 percent of Southborough under the jurisdiction of the Metropolitan District Commission, which makes an annual contribution to the town in lieu of taxes.

The last years of the nineteenth century saw the beginnings of a New England tradition that now brings worldwide attention to South Middlesex once every year. It began in 1896 when a delegation from the Boston Athletic Association (BAA) went to Athens, Greece, to observe the first of the modern Olympic games. One competition was based on a historic event in 490 B.C. On that occasion a messenger ran from the scene of victory at the Battle of Marathon to deliver the news at the Athens marketplace, roughly twenty-five miles away.

The BAA decided to hold a similar run every year in conjunction with field and track events in Boston. The starting point of the race was set twenty-five miles into the countryside, at the beginning of a route that encountered the least interference from railroads. The best route seemed to be one parallel to the Boston and Albany line, which took officials out as far as Metcalf's Mill in Ashland. The first run of the Boston Marathon was on April 19, 1897. Fifteen runners showed up at Ashland and eleven crossed the finish line in Boston. The winner was John J. McDermott.

Above: For the Framingham Bicentennial in 1900, the new Hotel Kendall was decorated with flags and bunting. The Kendall offered all the amenities of a big city hotel. Shaker Lemonade was sold during the parade below the parade reviewing stand at the left. Courtesy, Framingham Historical Society

Right: Two columns of spectators in South Framingham line the route of the Boston Marathon circa 1900. Brave spectators got a bird's-eye view from the top of a telephone pole. A trolley car of the Middlesex and Boston Street Railway Company passes behind the crowd. Courtesy, Framingham Historical Society

Later, the starting point of the race was moved to different parts of Ashland as the location of the finish line was moved and other minor adjustments were made. Then in 1925 the BAA adopted a new distance for the run. The distance of 26 miles and 385 yards had become the standard marathon length, based on the 1908 Olympics run from Windsor Castle to London. The extra distance pushed the starting point out to Hopkinton where, with minor variations as the Boston finish line shifted from place to place, it has remained. Today thousands of runners partake in this classic spring event, the most prestigious of all American marathons.

The end of the nineteenth century coincided with the 200th anniversary of the Town of Framingham. The board of trade used this occasion to stage a grand celebration, emphasizing South Framingham businesses. The business blocks of South Framingham were covered with bunting, and the larger companies had elaborate floats in the main parade. The festivities, which lasted for several days in June 1900, included speeches, exhibits, and banquets. The new town seal with its railroad hub design was introduced. President McKinley was invited to attend, but he sent a telegram expressing his regrets.

The Framingham Bicentennial was as much a celebration of the future of Framingham as a celebration of its past. The population at that time was approaching the magic number of 12,000, which would allow the town to become a city. (One bicentennial speaker mentioned this fact and recommended that the future city hall be named Danforth Hall.) New factories and business blocks of durable and fire-resistant brick and stone were being built. A "first class" hotel, the Kendall, had just been constructed in South Framingham. It offered billiards, bowling, steam heat, and a barbershop. There were three Framingham newspapers at the time, the weekly *Gazette* and *Tribune* and the daily *Evening News*. All promoted the virtues of the town.

But the future of Framingham as an urban center with the other South Middlesex towns as suburbs was only as solid and promising as the future of the railroad.

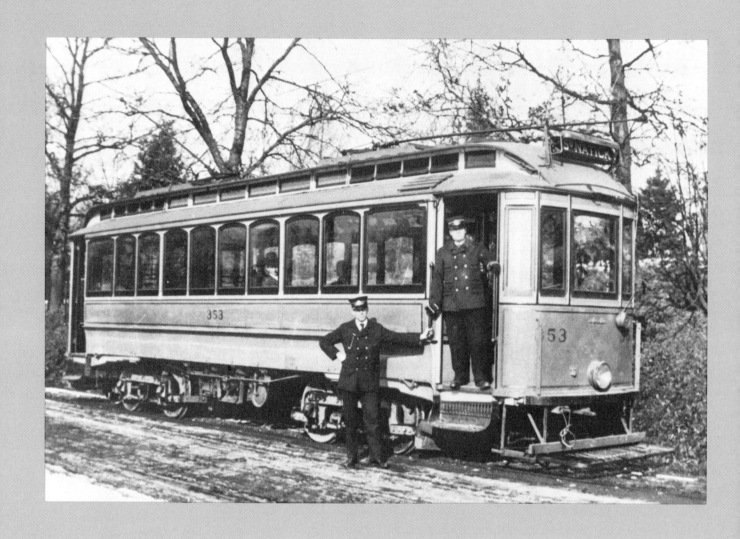

5 AGE OF TAGS AND TROLLEYS (1900-1945)

The South Middlesex that emerged from the smoke and upheavals of the late-nineteenth century was a geographic sandwich. Natick, Framingham, and Ashland were the central layer, composed of factories and stores. These towns were enclosed in the rural and farm layers of Wayland, Sudbury, and Southborough to the north, and Sherborn, Holliston, and Hopkinton to the south.

At the very center of this sandwich was the mighty Boston and Albany trunk line. In 1900 the operation of the Boston and Albany came under the extensive New York Central system by means of a leasing agreement. (The name New York Central was actually put on all the equipment until regional indignation forced a return to Boston and Albany in 1912.) The system included the branch line from Natick to Saxonville, and the Milford branch that ran through Ashland and Holliston. In a similar move, the north-south lines that had been a part of the Old Colony Railroad came under the control of the New York, New Haven and Hartford system. Thus the rail network of South Middlesex at the beginning of the new century was based in New York City rather than in New England. The New York Central's fabled Twentieth Century Limited was inaugurated in 1902, and a Boston section was soon added, thundering through South Middlesex every day. The age of steam railroading was entering a phase of maturity and power that would support the consolidated local industries of South Middlesex for another half century.

The regional bond of iron rails that brought the towns of South Middlesex together in the 1860s and 1870s was further tightened at the turn of the century with copper wire—electrified trolley wire. A variety of small, horse-drawn streetcar lines first began appearing in the 1880s. These complemented the local service provided by the railroad lines and connected villages where previously the only public transportation had been stagecoaches. In the 1890s the development of electric traction motors put the horses out to pasture and caused wires to be strung over every main street in the region. In 1892 you could take the "electric cars" from Natick to Cochituate for five cents. By 1899 this line went as far as Wayland Center, drawing residents of that community

Electric trolleys began to replace the horse-drawn variety by the 1890s, and their appearance further strengthened the unity of the South Middlesex region. Trolleys like the one pictured above circa 1910 branched out to South Natick, Cochituate, and Wayland Center, bringing shoppers to the urban centers of Natick and Framingham. By 1912 trolley freight service had begun serving some areas. Courtesy, John A. Morris

Above: In Framingham Center at the turn of the century, Curtis F. Jones posted himself with a signal flag in front of the railroad shack at the Pleasant Street crossing, where New York, New Haven and Hartford Railroad cars passed on their way from South Framingham to Fitchburg. Jones said many market-men and milkmen slept on their horse-drawn wagons while on their homeward trips, and he "saved their necks" by waking them at the crossing. Courtesy, Framingham Historical Society

Below: The Boston and Albany Railroad had come under the control of the New York Central system when this picture was taken at the Cordaville depot in Southborough circa 1915. In the background one of the few remaining structures of the Cordaville Woolen Mills can be seen. Courtesy, Southborough Historical Society

Passersby watch the progress as workmen lay track through Irving Square in South Framingham for the Milford, Holliston and Framingham Street Railway just before the turn of the century. The new track is curving toward the railroad depot, which was becoming the center of a network of train and trolley lines that would connect all of South Middlesex and beyond. Courtesy, Framingham Historical Society

into the shopping areas of Natick and Framingham rather than into Waltham and Watertown.

The trolley lines could not operate efficiently as small independent companies. The opportunity to consolidate came in 1901 when a new company called the Boston and Worcester Street Railroad Company was incorporated. The primary purpose of this company was to build a high-quality interurban rapid transit line between the two largest cities of Massachusetts. This line would use the route of the old Boston-Worcester Turnpike wherever possible, thus passing through Natick, Framingham, and Southborough. By the time the Boston and Worcester trolley line was ready for business in 1903, it had absorbed short lines that provided connections with South Framingham, Saxonville, and Southborough Center.

A similar consolidation occurred when a trolley line that lay parallel to the Boston and Albany tracks merged with the Natick and Cochituate line to become the Middlesex and Boston Street Railroad Company.

The only trolley line in South Middlesex not included in these mergers was the Milford, Holliston and Framingham Street Railroad Company, although this line was extended as far as Uxbridge in 1902.

Of all the trolley companies, it was the Boston and Worcester (B&W) that would have the most impact on South Middlesex. Framingham, at the midpoint of the route, became the location for the B&W headquarters, powerhouse, car barns, and junction station (Route 126 and Route 9). In 1903 the fare from Boston to Framingham Center was twenty cents, and the ride took one hour and fifteen minutes. The

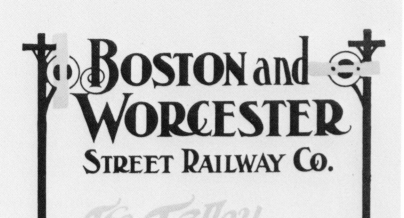

BOSTON and WORCESTER
STREET RAILWAY CO.

The Trolley Air Line

DOUBLE TRACK
PROTECTED BY AUTOMATIC BLOCK SIGNALS
OPERATED BY TRAIN DISPATCHERS

• LIMITED SERVICE •

FALL TIME TABLE SEPT. 9, 1914

E. P. SHAW JR.
GENERAL MANAGER

A. E. STONE
GEN'L PASSENGER
AND TICKET AGENT

GENERAL OFFICE
SOUTH FRAMINGHAM, MASS.

TELEPHONE CONNECTION

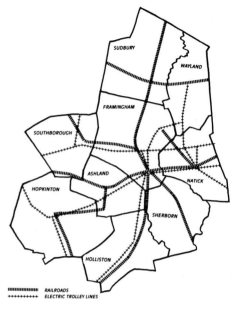

RAILROADS
ELECTRIC TROLLEY LINES

company received invaluable publicity that year when Governor John L. Bates took the B&W, rather than the train, to the state militia review at the Musterfield. The B&W also promoted itself heavily, using the motto "The Trolley Air Line." In 1912 the B&W increased its competition with the railroads when a freight service was started using enclosed trolley "box cars." The depots for this service were identified with the large bold words: ELECTRIC FREIGHT.

The mature railroad system of South Middlesex and its auxiliary network of electric trolley lines opened the way for a new generation of industries and industrialists. This new generation would not be dominated by the ethnic Yankee of English stock. The businessmen who were to hold center stage both economically and socially during the first half of the twentieth century represented an ethnic mixture, some coming from families that had immigrated during the previous century, thus fulfilling the potential of the American dream.

Regardless of their backgrounds, the new industrialists continued a Yankee tradition of inventiveness that dated back to the days of Eli Whitney. Some of them also carried on a tradition of surprisingly liberal management, first seen in such nineteenth-century industrialists as Michael H. Simpson and James M. Bent.

The man whose business best represented the successful transition from the fading shoe industry to the exciting new opportunities of the twentieth century was Richard H. Long (1865-1957). Long was the son of an Irish immigrant who found success in shoe manufacturing in western Massachusetts. Richard had joined his father's company as a boy in South Weymouth and, like Henry Wilson, learned the business from the bottom up. By 1900 Long had his own company and was making two popular styles of shoe—the Waldorf and the Traveler, distributed and sold in twenty-two states. While looking for a larger factory in 1902, Long was riding the train through Framingham when he noticed that the Coburnville shoe factory was available. It is said that he got off at the next stop and bought it.

The R.H. Long shoe company quickly outgrew the Coburnville building and built a new 500-foot reinforced-concrete building in 1910. The new factory was located right next to the railroad, near the forgotten village of Park's Corner. But shoe production did not last long in the new quarters. With the onset of the First World War, Long diversified into leather and canvas products, which were supplied to the British and then to the American forces. He had been unhappy with conditions in the shoe industry, particularly with the monopolies among the shoemaking equipment suppliers. Long had actually started a newspaper, the *Boston Telegram*, as a means of expressing his views.

Facing page, left: The premier trolley line of South Middlesex was the Boston and Worcester, which proudly boasted of its double track and sophisticated signaling equipment in this 1914 timetable. Billed as "the Trolley Air Line," the B&W used the highest quality equipment to assure passenger comfort. Courtesy, Framingham Historical Society

Facing page, top: The regionalization of South Middlesex can be seen in this map showing the railroad and trolley network circa 1910. All the towns and most of the villages are connected via the nerve center of South Framingham. Today all the trolley lines have disappeared and many miles of railroad track have been abandoned. Courtesy, Framingham Historical Society

Facing page, bottom: Unlike the other South Middlesex shoe companies that produced the brogan and other work shoes, Richard H. Long was best known for his fancy dress shoes such as the Traveler, and the Waldorf, pictured in this 1910 ad. Courtesy, Framingham Historical Society

Above: Henry S. Dennison led the Dennison Manufacturing Company to world-wide recognition during the first half of the twentieth century, and helped Framingham earn the nickname of "Tag Town." Like Richard Long, Dennison had a political philosophy much more liberal than most industrialists of his time. Courtesy, Framingham Historical Society

The success of Henry Ford and his Model T may have influenced Richard Long to jump into the new industry of automobile production, where no monopolies dominated. From 1922 to 1926 Long manufactured as many as 4,000 automobiles called the Bay State. But the large-scale mass production of Detroit was difficult to compete with, and Long realized that if he could not fight them he might as well join them. In 1927 he started a General Motors dealership specializing in the Cadillac and later the Pontiac models.

Long had strong Progressive political feelings, and he was an admirer of William Jennings Bryan. He became very active in the Massachusetts Democratic party, earning his party's nomination for governor (only to be defeated by Republican Calvin Coolidge, later president of the United States). He allowed his large Framingham estate, Longford, to be used as a summer camp for handicapped city children, and he also promoted baseball among his workers and in the town. In 1915 Long gave the town twenty-three acres to be used for baseball fields. His baseball team was fiercely competitive with the rival team from the factory down the track—Dennison Manufacturing.

Henry S. Dennison (1877-1952), like Richard Long, was another Progressive industrialist. He joined the Dennison manufacturing Company in 1899 (the firm had been started by his grandfather in 1844). By 1906 Dennison was manager of the Framingham operation, and by 1917 he was president of the company. Dennison came from Yankee stock, but he had little use for his Harvard classmates who

were assuming conservative roles in their respective fields. He promoted the ideas of unemployment insurance, employee ownership, and profit sharing long before the business world was ready to consider them. By applying these ideas to his own company, Dennison was able to soften the blow of the Great Depression in South Middlesex. During that depression he supported Franklin D. Roosevelt and the New Deal. In 1936 economist John Kenneth Galbraith considered Henry Dennison "the most interesting businessman in the United States."

Under Dennison's leadership, the company went from sales of $7.5 million in 1917 to $16 million in 1925. One of the company's largest and most visible product lines was shipping tags, and as the company grew in size and influence, "Tag Town" became a popular nickname for Framingham.

While Framingham was becoming known as Tag Town, its neighbor down the line, Ashland, was earning the nickname "Clock Town." During the nineteenth century Ashland had suffered more than its share of troubles getting started as an industrial town. By the turn of the century there were many empty factories and about a hundred empty houses. As the twentieth century unfolded, however, a whole new chapter in the life of Ashland opened up. Ashland would become the home of several new industries, ushering in the era of advanced technology so important to the economy of South Middlesex in the latter part of the century.

Ironically, it was the old-fashioned waterpower of the Sudbury River that attracted the first of the new-technology companies to Ashland. The Lombard Governor Company of Boston made devices that regulated water-driven equipment, and in 1904 it moved to Ashland where the river would enable convenient testing of their devices. The superintendent and engineer of the Lombard company was Henry Ellis Warren (1872-1957). His inventive genius and community spirit guided the fortunes of Ashland for half a century.

Henry Warren was intrigued by the idea of a clock driven by electricity. His experiments led to the formation of the Warren Clock Company in 1912, and he made crude battery-driven clocks in an old barn on Chestnut Street. By 1916 he had developed a successful clock motor using the alternating current supplied by power companies. But the output of the electric power companies of that time was often inconsistent, so Warren developed a "master clock" and convinced most of the larger electric companies to use it to regulate their current. (The first of these master clocks is now at the Smithsonian Institution.) In 1920 Warren resigned from Lombard to devote more time to electric

Above: Richard H. Long's liberalism is clear in this poster from his 1919 election campaign for Massachusetts governor. Though Long was defeated by Republican Calvin Coolidge, Long's campaign manager, James Michael Curley, went on to become a controversial Boston mayor and governor of the Commonwealth. Courtesy, Marjorie Long Maish

Facing page, bottom: One of Dennison Manufacturing's many operations was cardboard box manufacture. In this 1921 interior view, women assemble boxes under the stern eyes of their male supervisors. Courtesy, Framingham Historical Society

Right: A parade float for the Lombard Governor Company, circa 1916, displays one of the earliest pieces of "high technology" equipment manufactured in South Middlesex—a hydraulic regulator. The Lombard Company was the first of several Ashland businesses to utilize scientific technology. Courtesy, Ashland Historical Society

Bottom,left: Ashland's Henry E. Warren, "the father of electric time," developed the first successful electric clock, and his Telechron Company manufactured so many electric clocks that Ashland soon earned the nickname "Clock Town." Courtesy, Ann Thurston, Ashland

Bottom, right: The modern electric clock was born in an old red barn on Chestnut Street in Ashland. Prior to World War I, Henry Warren conducted experiments there on clocks using both battery power and electric current supplied by power companies. Courtesy, Ann Thurston, Ashland

clocks. By 1925 an estimated twenty million of his "telechron" clocks were in use. The next year the Warren Telechron Company was formed. Opening a decade of growth and expansion, the company employed over 1,000 in Ashland and surrounding towns.

In 1937, having earned the distinction as "the father of electric time," Henry Warren found himself in a position to purchase his old firm, Lombard Governor. He ran Lombard as president during the World War II years, when the company's engineering and manufacturing resources were adapted to military and wartime projects. Also during this time Warren became a principal of the Fenwal Company, a manufacturer of thermostats and other industrial control devices. Fenwal began business in Danvers in 1935. The name Fenwal is derived from the names of two of its founders—T. Legare Fenn and Dr. Carl Walter. In 1935, upon the invitation of Henry Warren, Fenwal moved to Ashland where unused buildings of Lombard Governor were available.

Meanwhile, electric clock manufacturing was still king of Ashland industry, although by 1943 it had come completely under the control of

B. Perini's first construction company office was in Ashland, on the second floor of the building shown in the center of this 1890 drawing. Courtesy, Framingham Historical Society

111

Right: A group of Natick old-timers gathers in front of a Northway Motors Company truck—one of several hundred that were assembled in Natick from 1919 to 1923. Northway was one of Natick's new businesses that replaced the shoe companies during the 1920s. Courtesy, John A. Morris

Below: Perini workers dig at an early reservoir construction site, circa 1890. Using hand tools and horses, these men would have appreciated the powerful construction machinery used today. Courtesy, Perini Corporation

the General Electric Corporation. In addition to being known as Clock Town, Ashland adopted the motto "Where Time Begins."

Another company that operated out of Ashland, and later Framingham, was the construction firm owned by Bonfiglio Perini. Born in Gotolengo, Italy, in 1863, Perini arrived in America in 1885 as a laborer. His company was formed in 1900, and one of its first major contracts involved work on the B&W trolley line. Perini gained a reputation for high-quality work on large projects such as highways and bridges, and eventually the company received national and international recognition. Incorporated in 1918 as B. Perini and Sons, the firm came under the leadership of one of the sons, Louis Perini, in 1924. The connection between South Middlesex businessmen and

In Natick circa 1900 the Park Cafe—a horse-drawn diner—was often parked on Main Street beside the town common, with its electrical equipment plugged into a box mounted on a light pole. The Park Cafe was busiest in the evenings, often staying open until 1:00 A.M.. The man standing by the diner is Wynn Daniels. This diner was the predecessor of Casey's Diner, now on South Street. Courtesy, John A. Morris

baseball is seen again when, in 1943, Louis Perini became a part owner of the Boston Braves (sold in 1962 after the team had become the Milwaukee Braves).

The third town in the industrial and commercial layer of the South Middlesex sandwich was Natick. It continued as the second-largest South Middlesex town, although it did not have a prominent large-scale employer such as Dennison or Telechron. Natick survived by diversifying as its shoe factory base dwindled. Saws, boxes, baseballs, and specialized shoe parts were some of the products made in Natick in the early twentieth century. In 1918, truck assembly began at Natick's Northway Motor Corporation. A New England tradition was started at the Whipple Company, where Grandmother's Mincemeat was produced by Harrison L. Whipple, a Natick grocer, using his grandmother's recipe. The Whipple Company expanded and eventually moved into one of the old shoe factories.

Natick had an advantage on the commercial side. The great fire of 1874 had stimulated a rebuilding in brick and stone that created a Victorian urban center of shops and services which could otherwise only be found in such cities as Marlborough and Milford. This down-town atmosphere still exists in Natick Center, where North Main Street is dominated by the ornate Victorian Clark Block.

South Framingham was catching up with Natick Center as the new century began, with several new business blocks filling in the spaces around Irving Square south of the depot and Concord Square north of the depot. One of these blocks was the Amsden Building. On July 13, 1906, as the construction of the Amsden building was nearing completion, the building suddenly collapsed, killing thirteen workmen

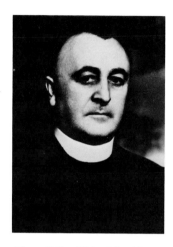

Above: Father Pietro Maschi came to South Framingham from Boston after his brother was killed in 1906 in the Amsden Building collapse. Father Maschi decided to stay, and he established a parish for the growing Italian community, which led to the establishment of St. Tarcisius' Church. Courtesy, St. Tarcisius' Church

Right: On July 13, 1906, the Amsden Building collapsed while still under construction, killing thirteen workmen. The disaster occurred as South Framingham was building a commercial building to rival those of Natick Center. It may have been caused when an old cistern under the building gave way. Courtesy, Framingham Historical Society

and injuring over thirty others. The collapse was one of the worst disasters in South Middlesex history. Many people outside South Framingham rushed to help, demonstrating the closeness of the regional community. The fire department and hospitals provided immediate support. Troops from the Musterfield hurried down Concord Street to lend assistance, and B&W construction crews came from as far away as Southborough to offer aid.

One of the workmen who was killed when the Amsden Building caved in was Romualdo Maschi. His brother was Father Pietro Maschi, a priest in Boston's Italian North End. Father Maschi arrived in Framingham to administer the last rites of the church to his brother. This tragedy led Father Maschi to establish a mission church in South Framingham, which served the growing Italian community and later became Saint Tarcisius' Church.

A new Amsden Building was soon constructed on the site of the disaster, and the Framingham Board of Trade moved its offices there and continued to lure new industry. Between 1895 and 1945 the board of trade "secured" at least thirty-seven companies. Framingham was not as affected by the fires, depressions, and labor problems of the late-nineteenth century because it was diversified while the other towns concentrated on shoemaking. The board of trade continued this pattern of diversification by bringing in such firms as American Roller Bearing, Robb-Mumford Boilers, Minard Liniment ("the king of pain"), Ames Plow, and Gurney Heater. They also helped negotiate labor problems, promoted pro-business legislation, and sponsored Christmas lighting for downtown streets. In 1927 the board of trade changed its name to the Framingham Chamber of Commerce.

Although shoe factories were generally declining as South Middlesex moved into the twentieth century, one company made a bold effort to survive and lasted past the midpoint of the century. The Arthur Ashley Williams Company was one of the few remaining Cochituate shoe firms when fire finally struck in 1909. Rather than close down as so many other companies had done, the firm moved to Holliston into one of the unused factories built by public subscription back in 1891. Williams' factory made work shoes in the tradition of the old brogan. The most popular style was known as the Goodwill shoe, and the company later changed its name to Goodwill Shoe. Arthur Williams (1879-1956) was a noted philanthropist, and he had a high regard for his workers and their community. In 1933 Williams donated land to Holliston to be called Goodwill Park. Today the Arthur Ashley Williams Foundation supports community improvement projects in Holliston and other South Middlesex towns.

Factories such as Goodwill Shoe were the exception to the rule among the six towns that made up the outer layers of the South Middlesex sandwich. A 1900 postcard showing a totally deserted Sherborn Center carried the caption: "Busiest part of the day." In 1907 Nabby Morse of Hopkinton, a local character who was then seventy-seven, wrote a brief "history" of the area filled with sharp Yankee wit. Business and industry was all wrapped up in one sentence, "The occupation of the people is mostly pickin' berries and potato bugs."

The actual occupations of the people of rural South Middlesex involved dairy farms, greenhouses, apple orchards, and small farms where sheep and hogs were raised. But they were not as isolated from

A rural way of life was reflected by the Nobscot Volunteer Fire Department in north Framingham at the turn of the century. The "hand tub," inherited when a more populous part of town acquired steam pumpers, pumped water from a stream or well onto a fire. Courtesy, Framingham Historical Society

Above: Mary E. Cutler of Holliston, who started the Winthrop Gardens nursery on Highland Street, is shown at work in her greenhouse circa 1904. Greenhouse horticulture was then becoming a popular business in many parts of South Middlesex, producing carnations and orchids as well as vegetables. Courtesy, Holliston Historical Society

Right: A circa 1910 postcard shows the first movie theater in South Framingham alongside the Hotel Kendall, the region's first elegant hotel catering to railroad travelers. This was the day of the "nickleodeon" theater, and signs in front of the Princess advertised "New Pictures," "New Songs," and a minstrel show with "Not One Dull Moment." Courtesy, Ralph Maish collection

civilization as their South Middlesex ancestors had been. The shopping emporiums of Natick and South Framingham were only a trolley ride away. There were also pleasure parks such as Waushakum Park near the Ashland-Framingham line, Wayside Park on the trolley route to Saxonville, and Sunnyside Park in Natick. In Holliston, Pleasure Point offered a dance pavilion and baseball fields. In South Framingham, the Gorman theater presented legitimate drama by traveling companies, and the small Princess Theater began exhibiting the novelty of moving pictures.

****

By 1913 South Framingham had grown to sufficient size to warrant officially dropping "South" from its name. Since then it has been known as downtown Framingham to avoid confusion with Framingham Center.

The bustle of activity in Framingham intensified when the United States was finally drawn into the Great War in Europe in 1917. Up to 6,000 Massachusetts soldiers crowded the Musterfield (it was officially called Camp Edgar at the time), and as many as 5,000 workers filled R.H. Long's factories making knapsacks, harnesses, and other equipment for the Allies. This influx of troops and workers created a housing shortage, and many of Long's employees were put up at the Kendall Hotel where Long had shut down the liquor service for the war's duration.

The year 1918 was a difficult one for South Middlesex. While thousands of local boys were fighting in Europe, epidemics of scarlet fever and Spanish influenza created a health crisis at home, reminiscent of the Memorable Mortality of olden days. These epidemics claimed more South Middlesex lives than the war. Overcrowded health facilities forced workers to set up tents as field hospitals, similar to those near the front lines in France.

The year after World War I came to an end, troops were once again assembled at the Musterfield, but this time the objective was Boston rather than France. The Boston Police Strike of 1919 propelled Governor Calvin Coolidge to national attention when he sent in militia units to replace the police force. The attention Coolidge gained helped him win the Republican vice presidential nomination the next year.

The 1920s brought peace, prosperity, and a renewed interest in the automobile as the only way to travel. In 1923 a traffic "beacon" was installed in downtown Framingham. During this decade the electric trolley lines faded into nonexistence. The B&W line, so promising in 1903, went into receivership in 1925 and began phasing buses into operation the same year. The automobile helped South Middlesex finally see some success in its effort to promote itself as a resort area. Summer camps sprang up near the ponds and streams of Natick, Holliston, and Wayland. For the middle-class city dwellers, summer cottages in the country became popular. South Natick became a prestigious place to relax and be seen. Bailey's Hotel, popular with bicyclists since the 1890s, became a resort hotel with open porches

C.S. Oaks in the Concord Building was one of many grocery and dry goods stores that made South Framingham a busy shopping area before the days of the automobile, shopping mall, and supermarket. Courtesy, Framingham Historical Society

Above: Natick's first permanent fire chief, John H. Neary, poses proudly in 1923 by his new Buick roadster, equipped with a fire bell mounted in front of the radiator and a siren on the running board. Courtesy, John A. Morris

Right: In the 1920s the New Haven Rail Road used a few of these railroad coaches—which had a truck-type gasoline engine mounted in front—to service the Marlborough branch. This snapshot was taken at Framingham on the New Haven tracks, looking eastward toward the Concord Street crossing. Courtesy, Charles A. Brown

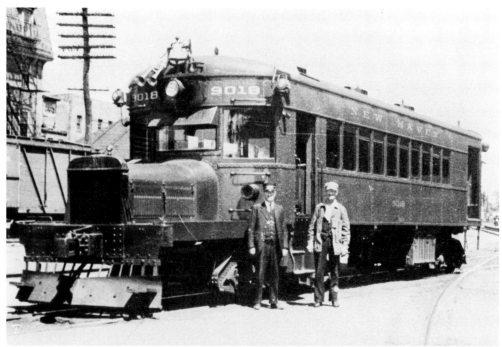

In South Natick in the 1920s, Bailey's Hotel, overlooking the Charles River, offered broad verandas, colorful striped awnings, and flowered window boxes. Resort hotels of this type sprang up in several parts of South Middlesex as the automobile gave wealthy Bostonians greater mobility. Courtesy, John A. Morris

overlooking the Charles River and the site of John Eliot's Indian village.

Some celebrities began discovering the rural charms of South Middlesex. Swedish film actor Warner Oland, who became famous in the role of Chinese detective Charlie Chan, had a country home in Southborough. (He was buried in Southborough after his death in 1938.) Baseball legend Babe Ruth owned a house and eighty acres in Sudbury from 1916 to 1926 (he was pitching for the Boston Red Sox in 1916). He got to know the people in town and would practice throwing with George Wilson near the mill in South Sudbury. The Babe's pitching arm was so strong, it has been said, that poor George would often get knocked over making a catch.

Another living legend of that era to discover South Middlesex was Henry Ford. Ford's wealth allowed him to indulge in a nostalgic search for America's roots. He collected historic structures around the country and had them moved to his "Greenfield Village" in Michigan. In Sudbury, Ford discovered the Wayside Inn and bought it in 1923. As he could not send the Wayside Inn to Michigan, he set up a little Greenfield Village in Sudbury. Ford had a tiny schoolhouse (supposedly from the poem "Mary Had a Little Lamb") moved from Sterling, Massachusetts, to the grounds of the inn. He also had an authentic operating gristmill built nearby. His mill used the gearing mechanism from an eighteenth-century mill in Hopkinton, and he hired its miller, Edwin R. Smith, to work it. When the old Boston Post Road was to be upgraded to a state highway (Route 20), the section of the road that ran in front of the inn was preserved in its rustic appearance by Ford; he had B. Perini and Sons build a bypass at his own expense.

Henry Ford had even bigger plans for Sudbury. He wanted to put

The rustic charm of Sudbury's Wayside Inn—originally known as the Red Horse Tavern—is captured in this nineteenth-century drawing. Henry Ford must have recognized this quality in 1923 when he purchased the inn and restored it for the enjoyment of later generations. Courtesy, Framingham Historical Society

Facing page, bottom: The old gristmill at the Wayside Inn in Sudbury, built by Henry Ford, used the gearing mechanism from an eighteenth-century mill in Hopkinton. Ford hired the Hopkinton miller, Edwin R. Smith, to run the new mill. Flour and grain ground by the mill can be purchased today in the Wayside Inn gift shop. Courtesy, Middlesex News

in an auto-assembly plant, build a dam, and create a model community combining modern technology with the virtues of early American living. The plan never materialized, although the dam was built. The fifty-foot dam, deep in the woods near the Sudbury-Framingham line, could never hold more that two feet of water. It has since been known to locals as "Ford's Folly."

In the year that Henry Ford purchased the Wayside Inn, Wallace Nutting, in the same spirit of colonial nostalgia, published his *Massachusetts Beautiful, Connecticut Beautiful,* and *New Hampshire Beautiful* travelogues. Nutting (1861-1941) had taken up residence in Framingham Center in 1912. He had already established himself as a photographer of sentimental scenes often with a colonial theme. Nutting had built up a business selling prints of these photographs handtinted by young ladies called colorists. He also began manufacturing early American furniture reproductions in 1917 in Saugus. In 1920 both the coloring and furniture operations were moved to an old shoe factory in Ashland. Then in 1925 the businesses were moved to downtown Framingham in the former Barber straw goods factory behind the Park Street Baptist Church.

After glorifying the charms of rustic New England in his 1923 books, Nutting traveled and wrote similar books on other parts of America, and England and Ireland. He also wrote authoritative books on early American furniture and in 1936 wrote his autobiography. His colored prints and furniture have become highly collectible, and his admirers are disappointed to learn that his Framingham home, Nuttingholm, no longer stands.

While the Wayside Inn was being preserved and improved by Henry Ford, another old tavern along the Boston Post Road had a less fortunate fate. The Pequot House in Wayland Center dated back to the days of the Revolution and had a long history in the annals of local entertainment. There was a ballroom, and the inn was a favorite spot for sleighing parties after a ride. An unsavory reputation developed, however, when it was found that forbidden beverages could be had there although the town had voted "no-license." In the twenties (after it had changed its name to the Wayland Inn) the new morality encouraged by the automobile brought the old Pequot House down to the level of a "roadhouse." Finally in 1928 some prominent local citizens banded together, bought the place, and had it torn down.

The new personal freedom brought by the automobile flew in the face of national prohibition. Roadhouses along the highway and stills on the farms were as common in South Middlesex as in any other part of the country. The venerable Wilson House hotel in Natick Center was destroyed by fire supposedly after a still exploded in the basement. Stills in the country, including one at the Stannox farm in teetotaling Sherborn, were raided by federal agents. More than half the arrests made by the Framingham Police Department during the 1920s were for drunkenness or liquor law violations.

Downtown Framingham, where all the growth of the previous fifty years was concentrated, was wedged between Ashland and Sherborn. Residents flowing over into the smaller towns created problems,

Above: While Henry Ford's interest in colonial nostalgia was only a hobby, Wallace Nutting turned it into a business. Nutting produced hand-colored prints with colonial themes and made high-quality reproductions of colonial furniture in both Ashland and Framingham. This portrait is from Nutting's 1935 autobiography. Photo by Grady. Courtesy, Framingham Historical Society

Right: A silhouette greeting card, circa 1920, shows Wallace Nutting and Marietta Griswold Nutting seated on Windsor chairs. Wallace Nutting was the author of numerous authoritative books on Early American furniture, and his valuable furniture collection was purchased by J.P. Morgan in 1925, and is now housed in Hartford's Wadsworth Atheneum. Courtesy, Framingham Historical Society

Below: The Pequot House, built by Elijah Bent along the Boston Post Road in Wayland Center in the eighteenth century, was still an active public house by the end of the nineteenth century when this photo was made. It was torn down in 1928 after gaining a shady reputation as a roadhouse. Courtesy, Wayland Historical Society

especially for Sherborn. Residents of northwest Sherborn worked, shopped, and found entertainment in Framingham. Yet they depended on Sherborn for town services such as fire protection. Framingham could provide these services more efficiently, and efforts to have the northwest corner of Sherborn annexed to Framingham had been going on since the 1880s. This was a much-debated and often hot issue in both towns, and it was not until 1924 that the 575 acres in question were finally transferred.

At the turn of the century, Natick's Wilson House on South Street was a popular railroad hotel. In the 1920s the hotel was destroyed by a fire supposedly caused by the explosion of an illegal still in the basement. Courtesy, John A. Morris

In addition to 600 new residents, the annexation gave Framingham the Women's Reformatory (old-timers still call it the Sherborn Reformatory) and Teddy Gould's farm. In acquiring Gould's farm, Framingham would have one of two encounters with aviation. Teddy Gould leased his land to various air service companies from 1930 to 1946. Gould's airport was also used for air meets, demonstrations, and shows. The other encounter with aviation in Framingham was at the Musterfield, which was used by the U.S. Army Air Service after World War I, and where some of the first airmail deliveries were made. During this period there were also "flying fields" in Natick, Wayland, and other parts of South Middlesex.

It was during the 1920s that the time seemed ripe for Framingham to graduate from its ancient township organization to the status of a city. With a population of 20,000, Framingham was twice as large as Natick and was beginning to experience city-like problems. In 1925 a bill was actually passed incorporating the City of Framingham. The bill was signed by Governor Alvin Fuller, and all that was required was confirmation by the town. But the town would not cooperate and the change was defeated.

Although it had not become a city, Framingham did in effect build a city hall for itself. Town meetings had been held in the downtown

Above: Framingham's new town hall was completed in 1928 as a memorial to its "citizens who served in the nation's wars." It is seen here shortly after it was opened. The building's large auditorium was used for town meetings, and was named after David Nevins, a nineteenth-century industrialist who had bequeathed $100,000 for its construction. Photo by Cokell. Courtesy, Framingham Historical Society

area for many years, often in social halls and theaters. But these halls could not accommodate the open town meeting after the population tripled between 1880 and 1920. A new hall with a large auditorium was completed in 1928 on Concord Square. It was called the Memorial Building.

In the same year that the Memorial Building was completed, a business block born from an unusual new idea was constructed right across the street—the Arcade Building. It included a central arcade with a skylight overhead and about a dozen stores. The Arcade was a forerunner of the enclosed shopping mall of a later generation.

But business in 1928 was headed for problems. No one had any idea that the slump that started in 1929 would lead to such a long and deep period of economic depression. South Middlesex entered this period as a toughened survivor. The fires, depressions, and labor troubles of the late-nineteenth century had already weeded out weak and marginal businesses. The regrouped and consolidated business base of South Middlesex was better equipped to withstand a long economic downturn than many other areas of the country. Dennison and Telechron stayed open, providing economic anchors for the retail and service businesses in their towns. There was actually a small building boom in 1930 when a new main post office and a telephone facility were built in Framingham. And work was started to convert the old Boston-Worcester Turnpike into a major state highway (Route 9). The Perini company, which moved its headquarters from Ashland to Framingham in 1931, got the contract for much of the Route 9 work, including the dismantling of the B&W trolley tracks and poles. The last B&W trolley ride was on January 11, 1931.

Hardest hit by the Great Depression were Natick and Wayland. Natick did not have a major industry with products protected by patents, such as Dennison's tags and Telechron's clocks. Many small and medium-sized companies closed down, quickly swelling Natick's welfare rolls. By 1934, 10 percent of the workers of Natick were unemployed. City folk who had lost their jobs fled to their summer cottages in Natick and Wayland. These cottages, crowded along the banks of ponds and streams, were crudely winterized, and many owners turned to the towns for food, fuel, and clothing.

As the Depression deepened it appeared that the resources of the town welfare agencies would become exhausted. Welcome relief came in 1933 when the New Deal brought federal aid and began putting people to work under the Work Progress Administration (WPA). There was also a Civilian Conservation Corps (CCC) camp nearby, providing robust employment for younger men. Under the WPA a new dam and

Facing page, bottom: Two men grasp the propeller as they prepare to start up the Avro at Framingham's Musterfield airport shortly after World War I. The biplane was flown by local aviators such as Harland Banks and Ray Brooks, who had distinguished themselves as "aces" during the war. Photo by Robert Edgar Mayall. Courtesy, Framingham Historical Society

Above: The new Route 9 "super-highway" in Framingham in the early 1930s was lined with beautiful trees and quiet residences. Within twenty years, however, the solitude would be replaced by stores, parking lots, neon signs, and restaurants. This highway had been the route of the Boston-Worcester Turnpike and the B&W trolley line. Courtesy, Framingham Historical Society

Right: The New Deal's Works Progress Administration left its mark in several places in South Middlesex. This plaque is on a stadium built at Bowditch athletic field on Union Avenue in Framingham. Courtesy, Framingham Historical Society

bridge were built at South Natick; a Farm Pond beach was cleared and tennis courts were installed in Sherborn; early documents and records in many towns were transcribed; and WPA writers did town histories for Ashland and Sudbury.

Along with the New Deal came the repeal of national prohibition. Perhaps in an effort to relieve its Depression doldrums, Natick almost immediately issued liquor licenses, soon earning a reputation for its many saloons. By contrast, Sherborn remained steadfastly dry and would maintain that standard until a "package store" was finally allowed in 1976, 154 years after Galim Bullard's wild party. Natick sobered up in 1938 when it limited liquor sales to package stores and private clubs.

While President Roosevelt was making national news, a good deal of local interest was stirred when the president's eldest son, James Roosevelt, bought a home on Salem End Road in Framingham. The younger Roosevelts lived in Framingham from 1938 to 1941, and they were visited by James' mother, Eleanor Roosevelt, who also visited and spoke at the women's prison.

* *

As if the problems of depression were not enough, in 1938 New England was prostrated by a major hurricane. The storm took 600 lives, mostly in the coastal areas, and thousands of trees were felled in South Middlesex. Crews from the CCC camp helped clean up the mess, and in true Yankee spirit a brief but booming lumber industry was enjoyed. The hurricane cleared a hill near the Wayside Inn where Henry Ford decided to build a chapel. The white classical Martha-Mary chapel with its tall slender spire represented the best traditions of the New England meetinghouse. While the names Martha and Mary have apparent religious connections, they were actually the first names of Henry Ford's mother and mother-in-law.

In Southborough the Sudbury Reservoir and the Wachusett Reservoir to the north of it had been running dangerously low. Boston was once again on the trail for new sources of water. This time the quest went well beyond South Middlesex to the Swift River valley some sixty-five miles west of Boston. The construction of the Quabbin Reservoir during the 1930s was on a much larger scale than anything done before. The flooding of the valley actually eliminated several old Massachusetts towns and villages, including Enfield and Dana. It was in this valley that Hopkinton native Daniel Shays was living when he started his rebellion back in the 1780s. The Daniel Shays Highway is one of the new roads built around the perimeter of the reservoir.

An automobile travels under the arch of a fallen elm tree on Central Avenue in Framingham after the 1938 hurricane. Parts of Gordon's bridge can be seen in the foreground. Courtesy, Framingham Historical Society

Completed in 1939, it took seven more years for the Quabbin to reach full capacity and cover thirty-eight square miles with water. South Middlesex was not entirely exempted from this new chapter in the history of Boston's search for water. New aqueducts were added to the existing network, including the Hultman Pressure Aqueduct through Southborough, Framingham, and Wayland. Completed in 1940, this aqueduct, and the earlier Weston Aqueduct, ran through South Middlesex at ground level. The aqueducts are concealed under an embankment of earth that makes them look like abandoned railroad beds. Today these aqueducts are tempting routes for the dirt bike and the snowmobile.

While construction of the aqueduct, highways, bridges, and dams provided jobs for South Middlesex workers, the unemployment problem was not fully solved until the United States was once again involved in global warfare. Local registration for the Selective Service began in 1940, and the registration rolls carried twice as many names as the unemployment rolls.

Although militia encampments, Governor's Day, and other func-

Above: The Swift River valley was flooded in the 1930s to become the Quabbin Reservoir. Thirty miles west of South Middlesex, the Quabbin project and its aqueducts provided many Depression-era jobs for local men. This vantage point once overlooked the town of Enfield, now at the bottom of the reservoir. Photo by Jack Swedberg.

Left: Henry Ford built the Martha-Mary Chapel not far from Sudbury's Wayside Inn after this hill was cleared by the high winds of the 1938 hurricane. The Chapel's classical lines and picturesque New England setting have made it a popular wedding site for almost fifty years. Photo by Zaharis. Courtesy, Wayside Inn, South Sudbury

Built specifically as a wartime military hospital, Cushing General Hospital later served as a Veteran's Hospital and a state hospital for the elderly. This 1941 postcard view shows the hospital as it looked after the start of World War II. Courtesy, Framingham Historical Society

tions of the Musterfield had been transferred to Fort Devens (near the town of Ayer) back in the twenties, the old Musterfield was activated for the last time as a recruit training camp for the new war.

The Second World War involved many more South Middlesex men and women in the armed services over a longer period than the First World War. While unemployment disappeared, the kind of hardship that everyone had gotten used to during the Depression continued. Scraps of aluminum and other war materials were scrupulously saved. Farm production was supplemented with "victory gardens" in almost every backyard. Basic commodities from sugar to gasoline were tightly rationed. And there were the regular announcements of fatalities from overseas. A large board hanging on the front of the Memorial Building in Framingham showed two numbers—one next to a blue star for the number of residents in the service, and one next to a gold star showing the number of those who had given their lives.

For the wounded who had to be returned "stateside," the army constructed a major New England medical center right in the middle of South Middlesex. The army hospital, built in 1941 on the west side of Farm Pond in Framingham, was named for Dr. Harvey Cushing, a noted Boston surgeon who had died in 1939. Dr. Cushing was also the father of Mrs. James Roosevelt.

For thousands of men and women serving overseas, one of the nine South Middlesex towns was "home." And home is never more appreciated than when one has endured the hardships of war. Leonard

Crawford, a Framingham Marine, wrote home from Guadalcanal, "Sitting in the shade of a coconut tree and occasionally bathing in the surf, it really is a nice place—but I wouldn't trade good old Framingham for all the South Sea Islands."

When the men and women of South Middlesex returned home in 1945 they had little idea that the forests, orchards, farms, meadows, and villages that they had longed for while in strange foreign countries would soon be invaded by a different sort of army—an army of developers and suburbanites.

In the days of horse-drawn vehicles when horse troughs were in the middle of town, Natick was the only South Middlesex town that could boast a main street in the true urban sense. Tall commercial "blocks" concentrated along North Main Street made Natick Center an attractive place for banking, shopping, or enjoying a soda at the corner drugstore. During the early twentieth century, Natick Center was served by several trolley lines as well as the Boston and Albany Railroad. Courtesy, Morse Institute Library, Natick

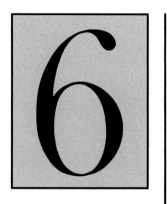

6

AGE OF MALLS, SUBURBS, AND SEMICONDUCTORS
(1945-Present)

The Second World War was also the first nuclear war. The atomic bomb that brought an abrupt and welcomed end to the war was just one of several technical triumphs that used Yankee ingenuity to help defeat both Germany and Japan. There were also developments in rocketry, radar, and electronic guidance systems. While the term "Yankee" had come to apply to all of the United States, much of the Second World War's Yankee ingenuity came from New England, particularly eastern Massachusetts with its base of intellectual and scientific institutions.

The application of specialized branches of science to wartime business meant that these sciences could also be applied to peacetime and Cold War business. South Middlesex, at the center of eastern Massachusetts, was well positioned to benefit from the potential success of any such industries. Although a small part of the Manhattan Project (development of the atomic bomb) was conducted behind a Natick storefront, it would be ten years before the growth of "high technology" industry would have a significant impact on South Middlesex. Meanwhile, more down-to-earth forces got South Middlesex started on its phenomenal and unprecedented pattern of growth.

In 1945 the population of South Middlesex was 59,696. By 1980 that number had reached 159,914. For every 1945 resident, more than two newcomers had arrived by 1980. Also, this near tripling of population over thirty-five years was fairly evenly distributed through all nine towns. But this growth did not occur simultaneously in all the towns.

During the first decade of postwar growth the spotlight was on Natick, the "Home of Champions." This motto emphasized a sense of community spirit based on athletic rivalries that went back to the days of the Natick Mystics baseball club. In the twentieth century Natick was proud to be strongly represented in the champion Harvard football team of 1919. Natick was also proud of 1946 champion amateur golfer Ted Bishop, and 1948 Boston College stars Bobby Paladino and Ed Clasby. At Casey's Diner, a Natick institution since the 1920s, local sports have always been a major topic of conversation. This

This small South Natick park, today a popular summer recreation area, was the location selected by John Eliot for a praying Indian town in 1651. Courtesy, Framingham Historical Society

133

Casey's Diner is a popular spot for local sports talk in Natick. Famous for its steamed hot dogs, Casey's has been a Natick Center institution since the 1920s. It seats only a small number of guests, and during busy hours customers wait in line for seats at the counter. Courtesy, Framingham Historical Society

"hometown" spirit plus Natick's position as the closest South Middlesex town to Boston via Route 9 made it very attractive to veterans returning to the confined spaces of metropolitan Boston.

The Serviceman's Readjustment Act of 1944, better known as the GI Bill, offered the new generation of veterans low-cost loans. These loans plus the stimulus provided by the Federal Housing Administration began a stampede to the South Middlesex towns that has never really stopped.

One of the first businessmen to recognize the potential for Natick was Martin Cerel, a Natick realtor who became a developer of homes, shopping centers, and industrial parks. One of Cerel's first projects was a development called Sherwood-at-Natick where single-family homes were offered for $12,990. Some smaller homes in the early developments were priced as low as $4,500. By 1950 Cerel had built about a fourth of the 1,200 new homes that sprouted up in Natick.

Within South Middlesex the automotive industry also provided an impetus to the local economy. In 1946 Teddy Gould gave up on aviation and sold the 200 acres of his Framingham airfield to General Motors, where a sprawling assembly plant was put up within two years. Located right on the Sherborn boundary, the GM plant attracted thousands of workers who would seek housing in Framingham, Natick, Sherborn, and Ashland. In 1951 the Ford Motor Company put a large parts warehouse and distribution center on Route 9 in Natick near the Framingham line.

Framingham was also growing rapidly at this time, although not as fast as Natick. In response to a severe housing shortage Framingham built apartments for veterans on part of the old Musterfield. The new roads in this development were given World War II battlefield names such as Normandy, Anzio, and Guadalcanal. Framingham had a

Much of the Musterfield at Framingham was used for veterans' housing during the post-World War II population boom. A small portion of the complex is seen here. Apartment buildings accommodated the ex-GIs while their families were small, but soon they were looking for single-family homes. Courtesy, Martha E. Dewar

long-term advantage over Natick—the advantage of space. Space became of greater importance than rivers, railroads, and even highways as developers gobbled up farms and meadows. Framingham has more space (over twenty-five square miles) than any other South Middlesex town except Hopkinton, while its old industrial partners, Natick and Ashland, are much smaller. (Natick has fifteen square miles and Ashland, the latecomer among South Middlesex towns, is the smallest at twelve square miles.)

The open spaces of northwest Framingham, with its rolling hills and winding roads, was attractive enough to interest a group of international delegates who were looking for a permanent home for the new United Nations organization. In 1946 these delegates, along with Governor Maurice Tobin, visited Henry Dennison at his Doeskin Hill estate in northwest Framingham. There Dennison informed them, in no uncertain terms, that he would not have the UN in his backyard. The UN had to settle for New York City as its permanent headquarters, and northwest Framingham still remains largely untouched by developers.

Where there is a housing boom, shopping centers are sure to follow. The commercial potential of South Middlesex was early recognized by developers ready to try a bold new concept in retailing. Old Framingham sewer beds along Route 9 were bought up, filled in, and developed as a major shopping center featuring two levels of stores surrounding a landscaped mall. Opened in 1951, Shoppers World contained almost fifty stores and provided free parking for 6,000 cars. The only other shopping center of this type in the country had just opened up a few months earlier near Seattle. Shoppers World was a direct challenge to downtown shopping areas where, five years before, the first parking meters had been installed. Shopping was no longer a matter of hopping on and off a trolley—now you had to put your car somewhere.

Martin Cerel was quick to seize the opportunity for commercial development. In April 1952 he announced that he had formed a company with Huston Rawls to develop Route 9 properties. The company was called United Sherwood. Eventually a shopping center called Sherwood Plaza opened on Route 9 within view of Shoppers World.

Route 9 in Framingham also became a popular place for restaurants and night spots. The staid Abner Wheeler House and 1812 House restaurants in Framingham Center were upstaged by such colorful places as the Maridor, Ken's Steak House, Giovanni's, Sea'n'Surf, Armand's Beacon Terrace, and The Meadows. (It was from The Meadows that singer Vaughn Monroe began broadcasting his Camel Caravan radio show in 1946.) Also as a portent of things to come for Route 9, Framingham issued its first motel permit on September 21, 1951.

The intense commercial development of the eastern end of Route 9 in Framingham, flowing over into Natick, earned that area the nickname "Golden Mile."

The growth of Framingham and Natick during the first postwar decade put a strain on the traditional town meeting form of government. Framingham's 1928 Memorial Building was filling up for town meetings, and Natick (notorious for its lack of centralized town administration) was improvising, using loudspeakers and microphones to hold a town meeting simultaneously in various social halls, theaters, and schools. With a Framingham population of 28,000 and a Natick

These Cape Cod-style homes on a Framingham street were typical of many single-family dwellings that appeared in Natick, Framingham, and Wayland in the early postwar period. Courtesy, Framingham Historical Society

The Jordan Marsh dome anchored one end of Shoppers World, which included nearly fifty stores and a movie theater when this aerial photo was taken soon after its opening in 1951. Courtesy, Middlesex News

population of 20,000, clearly something had to be done to accommodate participants in the town meetings.

In 1951 Framingham was first to convert to a "limited town meeting" form of government, with 200 town meeting members elected from the various precincts. Natick followed in 1952 with a limited town meeting membership set at 240. The third largest South Middlesex town in 1950 was Wayland with only 4,400 people. By 1985 none of the seven smaller towns had reached Natick's 1950 population, and the open town meeting system still prevails in all of them.

Wayland, however, did have something in common with Natick. Its proximity to Boston (and the new Brandeis University in Waltham)—with connections via Route 20, Route 30, and the Boston and Maine commuter railroad—made Wayland the next natural target of the developers. Between 1950 and 1955 Wayland almost doubled in size, causing the town fathers to dust off the 1931 zoning laws set up to avoid a repeat of the uncontrolled summer cottage growth of the 1920s.

In the second postwar decade (1955-1965) Natick's growth began to slacken while Framingham was just building up steam. Wayland continued building at a healthy rate, joined by Sudbury, a town with almost as much space as Framingham. Feeding this growth was a new highway that did not actually enter South Middlesex—Route 128. Governor Tobin was ridiculed when he promoted this outer belt highway for Boston, as it would pass through a depressed area filled with bogs and gravel pits, bypassing the coastal industrial centers.

Route 128 was constructed nevertheless, creating a region that would become "a foremost world center of space—missiles—electronics technology." By 1975 Route 128 was lined with thirty industrial parks and over 700 firms. Many of these firms were industrial "spin-offs" from the scientific think tanks of Cambridge—Harvard University and the Massachusetts Institute of Technology (MIT).

The high technology development along Route 128 soon spilled over into South Middlesex, only a few miles to the west. In 1954 Wayland had to bend some of its zoning rules to allow the Raytheon Corporation to build a research center. Raytheon was established in 1922 in Newton. During World War II it worked with MIT in the development of radar. In 1958 Raytheon also bought fifty acres of the Hood farm in Sudbury, where an electronics laboratory was built.

Another technology-oriented establishment to enter South Mid-

A favorite 1940s night spot was The Meadows in Framingham, where singer Vaughn Monroe broadcast his radio program. The building burned in 1980 and five years later an office building was built on the site. Also named The Meadows, the new building uses the same double-yoke trademark. Courtesy, R. Maish Collection

Facing page, top: Route 128 was completed in the 1950s as Boston's "outer belt." It exited directly into South Middlesex, and became the ideal location for industrial parks and high-technology firms, whose employees found homes in South Middlesex towns. Courtesy, Massachusetts Turnpike Authority

Facing page, bottom: After 250 years of open town meetings, Framingham held its first limited town meeting on March 14, 1951. The rapid postwar growth in Natick and Framingham forced the change from the traditional form of New England town government to a representative system. Courtesy, Framingham Historical Society

dlesex was the U.S. Army Quartermaster Research and Engineering Command Headquarters, better known as the Natick Army Labs. The $15-million complex covering 100 acres on the shores of Lake Cochituate was dedicated in 1954. It brought over 1,300 jobs to South Middlesex, mostly for civilian engineers and technicians.

As the federal government was moving into Natick it was moving out of Framingham. Cushing Hospital had been converted to a Veteran's Administration hospital after the war, but in 1955 it was turned over to the state for a very different purpose. Cushing became one of the largest public hospitals in the nation that specialized in the care of the elderly. Although the minimum patient age was set at sixty-five, in 1985 the average patient age was eighty-three. Among its patients have been a ninety-three-year-old set of triplets.

Another new employer for the Natick-Framingham area, also on the shores of Lake Cochituate, was the Carling brewery. Opened in Natick in the spring of 1956, the huge windowless main building

containing vats and fermentation tanks loomed over Route 9, becoming a local landmark. The company softened its image by landscaping the area around the brewery and creating a picturesque park with a waterfall—a scene enjoyed by Route 9 motorists as they approached the Framingham line. Carling manufactured Black Label, Red Cap, and Tuborg beer, promoting its location on Lake Cochituate much as the builders of the Boston waterworks touted the lake's waters in 1848. But Carling did not use lake water for its beer. Well water went into the beer while lake water was used in the cooling process and cycled back into the lake through the waterfall.

Right: High-technology development along Route 128 prompted the area's designation by the state as "America's Technology Region." Route 128 has also attracted shopping centers, hotels, and convention centers. Courtesy, Framingham Historical Society

Below: The U.S. Army Natick Research and Development Center (Natick Labs) has been one of the largest employers for Natick and nearby towns since it opened in 1954. Natick Labs has been improving the lot of the U.S. Army soldier by developing improved uniforms, food storage methods, and other logistical support. Courtesy, Framingham Historical Society

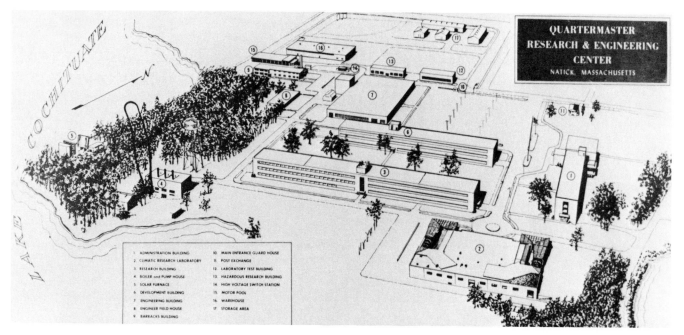

QUARTERMASTER
RESEARCH & ENGINEERING
CENTER
NATICK, MASSACHUSETTS

1	ADMINISTRATION BUILDING	10	MAIN ENTRANCE GUARD HOUSE
2	CLIMATIC RESEARCH LABORATORY	11	POST EXCHANGE
3	RESEARCH BUILDING	12	LABORATORY TEST BUILDING
4	BOILER and PUMP HOUSE	13	HAZARDOUS RESEARCH BUILDING
5	SOLAR FURNACE	14	HIGH VOLTAGE SWITCH STATION
6	DEVELOPMENT BUILDING	15	MOTOR POOL
7	ENGINEERING BUILDING	16	WAREHOUSE
8	ENGINEER FIELD HOUSE	17	STORAGE AREA
9	BARRACKS BUILDING		

The specter of rapid development in Natick, Framingham, and Wayland started ringing alarm bells in the other South Middlesex towns. In 1955 new zoning laws were passed in Sherborn, Holliston, Ashland, and Southborough. Growth in the smaller towns was not prevented, but it progressed at a more moderate pace.

In 1957 part of the new interstate highway system was constructed through the middle of South Middlesex. For years people had been talking about "the new east-west tollway," that, as part of the interstate highway system, would be called "I-90." But when it was opened everybody came to know the highway as the Massachusetts Turnpike, marked with signs showing a green pilgrim hat pierced by a large arrow.

The "Mass Pike" ran from the New York border in western Massachusetts as far east as Route 128, then stopped. It would be another eight years before the turnpike would penetrate the dense layers of metropolitan Boston. In South Middlesex the turnpike roadway actually involved six of the nine towns: Natick, Wayland, Framingham, Ashland, Southborough, and Hopkinton; but its two South Middlesex exits were both in Framingham. Exit 12 was constructed at the west end of Framingham where the turnpike crossed over Route 9, and Exit 13 was built at Framingham's east end near Natick and Route 30.

The turnpike exits became the centers for new development. In 1958 a large tent theater called the Carousel was set up just north of Exit 13. Here big name entertainers such as Liberace and Danny Kaye helped draw crowds to the shopping and dining offered along the

The scope of the Natick Army Labs' activities is suggested in this early sketch of the buildings and grounds. A solar furnace was built near the shore of Lake Cochituate long before solar energy came into fashion. Courtesy, Framingham Historical Society

Golden Mile. Trucking companies set up depots there, and in 1964 one of the nation's largest bakeries went into operation producing carloads of Wonder Bread and Twinkies.

Martin Cerel got involved in industrial parks by teaming up with the Perini construction company. In 1958 a broad hill near Exit 12, locally known as "the Mountain," was partially leveled and developed as the Cerel-Perini Industrial Park (later the Framingham Industrial Park). Not far away, in Southborough, Cerel-Perini Associates acquired eight million square feet of farmland that same year. A small industrial park was also tucked in behind Cerel's Sherwood Plaza on the Golden Mile.

The new, smaller, often technical businesses that moved into the industrial parks only fed the demand for more houses, particularly in Framingham. From 1955 to 1960 Framingham's population grew by an incredible 13,000. In addition to Martin Cerel, other developers such as the Campanelli Brothers and Paul Livoli became visible and prominent during this time. As the fifties were ending it became apparent that a vast change had come over Framingham. In August 1958 *Framingham News* reporter Charles Ayer wrote:

For those addicted to nostalgia, gray days have come. The familiar sights of forest and rolling meadow are fast fading from view. It was not too many years ago when such beauty spots as the 'Barney', the Prior Estate off Cherry Street, Dorrfield, the Roger Smith Estate, and the upper end of Lake Cochituate, the Winter Street dam and Salem End Road area, and the gently sloping hills and reservoir border lands along Pleasant Street near Waveney Farm still retained their country-side aura.

The extension of the Massachusetts Turnpike into Boston in the 1960s furthered the railroad's displacement by the automobile. The Boston and Albany Railroad trunk line enjoyed the wide berth of four parallel tracks, as seen in the older photo at top, taken near the turn of the century in Newton. Half of this right-of-way was given up to the new turnpike, as seen in the lower photo taken in 1984, also in Newton. Courtesy, Norton D. Clark

For those who believe that a town like Framingham must grow, even at the expense of losing such treasured things, the dramatic metamorphosis indicates a move in the right direction.

The threat that overdevelopment posed to the attractive qualities of South Middlesex was recognized when the state, in 1957, passed legislation providing for town conservation commissions. By 1963 most of the South Middlesex towns had set up such commissions, and Sudbury and Wayland initiated floodplain zoning. Also, private watershed protection associations for the Sudbury River, the Charles River, and Lake Cochituate became active.

The need for conservation and recreation as well as good schools

The exit interchanges of the Massachusetts Turnpike became the centers of new development. At Exit 12 in Framingham, where the turnpike passes under Route 9, hotels, restaurants, apartments, and condominiums have sprung up along the shore of a reservoir created in the 1870s for Boston's water supply. Photo by Ric Getter. Courtesy, Dave Granlund and Don's Flying Service

Facing page: The dustcover illustration for Conjuror's Journal, *by Frances Shine of Framingham, shows Joshua Medley, whose adventures were based on the life of Richard Potter, the early nineteenth-century magician who was born in Hopkinton and traveled throughout South Middlesex and beyond. Painting by Wendell Minor. Courtesy, Dodd, Mead and Company*

and services stimulated participation in town government, where old-timers and newcomers alike fought to preserve their quality of life. In Wayland, for instance, a busy Harvard law professor found time to participate in town government. Professor Archibald Cox, of later Watergate fame, had to give up his seat on the Wayland Board of Selectmen when he was appointed U.S. Solicitor General in 1961.

The 1960s brought new forces to bear on the burgeoning South Middlesex area. Cold War tensions were high during 1961—the year that the Berlin Wall went up—when Charles Ayer wrote,

From the distant rumbles of Berlin to the hearing halls of Framingham there has been an uneasy ferment, with promise of more to come.

In the shadow of a world growing in population and complexity is a growing Framingham, which more and more, day by day, becomes the central nexus of a new metropolitan area.

It was in 1961 and 1962 that Cold War fears spawned a craze for fallout shelters across the country. In March 1962 the state of Massachusetts started constructing its own fallout shelter—an underground bunker on part of the old Musterfield, which became the state's Civil Defense headquarters. The Cold War also brought government contracts to Route 128 firms specializing in military and weapons technology. In 1962 a contract for a Polaris missile guidance system went to Raytheon in Sudbury.

Also in the early 1960s, once President Kennedy set his sights on the moon, the government handed out contracts for aerospace projects. Many of these contracts went to Route 128 firms and such South Middlesex enterprises as Microwave Development of Natick.

In 1964 Raytheon, one of the few companies to recognize the

CONJUROR'S JOURNAL

Excerpts from the Journal of Joshua Medley

Conjuror, Juggler, Ventriloquist, and Sometime Balloonist

A Novel by FRANCES L. SHINE

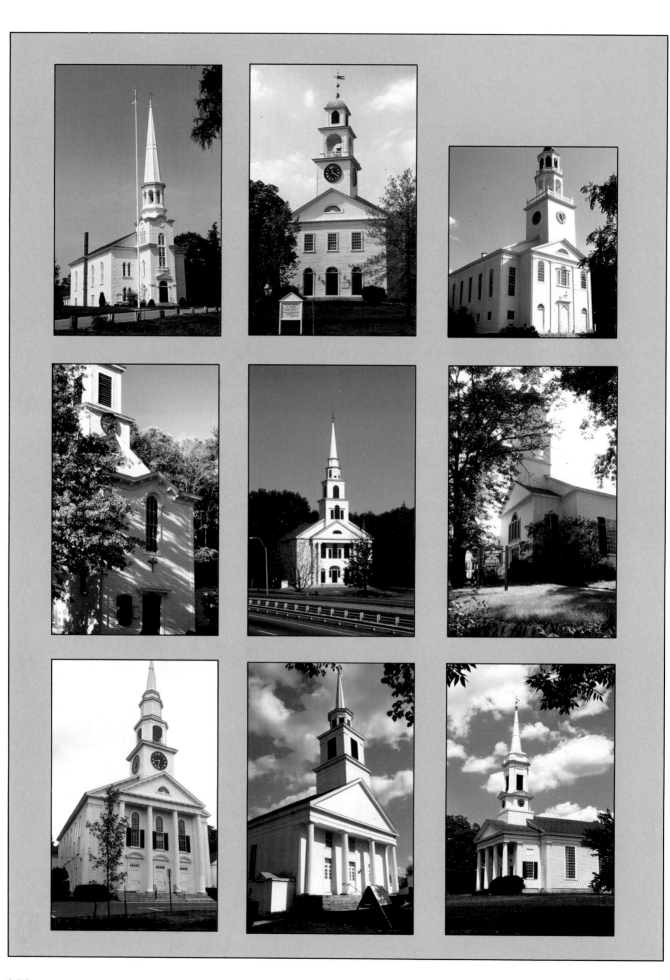

IN THIS LITTLE SHOP
HENRY WILSON
20ᵗʰ VICE PRESIDENT OF THE UNITED STATES
LEARNED TO MAKE SHOES
WAS KNOWN AS THE NATICK COBBLER

Facing page: All nine South Middlesex towns contain at least one church that reflects traditional New England religious architecture. While most of these houses of worship date from the nineteenth century, the oldest is the Sudbury First Parish Church, built in 1797. On facing page, from top left: the Pilgrim Congregational Church in Southborough; the First Parish Church of Sudbury; the First Parish Church (Unitarian) of Wayland Center; the Woodville Baptist Church of Hopkinton; the First Baptist Church of Framingham Center; the Eliot Church in South Natick; the First Congregational Church of Holliston; the Federated Church of Ashland; and the First Parish Church (Unitarian) of Sherborn. Courtesy, Framingham Historical Society

Above: Henry Wilson, "the Natick cobbler," began his shoe manufacturing career in this small shop on West Central Street in West Natick. Today this site is a patriotic shrine complete with liberty bell and town honor roll. Courtesy, Framingham Historical Society

Right and far right: Elias Grout was a teacher and gentleman farmer in Ashland and a president of the Middlesex South Agricultural Society. Grout's father was one of the youngest soldiers at the Battle of Bunker Hill. Mrs. Harriett Fiske Grout had her protrait made at the same time as her husband, circa 1850. Courtesy, Ashland Historical Society

Below, Left: James Jackson, one of Ashland's founding fathers, had been promoting township for his village of Unionville for many years before incorporation was finally granted in 1846. Jackson's political idol was Henry Clay, whose Ashland estate in Kentucky was the inspiration for the name of the new town. Courtesy, Mrs. Ann Thurston

Far right: The Reverend Edmund Dowse of Sherborn served as pastor for sixty-seven years. As a state senator he initiated legislation that brought about the Reformatory Prison for Women at Sherborn, now Massachusetts Correctional Institute (MCI) at Framingham. Courtesy, Sherborn Historical Society

The Noyes-Parris house in Wayland was built about 1669. The Reverend Samuel Parris, former minister at Salem Village and prominent in the witchcraft trials of 1692, lived out his life here. Many of the families persecuted by Parris and his family moved only a few miles down the road to Salem End in Framingham. Courtesy, Wayland Historical Society

Fire Department, So. Framingham, Mass.

Above: The men and equipment of the Framingham Fire Department on Hollis Street proudly turn out for their picture. The brick station (with its hose drying tower in the rear) was just a few years old when this picture was made circa 1900. Courtesy, R. Maish Collection

Right: One of Henry Warren's early experimental electric clocks was housed under a glass dome. These clocks required cumbersome batteries, but this led Warren to develop the "telechron" clock motor powered by alternating current. Courtesy, Ann Thurston, Ashland

Facing page, top: The rural flavor of the villages of the early nineteenth century is captured in this 1850 watercolor of Wayland Center showing the Greek Revival town hall and the "old red store." Courtesy, Wayland Historical Society

Far left: The site of Hopkinton's first meetinghouse, chosen by lot in 1724, is now marked by a plaque that represents the early settlers of that town at prayer. Now runners pray here every year as they prepare for the grueling twenty-six-mile Boston Marathon, which starts nearby. Courtesy, Framingham Historical Society

Left: The pulpit from the Indian church of Natick that was used by Takawambait, the Indian minister who succeeded John Eliot, is now back in Natick. It contains a large drawer that may have stored the Indian Bible. Courtesy, First Congregational Church, Natick, and Mr. Henri Prunaret, Trustee

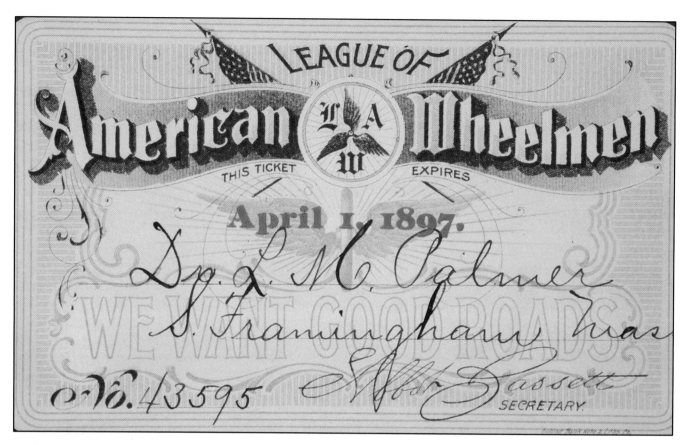

The popularity of the bicycle
near the end of the nineteenth
century encouraged enthusiasts
to organize into groups like the
League of American Wheelmen.
This membership card belonged
to Dr. Lewis Palmer, a prominent physician and superintendent of schools in Framingham.
On the card behind the signature are the words: WE WANT
GOOD ROADS. Courtesy, Framingham Historical Society

The incorporation of Southborough in 1727 is commemorated on this parade banner that also celebrated the agricultural heritage of that town. The original banner was badly worn from many years use, and this reproduction restored the color and detail that had been lost. Courtesy, Southborough Historical Society

Far right: In 1848, Boston celebrated the flow of water from Lake Cochituate with a new dance—the Cochituate Grand Quick Step. This hand-colored, lithographed illustration shows a Boston Common fountain that was part of the new water system. Courtesy, Framingham Historical Society

Right: At Old Path Village, a small shopping center in Framingham, a huge boulder and bronze plaque commemorate the Old Connecticut Path, which runs by it. The path was the route taken by the Reverend Hooker and his followers to establish the Connecticut colony in the 1600s. The stone was erected by Joseph and David Brossi, developers of the shopping center. Courtesy, David A. Brossi

154

Top: The Wayside Inn today looks much the same as it did in Longfellow's time, thanks to preservation efforts by Henry Ford, and to many generous contributions for restoration after a disastrous fire in the 1950s. Courtesy, Framingham Historical Society

Bottom: Sudbury's Red Horse Tavern looked like this about the time that Henry Wadsworth Longfellow's Tales of a Wayside Inn *was published in the 1860s, bringing the tavern popularity and a change of name to Longfellow's Wayside Inn. Courtesy, Goodnow Public Library, Sudbury*

Facing page, top: Captain John Stone built his hotel near the depot at Unionville (now Ashland) when the Boston and Worcester Rail Road was put through in 1834. The hotel may also have been a stop on the Underground Railroad when slaves were smuggled out of the South. The building is now a restaurant called John Stone's Inn. Courtesy, Framingham Historical Society

Above: This North Sudbury garrison colonial-style home, complete with a split rail fence, is evidence that New England architectural traditions are preserved in South Middlesex. Courtesy, Framingham Historical Society

Right: The Haynes garrison house was one of several fortified buildings on the west side of Sudbury that provided shelter when King Philip's warriors scourged the town in 1675. Courtesy, Goodnow Public Library, Sudbury

Above: Farming is still an important business in many parts of South Middlesex, such as northeast Southborough where Willow Brook Farm has been operating for many years. Courtesy, Framingham Historical Society

Left: Harold Hildreth stands in the door of his Sherborn barn in this 1978 photo. His lands have been farmed by the same family for generations. Once the dominant occupation of the region, farming is now practiced by only a small minority. Photo by Ruth DeMauro. Courtesy, Framingham Historical Society

Harvest time in Hopkinton finds farmers selling colorful potted chrysanthemums, pumpkins, and other produce at the many rural farm stands still found in South Middlesex. Courtesy, Framingham Historical Society

Left: The home of Henry Wilson still stands on West Central Street near Natick Center. This house, plus several other fine nineteenth-century dwellings, are now included in the Henry Wilson Historic District. Courtesy, Framingham Historical Society

Below: Once a year, Hopkinton, Massachusetts, becomes the center of attention as the area gears up for the famed Boston Marathon. WKOX, a Framingham radio station, was on hand at a recent running of the spring event to broadcast the action to South Middlesex communities.

A stone-arched bridge built by the WPA in the 1930s blends in with the park setting on the banks of the Charles River in South Natick. This is the site where John Eliot's praying Indians built a wooden footbridge, also arched, three hundred years before. Courtesy, Framingham Historical Society

With the rise of rapid development grew concern for the protection of wetlands like the Sudbury River watershed. In the 1950s private watershed protection groups were formed, followed by town conservation commissions. Courtesy, Jerry Howard

danger of overdependence on government contracts, began diversifying into commercial areas. That same year the Perini company was one of three construction firms contracted to push the Massachusetts Turnpike all the way to Boston harbor. Perini also built the new Prudential Center with its fifty-two-story tower—one of the first landmarks of the "new Boston." The turnpike ran right under the Prudential Center, not far from a newly painted finish line for the Boston Marathon. Access to Boston, once an all-day effort, was reduced to twenty minutes. Exit 13 saw more than five million cars pass through its booths in 1967, sending more traffic onto Route 30 and Speen Street (its direct link to Route 9). The corresponding development along Route 30 and Speen Street expanded the Golden Mile into a golden triangle.

The Route 30 side of the triangle soon had a new engineering headquarters for New England Telephone and a new regional post office. In 1965, at the Speen Street-Route 9 corner of the triangle, a new generation of shopping malls was introduced. The fully enclosed Natick Mall made leisurely and comfortable shopping possible during the long months of the New England winter. Shoppers World's open-air mall was a delightful place in the spring and summer—an oasis of green and bright floral color. But the harsh winds of fall and winter that swept

Above: The state's underground Civil Defense Agency at Framingham's old Musterfield is marked only by radio towers and a sign on Route 9. Built during the bomb-shelter craze of the early 1960s, the underground bunker can accommodate state government in the event of an emergency. Courtesy, Framingham Historical Society

Right: Christmas shopping is warm and dry at stores in the Natick Mall. Opened in 1965, Natick Mall introduced enclosed shopping malls to South Middlesex, and offered shelter from the New England winters. Photo by Linda Sussman. Courtesy, Natick Bulletin

down its ramps and walkways discouraged even the most hardy New England shoppers. By 1984, after several more enclosed malls appeared on the triangle and nearby, the owners of Shoppers World made plans to abandon the open-air oasis of flowers and summer concerts for the more comfortable and profitable accommodations of a larger, enclosed mall complex. The old structure, one of the nation's first large landscaped malls and a landmark of postwar resurgence, was thus to be consumed by its own success.

During the third postwar decade (1965-1975) growth continued in Framingham and increased in Sudbury and Holliston. By 1972 Holliston counted forty-eight developments of all sizes built since 1950. The town required a police force of eighteen to do a job that was done by one man in 1925.

It was probably some time during 1967 that Framingham became the largest town in Massachusetts. For several years Brookline and Arlington were larger, but as they were both mature, fully built-up sections of metropolitan Boston, it was inevitable that the rapidly expanding Framingham would surpass them. Framingham was twice the size of Natick and encompassed about 40 percent of the population of the entire South Middlesex region. The problems of running a city-sized town with a board of three part-time selectmen was recognized in 1965, when the position of executive secretary-coordinator (now executive administrator) was created to provide a full-time administrator for town business.

For some time the Framingham Chamber of Commerce had been involved with the needs and problems of the business communities of

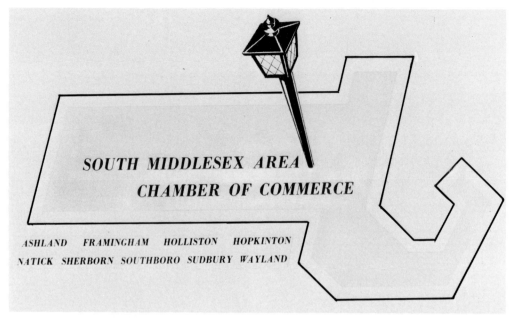

other South Middlesex towns. The extended scope of the chamber was recognized in 1966, when it changed its name to South Middlesex Chamber of Commerce.

When the recession of 1968-1969 hit hard in Massachusetts, it looked again like the end to the boom may have come. Space program cutbacks and the Nixon administration's anti-Massachusetts stance proved how unreliable government contracts could be. The number of Massachusetts employees in electronics slid from 103,000 in 1967 to 80,000 in 1971. There was a purge along Route 128, but South Middlesex was so well diversified and involved in private sector industry that it was able to withstand the blow. For instance, in 1968 Dr. Amar G. Bose used his MIT engineering background to start manufacturing high fidelity loudspeaker systems at the Framingham Industrial Park.

This was also a time when developments in data processing technology were opening up a major new opportunity for computer manufacturers. The transistor, introduced in 1948, evolved into an array of electronic devices called semiconductors. These became the building blocks for smaller but powerful computers called minicomputers. Three of the companies that were to become leaders in the field of minicomputers were closely related to the South Middlesex area: Digital Equipment, Data General, and Prime Computer.

Digital Equipment was founded in 1957 in Maynard, a mill town on the Assabet River incorporated in 1871. (Maynard had been created by combining parts of Sudbury and Stow.) Digital started business in a corner of one floor of the former American Woolen Company mill. It experienced a phenomenal growth rate, particularly after it introduced its first successful "professional data processor" in 1965, the PDP-8. The

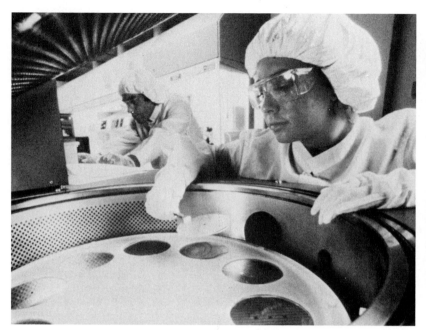

Above, left: Semiconductors are manufactured on silicon chips in a superclean environment at the Raytheon Semiconductor Division. Chips such as these are the heart of the minicomputer, manufactured by such South Middlesex firms as Digital Equipment, Data General, and Prime Computer. Courtesy, Raytheon Semiconductor Division

Above, right: Dr. Amar G. Bose poses with a speaker that earned the Bose Corporation a reputable name in the field of high-fidelity acoustics. In the 1960s, Bose Corporation, like many South Middlesex technological companies, relied less on government contracts and more on innovation. Courtesy, Bose Corporation

company eventually filled the mill and has expanded to facilities throughout eastern Massachusetts, including Southborough and Sudbury. Digital has grown worldwide to employ more people than the entire population of Framingham.

Some of the engineers working on Digital's successful PDP line decided to form their own company. In 1968 they founded Data General in the town of Hudson. Selling 100 computers during its first year, Data General soon moved into an industrial park in Southborough, then built its own large headquarters complex in Westborough in 1977.

While Digital and Data General built computers for scientific and technical customers, a need for more commercially adaptable minicomputers was seen by investors who started Prime Computer in 1972. Another fast-growing company, Prime soon occupied a large facility in the Framingham Industrial Park.

The future of South Middlesex as a center of technology and professional industry was assured in 1969 with the opening of another major highway. Route 495 was built roughly parallel to Route 128, ten miles farther west. The new highway started near the New Hampshire border and swept down to the Rhode Island border, cutting through the western parts of Southborough and Hopkinton. A new Massachusetts Turnpike exit (Exit llA) was created where the turnpike intersected Route 495. This exit was not far from a Marlborough computer complex built by RCA but later sold to Digital Equipment after RCA pulled out of the computer business in 1971.

The increasingly attractive economic atmosphere would have

fueled the housing boom indefinitely had it not been for the towns' efforts in zoning, conservation, and planning, as well as the simple exhaustion of available land. Twenty-five years after the Second World War ended, the growth finally leveled off. The effect of the limited supply was a corresponding increase in real estate prices.

In 1969 the state legislature became concerned over racial imbalance caused by high housing costs in such middle-class areas as South Middlesex. An "anti-snob" law was passed to give state housing agencies more power when dealing with local zoning disputes. However, the racial mix of the suburbs did not change significantly. This was pointed out in a 1975 state/federal report titled "Route 128: Boston's Road to Segregation." By 1980 the nonwhite population of the South Middlesex towns did not exceed 3 percent in any town except Framingham, where a large Hispanic community brought the nonwhite population to just over 5 percent. Although Framingham's black population is only just over 2 percent, since 1967 the town's school system has participated in a voluntary busing program called METCO. As of 1985, 122 inner-city students were involved in Framingham's

The spirit of high technology in South Middlesex is well represented in the name of this company located in a Natick industrial park. While the name suggests Albert Einstein's theory of relativity, the company actually makes memory storage units for computers. Courtesy, Framingham Historical Society

165

METCO. Sudbury, Wayland, Natick, and Sherborn also participate in the program.

In the early 1970s Framingham experienced a brief housing resurgence when large-scale apartment buildings were allowed. The Exit 12 area soon had a string of hotel-size units along Route 9 overlooking the reservoirs that had been put there one hundred years before. By 1974 it appeared that this type of development was getting out of hand, and the result was a moratorium on such building. These apartments and others in Ashland, Wayland, Hopkinton, and Holliston did not fulfill the promise of lower housing costs, as many of them were converted to condominiums in the later seventies.

The seventies brought increased regionalization to South Middlesex. High schools in the smaller towns, plus Framingham's vocational high school, were combined across town lines. In 1971 *The Framingham News* became *The South Middlesex News*, and expanded its circulation base not only to the nine South Middlesex towns, but to a wider area of about thirty towns it called MetroWest. As its readership approached 50,000 in 1979, the *News* joined Bose and Prime Computer at the Framingham Industrial Park. There the *News* built a sprawling $7-million plant and changed its name to *The Middlesex News*. By that time the old State Normal School had become Framingham State College. The only institution of higher learning in South Middlesex, Framingham State now offers both men and women of surrounding communities a wide variety of academic programs.

Along cultural lines, the Danforth Museum of Fine Arts opened in 1975 in a former Framingham high school building. Offering exhibits of

Below Left: Apartment buildings and condominiums built in the early 1970s near Massachusetts Turnpike Exit 12 in Framingham are pleasantly situated between a reservoir and the Framingham Country Club. An 1870s reservoir gate house can be seen in the lower right. Photo by Ric Getter. Courtesy, Dave Granlund and Don's Flying Service

Below Right: Since World War II, housing developments have spread throughout South Middlesex, underscoring the region's population increase since 1945. These developments began in Natick and Wayland and have reached to the western parts of Southborough and Hopkinton. Courtesy, Framingham Historical Society

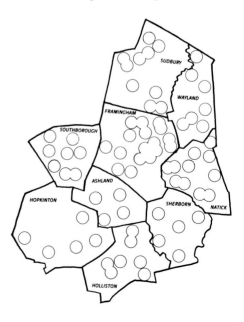

the works of nationally and internationally known artists, Danforth also offers classes in a variety of arts-related fields, as well as internships for students at the state college.

The national bicentennial activity that started in 1975 with the 200th anniversary of the Battle of Lexington and Concord helped stimulate an interest in local heritage. New town histories were published for Natick, Holliston, and Sherborn. Natick established the John Eliot Historic District in South Natick in 1974, and created the Henry Wilson Historic District along West Central Street a few years later. Sherborn had celebrated its 300th anniversary in 1974, introducing a new town seal featuring the pine tree shilling. Framingham observed its 275th anniversary in 1975 with a parade and special exhibits on local history.

As the bicentennial was primarily a celebration of the events of 1776, an enterprising young man in Sudbury took advantage of the fact that the zip code for Sudbury happened to be 01776. He had red, white, and blue bumper stickers printed celebrating Sudbury's patriotic zip code, and sold them. For a while it seemed that every car in Sudbury had one of these stickers, and faded specimens could still be seen ten years later.

A cloud hanging over the bicentennial celebration was the recession of 1974-1975. This one involved energy shortages, impacting the commuters and homeowners of South Middlesex. From 1974 to 1979 the local construction industry was virtually at a standstill. Inflation and increasing interest rates put South Middlesex houses and condominiums out of reach for many potential buyers. These buyers were forced to seek housing in the communities north, south, and west of the South Middlesex towns.

When construction resumed it took the form of shopping malls, condominiums, and professional office buildings. In rapid succession, landmarks of the early postwar period were replaced as the new commercial building boom progressed. The Natick Drive-In theater became a mall-hotel complex. The Carling brewery became the headquarters for Prime Computer. The Carousel Theater site was developed as a Prime Computer research and development complex. The Meadows supper club became an office building, also called The Meadows. One of the Exit 13 trucking depots was cleared out for Point West Place, a professional office building designed in the post-modern style by Robert A.M. Stern. A miniature golf course and driving range in Natick on Route 9 became the site of a glittering high-style mall called Apple Hill.

With the earlier housing boom, South Middlesex towns had

The Danforth Museum of Fine Arts has been a regional cultural institution since 1975. Located in a former Framingham high school building on Union Avenue, the museum offers classes in art-related subjects. Courtesy, Middlesex News

Boston Marathon runners in 1985 charge from the starting line at Hopkinton Center on their way to Ashland, Framingham, and Natick along Route 135. Only the stronger ones will make it through Wellesley and Newton to the finish line in Boston, in this annual rite of spring. Courtesy, Middlesex News

Office buildings surround the north end of Speen Street where it meets the Old Connecticut Path in Framingham. This area was once noted for its greenhouses and is near the site of an old Indian village. Courtesy, Framingham Historical Society

become known as "bedroom" communities, their wage earners mostly working in the Boston area. The later commercial and high technology boom, however, started reversing that trend, especially in Framingham and Natick. Since 1970 the number of new jobs opening up in South Middlesex has exceeded the number of new residents coming in by a ratio of three to one. A November 1984 report on commercial development appearing in *The Middlesex News* stated, "From an area once known for its farms and mills, MetroWest has catapulted its way into an urban conglomeration that has one of the nation's highest concentrations of high technology industries outside of California's Silicon Valley."

Ashland, the town that introduced scientific technology to South Middlesex industry in the early twentieth century, was not able to keep up with Framingham and Natick, its old industrial partners. Shrinking electric clock production was passed off from General Electric to Timex, then sold to its employees. The employees resurrected the name Telechron but had only a fraction of the work force of the 1940s. Also, the Lombard Governor Company gradually sold off its diversified product lines to interests out of town, until the company no longer existed. High technology, however, has been carried into the latter twentieth century by Fenwal (now a subsidiary of the Kidde

conglomerate) and smaller electronics firms.

The commercial development of the fourth postwar decade (1975-1985) helped South Middlesex become the largest retail center in New England outside of Boston, its stores and shopping centers doing an annual trade approaching one billion dollars. When the ancient Massachusetts "blue laws" restricting Sunday shopping were finally lifted in the early 1980s, thousands of shoppers who previously crossed the border into New Hampshire on Sunday flocked to the more conveniently situated malls and shopping centers of South Middlesex.

The spirit of economic revival even reached the aging downtown areas where an awareness of the heritage of older buildings has been evident. In downtown Framingham the former Barber straw goods factory became an office center, and the architecturally significant railroad depot was renovated as a restaurant. In Natick Center, the Harwood Baseball factory building was converted to condominiums.

On the negative side of the boom in commercial properties has been a mounting concern by residents over its impact on traffic, water, and sewerage. This concern grew into moratorium movements in Framingham and Sudbury that sought, in 1984, to ban further commercial construction. While the town meetings defeated the moratoriums, higher standards for traffic control were set for future developments. But as construction goes on, some predict that the only way to relieve the traffic burden on Route 9 will be to make it into a "double-decker" highway through the Golden Mile area.

With all the attention on development, it is easy to lose sight of the fact that most of the actual acreage of South Middlesex remains either undeveloped or agricultural. State parks, town forests, reservoirs, lakes, rivers, wetlands, and other protected properties constitute an average of 60 percent of the territory of the nine South Middlesex towns. Add to this the still respectable 8,759 acres devoted to farms, orchards, and nurseries, and the average "open" space total comes to almost 70 percent. Commercial and industrial space, for all its congestion and controversy, constituted less that 5 percent of South Middlesex area in 1985.

The open areas provide a wide range of contributions to the quality of South Middlesex life, including recreational activities such as hiking and swimming at the state parks in Wayland, Framingham, Ashland, Holliston, and Hopkinton; nature walks in the Broadmoor Wildlife Sanctuary in Natick and in the Garden in the Woods in Framingham; seasonal produce available at roadside stands run by local farmers; riding stables; and canoeing on the rivers and ponds. In Southborough, although there is no longer a Deerfoot Farm, agriculture

Facing page, top: South Middlesex housing construction in the 1980s often took the form of condominium clusters such as these in the western end of Ashland. This development is not far from the sites of the old poor farms of Ashland and Holliston. Courtesy, Framingham Historical Society

Facing page, bottom: Natick Village, an apartment complex in West Natick, houses thousands of apartment dwellers. Courtesy, Framingham Historical Society

Historic preservation and awareness is represented in these two scenes from South Natick. At right, the Goin Bailey house of 1839, although "recycled" as a small shopping complex, retains its Greek Revival splendor. Above, a group of newly built office buildings has been built in the same classical spirit. Courtesy, Framingham Historical Society

traditions are carried on at Willow Brook and other active farms and dairies. Southborough is also home to some types of animals one would not expect to find in South Middlesex. One farm keeps a small herd of buffalo, and up on Pine Hill Road the behavior of monkeys and larger apes is studied at the New England Regional Primate Center.

An exciting moment in a 1982 baseball game continues a 100-year tradition in South Middlesex, where the manufacture of baseballs was once an important industry. Courtesy, Dave Granlund

The open areas have also allowed much of the area's heritage to be preserved. The view from the site of the first Sudbury meetinghouse, where it all began, is of a few cultivated fields stretching out to the great meadows of the Sudbury River—much as it must have looked over 300 years ago. Just off the main roads of Wayland and Sudbury can be found monuments to the battles of King Philip's War. In the old Boggestow area of Sherborn, a boulder in a small cemetery commemorates the place where the founders of Sherborn and Holliston first settled. In the same cemetery a 1754 headstone recalls the horrors of the Memorable Mortality. The waterfall at South Natick suggests Indian fishing weirs, Yankee mills, and the engineers of the WPA. Hostile Indians are recalled in a Framingham playground where a

Above: In tribute to Christa McAuliffe, the nation's first teacher-astronaut, a giant billboard was erected in Framingham Center, facing Route 9 and the college where she graduated. The billboard was a result of the collaboration of local businessman Paul Cohen, the state college, the Middlesex News, and the Coleman Sign Company. Standing, left to right: Dr. Joseph Lopes of Framingham State College; Dave Granlund, political cartoonist of the Middlesex News, who designed the artwork for the billboard; Chris Meli, sign painter for the Coleman Sign Company; and Jack Coleman. Courtesy, Middlesex News

boulder marks the place of the Eames Massacre. A few miles away, on Salem End Road, the house of accused witch Sarah Clayes still stands. And in the Ashland town forest are caves the Salem refugees may have used during that winter of 1692. From Route 495 passing through Hopkinton and Southborough can be seen endless acres of forest and wild land. This terrain looks much the same as it did to the Scottish immigrants of 1718 and the lessees of the Trustees of the Charity of Edward Hopkins.

While much of the heritage of South Middlesex is preserved in both its developed and undeveloped areas, it is also being carried forward by its people. Doug Flutie of Natick, the Home of Champions, won the 1984 Heisman college football trophy after a spectacular season as a Boston College quarterback. Christa McAuliffe, who grew up in Framingham and graduated from Framingham State College (the nation's oldest public teachers' college), became the first teacher chosen to travel in space. Her tragic death in the space shuttle disaster of January 28, 1986, taught the entire nation a lesson in courage.

The people of South Middlesex continue a tradition of Puritan independence and toughness plus Yankee ingenuity and enterprise that has spanned over three and a half centuries. Whether they are old-timers or postwar carpetbaggers, and regardless of religious or ethnic background, many of them would probably agree with the old-time preachers who selected as the text for their sermons this verse from the book of Psalms: The lines are fallen unto me in pleasant places; yea, I have a goodly heritage.

Facing page, bottom: Natick's reputation as the "Home of Champions" was strengthened in 1984 when native-son Doug Flutie won the coveted Heisman college football trophy. Flutie was further honored in 1985 when a new road connecting Shoppers World and Natick Mall was named "Flutie Pass." Courtesy, Middlesex News

Below: Despite the rise of suburban malls, downtown Framingham remained an active business center in 1967 when this picture was taken. At about that time, Framingham became the largest town in Massachusetts and was more populous than many of the state's cities. The Memorial Building, at right, continued as the center of town government. Courtesy, Framingham Public Library

7

PARTNERS IN PROGRESS

Framingham today is the heart of the second-largest commercial center in New England. Located in the center of eastern Massachusetts, it is the natural hub for transportation lines serving several states. Its commercial history began in 1806, when a private corporation built a toll road through town. The village now known as Framingham Center formed quickly along the new Boston-Worcester Turnpike and became home for several stage-coach companies and the town's first bank, opened in 1833. The village gained prestige twenty years later when America's first teachers' college relocated there. But business had already begun drifting away from Framingham Center and its stagecoaches, attracted to more convenient properties in South Framingham, which welcomed the arrival of the "iron horse" in the 1830s.

Framingham's first manufacturing plant—the Saxon Factory Company—opened in 1824 on the falls of the Sudbury River. Later known as the Saxonville Mills, it was busy during the Civil War producing uniforms and blankets for Union soldiers. Between the Civil War years and the turn of the century, life and business based directly on the land, such as mills, straw bonnet factories, and farms, gave way to mechanization. In the late 1800s the Para Rubber Shoe Company prospered on the site now occupied by the Dennison Manufacturing Company, employing up to 1,000 residents. A daily newspaper begun in 1890 survives today as *The Middlesex News*. In the 1920s Framingham became home for several automobile manufacturers. Waverly Electric cars were assembled near the Dennison factory, and the Bay State auto was manufactured on South Street by the R.H. Long Company. Franklin sedans were also built here by the Bela Body Company, and it is not surprising that when General Motors decided to manufacture cars in New England after World War II, it was attracted to Framingham, located on major highway and railroad trade routes. Construction of the Massachusetts Turnpike Extension with two convenient local exits cemented Framingham's position as the crossroads of New England in the 1950s. Shoppers World, the first regional shopping center east of the Mississippi, opened a dramatic new era of customer convenience in 1951—forty-four connected stores with ample free parking. Several businesses discussed in this chapter were born during the postwar baby boom, when families flocked to Framingham seeking homes, jobs, and consumer services. Since 1970, when it was learned that only 20 percent of area residents had daily business in Boston, the towns of South Middlesex County began drawing together, identifying themselves as a magnet. High-tech industries—once clustered along Route 128—now dot the hillsides of South Middlesex County, bringing new diversity to an already prosperous economic base. This chapter tells the stories of local entrepreneurs who have chosen to support this publication—large and small, new and old—who are not only good businesses, but also good neighbors.

One of several Framingham baseball clubs sets off for a game in the 1880s, using one of the old stagecoaches that hauled passengers between South Framingham and Framingham Center. Courtesy, Framingham Historical Society

METROWEST CHAMBER OF COMMERCE

Framingham merchants had a problem in the 1890s. One of the town's major employers—the Para Rubber Shoe Company—closed its doors in 1891, throwing about 1,000 workers out of jobs. In a village of 9,500, this caused a serious economic shock wave that was eventually felt at the cash drawers of every store in town.

Against this background, a local newspaper announced that a meeting would be held on July 9, 1895, to determine whether or not a businessmen's organization should be formed. Those who attended the meeting voted to establish the Framingham Board of Trade, hoping to revitalize the town's flagging economy.

The new Board of Trade hit the ground running. According to Henry S. Dennison, former president of Dennison Manufacturing Company, "We became interested in Framingham as an industrial location in 1895, through a circular sent out by your organization, enumerating many advantages of the town." Dennison soon moved its headquarters into the buildings vacated by the Para Rubber Shoe Company, and quickly became one of Framingham's major employers.

Encouraged by this major success, the Board turned its attention to other important issues affecting town businesses. For several years Framingham had been buying its water from a private concern. In 1896 the Board led a campaign to purchase the Framingham Water Company, which later became a town institution. Other innovations followed as the Board broadened the scope of its activities.

In 1900 merchants of the Board of Trade agreed to adopt uniform store hours. Seven years later the Board fought for and secured the widening

of the Framingham section of the Worcester Turnpike. During World War I the Board provided special services to the "boys" camping on the Muster Field in town. It first erected highway signs advertising Framingham in 1922, and in 1927 changed its name to the Framingham Chamber of Commerce, which was incorporated in 1931. This title would remain until its expanding influence in neighboring towns dictated a new signature, the South Middlesex Area Chamber of Commerce. Since 1985 it has been called the MetroWest Chamber of Commerce.

For nearly a century the Chamber has promoted the growth and welfare of the community by acting as the voice of business. Lobbying for better transportation and good sound planning, attracting and maintaining a labor force, promoting free enterprise, and sponsoring a business and education collaborative are present-day goals.

Today, from its modern offices at 600 Worcester Road, the Chamber continues to initiate and administer

Clifford Folger, the first president of the Framingham Board of Trade in 1895. The Board of Trade was the early predecessor of today's MetroWest Chamber of Commerce.

programs designed to improve the quality of life for all who live and work in the MetroWest area, and is an accredited Chamber of Commerce.

The Odd Fellows Block on Hollis Street in South Framingham. The building was erected in 1876 and remodeled in 1928. Photo circa 1881

ZAYRE CORPORATION

In 1956 the Max and Morris Feldberg family, owners of a chain of ladies' apparel stores since 1919, launched a new concept in retailing. They predicted that discounting would be the growth direction of the future and opened America's first neighborhood, self-service, general merchandise discount department store.

Today Zayre Corporation—named for the Yiddish expression "zehr gut" (very good)—has grown from its small experimental origins into one of America's biggest retail organizations, operating over 1,000 stores in 41 states from Maine to Florida and west to California.

Based in Framingham, Zayre Corporation now represents five separate retail businesses, each with a distinctive character. Zayre Stores, the largest division, boasts 360 full-line discount department stores. T.J. Maxx, established in 1977, is today the nation's second-largest off-price retailer, selling discounted brand-name family apparel in 31 states. Hit or Miss offers style-conscious career-oriented women high-fashion merchandise at low retail prices. BJ's Wholesale Club is a self-service, cash-and-carry warehouse, selling general merchandise and food at wholesale prices. BJ's serves small businesses, professional offices, institutions, and other groups on a membership basis. The newest Zayre division is Home Club, a chain of membership clubs offering high-quality brand-name home-improvement products at everyday low prices.

The corporate credo, "Zayre Cares," is manifested in both customer satisfaction and community service. Directed by its 16-year-old Office of Consumer and Community Affairs, the Zayre effort has been recognized by the White House Office of Consumer Affairs for its efforts in the field of consumer education. In addition, the firm provides financial support for the March of Dimes,

United Way, Save the Children, Toys for Tots, the Easter Seal Society, the Muscular Dystrophy Association, and many other charitable organizations in communities where its stores are located.

Nationwide, Zayre is responsive to the mounting concern about missing children. In Zayre Stores throughout the country, photographs of missing children are displayed on in-store posters and community bulletin boards. Zayre also has pictures of missing children printed on the inserts of one million picture frames it sells each year. A toll-free hotline number is provided so that customers

One of the largest discount store chains in the United States, Zayre Corporation represents several separate retail businesses. Clockwise, from upper left: Zayre Stores, T.J. Maxx, BJ's Wholesale Club, and Hit or Miss.

can help locate these lost children.

The Zayre good-neighbor policy has resulted in significant growth for the company. Extensive refurbishment and expansion continue to spur sales and earnings, and by 1986-1987 Zayre expects to see volume surpass five billion dollars, predicated by the opening of more than two million square feet of retail space to accommodate 1,200 stores.

NEW ENGLAND LAMINATING COMPANY

Ken and Linda Krupski are combining modern technology and Old World tradition in their family business—New England Laminating Company of Framingham. Their hand-crafted products—plaques, portfolios, posters, maps, photographs, wedding invitations, and menus—have been ordered by customers as far away as Alaska. They even produced a plaque for President Ronald Reagan when he was wounded—a "get well" telegram ordered by Western Union. Another, in Braille, was once designed for singer Stevie Wonder.

"Everything we do is custom made," emphasizes Ken Krupski, who worked for the company for five years—learning the business from the ground up—before buying it in December 1983. Linda, his wife and business partner, runs the office while Ken handles production. "We're a close family," Linda explains. Daughter Ashley, now one-and-one-half years old, has been at the plant almost daily since she was two weeks old. "She's our public rela-

tions expert," adds Linda.

New England Laminating takes obvious pride in a superior product. Using one of the largest laminators available—a Mylar 36—Ken does most of the work himself. "Nothing is ever farmed out," he explains, "and our wooden products aren't made with plywood, but only the highest-quality birch veneer. That way the edges are much more attractive."

Laminating is not a simple process. Both heat and pressure must be combined to bond sheet vinyl or mylar to both sides of subject material so firmly that the plastic actually penetrates the fibers of the item being laminated. But the advantages are obvious. Subjects may be viewed from both sides if necessary. Laminating may be hole-punched for use in a loose-leaf book. Mounting on wood or plastic also of-

Ken and Linda Krupski, pictured with their daughter, Ashley, manufacture their hand-crafted products in their New England Laminating Company plant in Framingham.

fers a wide variety of display possibilities. Best of all, lamination protects materials from dirt, moisture, or accidental tearing. It is a permanent process, and laminated subjects retain their original appearance indefinitely.

At New England Laminating, no request is too small. "We welcome individual orders," stresses Ken, "as well as quantity work." One of the firm's most popular specialty items is a personalized teak tray. "It's an ideal way to preserve a favorite family sketch or photograph," explains Linda, balancing Ashley on one knee, "and many people have found that it makes a unique and useful wedding gift." Each one is assembled by hand, with waterproof glue sealing every joint and all corners rabbeted for extra strength and beauty.

New England Laminating Company is an authentic "mom and pop" operation with a twist. Instead of a storefront, the firm occupies a 2,300-square-foot plant, but Ken and Linda Krupski still adhere to the Yankee motto that whatever is worth doing is worth doing well.

SHOPPERS WORLD

October 4, 1951—a mid-winter lull in the Korean Conflict was about to end. General Dwight D. Eisenhower, inspecting Allied forces in Germany, heard President Truman offer to step aside if he would run for President on the Democratic ticket in 1952. Closer to home, the New York Giants and Yankees were opening the first game of the World Series at Yankee Stadium.

And in Framingham, Massachusetts, State Treasurer John Hurley stood at attention while the Camp Edwards Army Band played "The Star Spangled Banner" and a detail of Marines raised the first flag over Shoppers World—the second planned regional shopping center ever built in the United States.

It was sunny on dedication day. Hurley, representing Governor Paul Dever, described Shoppers World as "one of the seven wonders of New England." A huge fence bearing the names of 2,400 men and women who worked on the project was unveiled, and then the 44 new stores all opened at once, welcoming thousands of visitors. "Ask Me" girls, employed by the mall, drifted through the crowds answering questions, giving directions, and even reporting the latest score of the World Series from portable radios.

Shoppers found pop-up toasters for $23, and 17-inch Motorola TVs (black and white only) for just $199.95. That evening most folks watched, *A Millionaire for Christy,* starring Fred MacMurray, at the Shoppers World Cinema—the first suburban mall theater in the country.

More than a third of a century later Shoppers World has become a living landmark. Men and women who came as children to sit on San-

The front page of the Boston Globe *proclaimed the opening of Shoppers World on September 30, 1951. One of the "Seven Wonders of New England," it captured media attention on the radio and in hundreds of papers and magazines. Reprinted courtesy,* The Boston Globe

ta's lap now bring their own boys and girls in April to see the Easter Barnyard. Ten thousand bulbs imported from Holland bloom in a splash of

brilliance on the mall each May, marking the beginning of spring for generations of area families and earning high praise from the Massachusetts Horticultural Society. The summer concert series has become as much a tradition in Framingham as the strolling carolers and live reindeer at Christmas which delight shoppers of all ages.

"The original developers who designed Shoppers World had tremendous foresight," comments George Aptt, mall manager. "With suburbs beginning to sprawl, they felt many shoppers would be attracted by a collection of quality stores and restaurants offering ample free parking—now known as a shopping center. And they were right."

In the beginning, Shoppers World had few neighbors. Ken's Steak House, Vaughn Monroe's famous supper club, The Meadows, and Wyman Nurseries were nearest. Today it is wedged snugly between other malls and businesses that comprise the so-called "Golden Mile" of Route 9. But it has not become lost in the crowd. More than a pioneer shopping center and forum for community involvement, Shoppers World put Framingham on the map, and Yankees appreciate that kind of legacy.

Many celebrities have appeared at Shoppers World. Here Bozo delights his audience.

R.D. SMITH, INC.

Family members involved in the day-to-day operation of the construction firm include Richard D. Smith (standing), president; (seated, left to right) Richard D. Smith, Jr., controller and clerk; Mark D. Smith, project manager; and Jeffrey L. Smith.

and steel-framed buildings for White Construction Company. In 1967 Smith helped launch a commercial division for G. Arnold Haynes, Inc.—a firm previously engaged in home building.

In 1978 Smith founded the Metal Division of his company, which is now located in a modern new facility in Northborough, Massachusetts. This important diversification resulted from his anticipation of customers' needs and the variety of services he should provide to meet those needs. The Metal Division in Northborough has the capacity to do miscellaneous

R.D. Smith, Inc., established in 1971, is a major building construction firm located in eastern Massachusetts, specializing in design, building, and management of office, commercial, and industrial developments.

Although the company's primary focus is to provide new construction and renovation of office complexes, other projects have included restaurants, apartments, condominiums, and institutional facilities.

The company was founded by Richard D. Smith, who serves as president and treasurer. He has 35 years of cumulative experience in the building, design, and construction fields. His experience includes creative structural design of buildings for specific uses; total package construction consisting of plan, design, and execution of building projects; management of renovations and additions; and architectural and structural concrete work.

Smith worked as an inspector on the Mystic River Bridge, the New Jersey Turnpike, and other major

heavy construction projects. He later worked for Esso Standard Oil Company as a designer of service station and bulk plant layouts. After graduating from Northeastern University with a degree in civil engineering, he was field superintendent for 13 years on many major reinforced concrete

A staff meeting is held every Monday morning to share ideas and discuss developments in the field. Shown here are Richard D. Smith (standing), president; with (seated, left to right) William G. Chapman, chief designer; John J. Lamb, Jr., vice-president; Thomas P. Burke, vice-president and general manager; Mark D. Smith, project manager; and Frank H. Barnhill, project manager.

Wells Research Center, Newton, Massachusetts. An aerial view of two construction management projects—the building complex at the bottom was completed in 1982, while the project still under construction is due for completion in 1986.

iron work and structural steel fabrication. Equally significant are the research and testing services it provides for the firm's building and design division.

"R.D. Smith, Inc., is really a family firm," explains Richard Smith. "My three sons all know how to use a shovel. They learned the business from the ground up, and each now holds a leadership role in the company."

Jeffrey L. Smith, a graduate of Springfield College, is active in the Steel Division, where he administers buying, job expediting, and employee relations. Mark D. Smith, who earned a civil engineering degree from Northeastern University, is a project manager and marketing advocate in the Construction Division. Richard D. Smith, Jr., who holds degrees in accounting, computer science, and taxation from Boston College and Bentley College, serves as controller and clerk of the company.

In addition to his responsibility for the financial and administrative functions of his father's firm, Richard Jr. also established his own firm—Smith

Realty Management, Inc.—in August 1982. Utilizing experience gained from several years with the international certified public accounting firm of Peat Marwick, Rick has brought his extensive knowledge of accounting and operational systems to bear on the design of management and financial plans for both large and small real estate operations.

R.D. Smith, Inc., has never tried to be the least expensive construction firm in the area. Describing Richard Smith's lifelong love of excellence, one customer has observed, "He'll never get rich because every building he puts up is a monument!"

"He was wrong about that," responds Smith with a smile. "We have

The Metals Division fabricates and erects miscellaneous and structural steel.

managed to make a little money." In fact, the company has achieved an annual average growth rate of more than 50 percent for the past decade. It netted over $8 million in fiscal 1985, boosting that to $18 million in fiscal 1986. Sales for 1987 are conservatively estimated at $25 million.

R.D. Smith, Inc., construction projects dot the landscape of eastern Massachusetts. Many Framingham residents will recognize the new building at 600 Worcester Road, which recently became home for the MetroWest Chamber of Commerce. In Marlboro a 112,000-square-foot office complex at 33 Boston Post Road was completed in 1984.

In Natick, a new four-story, 27,000-square-foot office facility on Commonwealth Road houses the corporate headquarters, as well as other tenants. These projects are just a few of the dozens recently completed or under construction by the firm.

The people at R.D. Smith, Inc., realize that a building project is more than just concrete and steel. "We strive to achieve the optimum in space, aesthetics, and quality—inside and out," explains president Richard Smith. "With our accomplished and experienced staff, together with many outside architectural and engineering consultants, we offer a balance of expertise, imagination, and experience that link proven methods and innovation with the latest in new ideas."

COHEN & GAFFIN

In 1959 the original firm of Cohen, Gaffin & Greb was formed with offices in Boston and Framingham. The MetroWest area grew so rapidly that their offices were expanded. In 1973 the law firm moved into its own building at 615 Concord Street, Framingham, directly across from the Framingham District Court. Five years later the firm was reformed into Cohen & Gaffin, which presently has six attorneys and nine support staff, occupying space on three floors including a library, conference rooms, and computer functions.

With the move of many businesses out of the Boston area and the influx of other companies from outside Massachusetts moving into Metro-

Jason J. Cohen, left.

Gerald E. Gaffin, right.

West, Cohen & Gaffin has continued to expand, keeping pace with its clients' needs in such areas as real estate, corporate and commercial, personal injury litigation, domestic relations, estate planning, criminal defense, and zoning.

The founding partners, attorneys Jason J. Cohen and Gerald E. Gaffin, have been active in both legal and community affairs over the years. Gerald Gaffin is counsel to the Metro-West Chamber of Commerce and

was co-founder of the Trinity Mental Health Association, a comprehensive mental health facility serving residents of Framingham and the surrounding towns. Both founding partners are past presidents of the South Middlesex Bar Association and have served in leadership positions in other bar associations. Jason Cohen is a respected authority on family law and active in a variety of local and national organizations.

Keeping clients "fully informed" is a cornerstone of the firm's philosophy. "Nine to five" is fine, in theory, but a client's problems don't always develop in that time-frame. "Flexibility and availability are the keys," says Gerald Gaffin.

WKOX RADIO

The sprawling beige house at 100 Mount Wayte Avenue looks much like a comfortable private home until you notice the twin broadcasting towers—each 450 feet high—that dominate the backyard. In fact, it's the home of WKOX, a dependable neighbor to radio listeners throughout the greater Framingham area for almost 40 years. Winner (more than once) of the coveted Associated Press News Station of the Year Award, WKOX recently received approval from the Federal Communications Commission to boost its power from 1,000 to 10,000 watts. Previously limited to daytime broadcasting, it is now authorized to provide MetroWest listeners with entertainment, news, and information 24 hours a day.

"Our three original owners, Dick Adams, Al Anderson, and Jim Shumaker, were young veterans who met during the war," recalls station manager Barry Sims. "They scoured the East Coast together, looking for a promising spot to locate a radio station, and eventually settled here in Framingham. It proved to be a wise choice."

Adams, Anderson, and Shumaker did much of the original work themselves, including laying underground cable and tower foundations. "We first signed on the air in April 1947," Sims continues, "on the day of the Boston Marathon. The towers were here, but our studios were then downtown by the railroad station, in the Smith Building on Route 135. Runners in the marathon came right past our front door."

To give listeners a step-by-step report of the annual race, former announcer Lee Emmerich sometimes dragged microphone wires from his studio up to the roof of the Smith Building, which offered a commanding view of the course through Framingham. In later years WKOX received permission from the Boston Athletic Association (BAA) to broadcast the race from a studio van just ahead of the front runner. As crowds increased and technology im-

The WKOX staff and mobile units in 1957.

proved, broadcasting was done from a police cruiser. Today WKOX is traditionally the only radio station allowed to broadcast from within the marathon. An announcer with state-of-the-art equipment now rides in the official BAA time car.

Company president Richard M. Fairbanks, whose ancestors in 1636 built the famous Fairbanks House in Dedham—the oldest wooden structure in America—is proud of his station's reputation for protecting listeners in times of possible disaster. In June 1953 a freak tornado twisted south from New Hampshire, turning east at Worcester and hitting Shrewsbury, Westboro, and Southboro before petering out near the Framingham town line. WKOX remained on the air 24 hours a day, with up-to-the-minute storm warnings and weather reports. "We did the same thing during the blizzard of 1978," remembers Sims, pointing out that the station has its own generators in case of a power failure.

Today WKOX is a full-time, high-power radio station. More than 50 people staff its modern studios on the shore of Farm Pond. "But we still like to cover high school football games," Sims adds with a smile, "because, like the kids on the playing field, we also grew up in Framingham."

WKOX Radio has grown with Framingham. Part of the staff is shown here with the mobile units and helicopter in 1986.

FRAMINGHAM STATE COLLEGE

The first building when the First State Normal School was moved to its permanent home in Framingham on December 15, 1853.

Wellesley College, graduated from Framingham Normal School in 1867.

Framingham Normal School also had links with two black institutions—Hampton Institute in Virginia and Tuskegee in Alabama. Elizabeth Hyde, class of 1875, taught at Hampton Institute for more than 20 years. As a result of this strong tie, Framingham teachers went south and

December 15, 1853, was a cold and snowy morning in Framingham. But on the chilly northwest slope of Bare Hill, state educators were gathering to mark the dawn of a new era—dedicating the "permanent home" of the first public training school for teachers in America.

During the early 1800s boys and girls in Massachusetts were taught eight months each year by a "schoolmaster" usually less than 20 years old and paid about $15 per month plus room and board. In the spring of 1838 Edmund Dwight, a wealthy merchant, met with Horace Mann, secretary of the newly formed Board of Education—to request state aid for teacher training. Dwight donated $10,000. The legislature matched his contribution, and on July 3, 1839, the first teacher-training school opened in Lexington.

Cyrus Peirce (pronounced "purse") was the first principal of the new "Normal School"—named after the French "ecoles normales" or professional school for training teachers. The original course took only one year. An extra six months were added in 1846, and by 1854 several curricula were available for women.

After five years in Lexington, the school moved to larger quarters in West Newton. These were outgrown

Normal class of household arts, circa 1905.

within nine years, and a new location became necessary. Many towns requested the Normal School, but Framingham offered a site on Bare Hill and $2,500 on condition that the school be located there forever.

The school grew steadily at its new location. In addition to teacher training, it dared to conduct an advanced program for women who aspired to careers in college teaching, medicine, and law at a time when few such educational opportunities were open to women. Lucretia Crocker, who taught mathematics at Antioch College and later supervised the schools of Boston, was educated at the Normal School. Maria S. Eaton, first head of the Chemistry Department at

black students came north. Olivia Davidson, class of 1881, later married Booker T. Washington, first principal of the famous Negro Normal School at Tuskegee. Washington's daughter, Portia, also studied at Framingham.

At the turn of the century Framingham was chosen as the site for the new "household arts" program under the terms of philanthropist Mary Hemenway's will. This newly endowed program included laboratories, making it possible to offer more instruction in chemistry and other sciences.

In 1932 Massachusetts Normal School became Framingham State Teachers College, and three years later began granting the bachelor of science degree in education. In 1959 the college was finally empowered by the State Board of Education to

S. Christa Corrigan McAuliffe
1948-1986

grant—in addition to baccalaureate degrees previously authorized—bachelor of arts and bachelor of science degrees. The following year all teachers colleges became state colleges, and Framingham, the only state college exclusively for women, admitted men for the first time in 1964.

Dr. D. Justin McCarthy, who was selected president of the college in 1961, helped shape this important transition. During his 24-year administration, Framingham State grew from an enrollment of 700 with only two majors—elementary education and home economics—to a comprehensive state college offering 27 undergraduate majors and 12 master's-level programs to over 5,500 students. Under his direction, the college achieved a multimillion-dollar facility expansion program including new academic buildings, dormitories, faculty and administrative offices, library, chapel, and modern college center used by all college constituencies and community groups. Midway in Dr.

McCarthy's administration, in 1972 the Board of Higher Education's Advisory Council on Education conducted an intensive study of state colleges. It pointed to Framingham State as the "outstanding example among state colleges."

In 1973 the college cooperated with community leaders in founding the Danforth Museum in downtown Framingham. The Danforth provides exhibitions and internship programs for Framingham State students.

Cyrus Peirce taught his nineteenth-century students to "live to the truth." These words have lived ever since as the school motto, and were incorporated by Dr. Martin F. O'Connor (president, 1936-1961) in a poem that became the college hymn.

"We've often said the sky is the limit," says college president Paul F. Weller, "but not any more." In 1986 Framingham State College graduate Christa Corrigan McAuliffe (class of 1970) was selected as the first civil-ian and teacher astronaut. The tragedy of her death in the explosion of the Challenger Space Shuttle rededicated the college to her vision and challenge to "reach for the stars."

In 1989 Framingham State College celebrates its 150th anniversary.

Framingham State College

Its handsome 73-acre campus has changed the face of Bare Hill, dotting it with 14 buildings including seven residence halls. President Paul F. Weller is optimistic about the future. "This school has a fascinating history of creative transitions. And I believe our challenge for the 1980s is to continue this flexible approach. Our strength as a college rests in the variety of possibilities open to our students—diverse academic programs that prepare them for the future, an excellent faculty, modern facilities, and a unique setting in the growing MetroWest area."

ANNIS CORPORATION

Keene Annis and Richard Morrill—like ham and eggs—belonged together. In the mid-1950s Annis was sales manager for a private Volkswagen distributor, while Morrill owned a fleet of Volkswagens as part of his Wellesley Fells Delivery Service. Annis, a skilled car salesman, was busy setting up new VW dealer organizations, and service-oriented Morrill wanted to own one. Together they scoured the area for a location with obvious growth potential, finally buying an acre of land from Wyman Nurseries on Worcester Road in Framingham. "They call that stretch of Route 9 the 'Golden Mile' today," remembers Annis, "but it was mostly

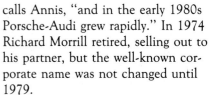

Keene Annis, president of the Annis Corporation.

open fields when we started. Vaughn Monroe's famous supper club, The Meadows, and Shoppers World, America's first shopping center, were both our neighbors, just across the street."

Annis-Morrill Volkswagen incorporated on October 13, 1959, just as Volkswagen's popularity was beginning to crest. The first car the firm

sold, a light-blue 1960 Beetle, had a sticker price of $1,602.81. (Ten years later the partners repurchased the car, and company employees still drive it today, in its original condition.)

The ubiquitous Beetle, lowest-priced car in America at the time, re-

More than 1,200 Volkswagen, Porsche, and Audi automobiles are sold each year from the Annis Corporation's modern showrooms on Route 9 in Natick.

mained Annis-Morrill's bread and butter for the next decade. As new homes sprang up in the area and young couples moved in, sales of the reliable, easy-to-fix "vee-dub-yah" were strong. But the folks at Annis-Morrill could foresee a time when families would become more affluent and demand upscale transportation.

In 1970 the company acquired three acres on Route 9 in neighboring Natick, and opened a small Porsche-Audi dealership. "Volkswagen sales leveled in the late 1970s," re-

calls Annis, "and in the early 1980s Porsche-Audi grew rapidly." In 1974 Richard Morrill retired, selling out to his partner, but the well-known corporate name was not changed until 1979.

The Annis Corporation consolidated at the Natick location in 1985, selling the Framingham property which had become very valuable. Today more than 1,200 Volkswagen, Porsche, and Audi automobiles are sold each year from Annis' innova-

tive split-showroom, designed by Mrs. Keene Annis, who joined the firm in 1975 and now serves as treasurer and director. Current prices range from about $7,000 for a Volkswagen Golf up to $54,000 for a Porsche 928S—like the one purchased by Natick football hero Doug Flutie. "And Doug's not the first celebrity I've met in this business!" explains Annis. "I once delivered a Volkswagen Beetle to Arthur Fiedler, when he was conductor of the Boston Pops Orchestra."

WESTON NURSERIES, INC.

Peter J. Mezitt immigrated to the United States from Latvia in 1907. Having attended agricultural colleges in Europe, he soon began work in commercial greenhouses around Lowell, Massachusetts. Two years later he had saved enough money to send for his wife-to-be, Anna, who was also a student of horticulture. Daughter Laura and son Edmund were born in 1913 and 1915, just before the Mezitt family moved to Weston where Peter became manager of Marion Case's Farm—now part of

Hopkinton, where Peter and Anna built their new home. When the new Massachusetts Turnpike was built through most of the Weston site in 1955, the move to Hopkinton was completed.

To supplement the selection process begun by his parents, Edmund Mezitt had started a plant-breeding program as early as 1943. One of his first crosses resulted in the creation of the world-famous "Rhododendron PJM" hybrids, named after his father, Peter J. Mezitt. Over the years the

nursery has introduced more than 50 new plants to the public—each one intended to meet specific needs for winter hardiness, low maintenance, improved color, or extension of bloom season. Laboratories at the nursery are also producing thousands of plants through tissue culture propagation—reducing by several years the time required to bring new plants and varieties to their customers.

Weston Nurseries today occupies about 900 acres in rural Hopkinton that are maintained by a seasonal labor force of over 200 employees. These include high school and college students, and contract workers hired from Puerto Rico through the Massachusetts Department of Labor. The nursery is still run on a personal basis by the Mezitt family. Each year they propagate more than one million new plants from seed, cuttings, and grafts, producing the largest variety of plants in the Northeast.

An aerial view of Weston Nurseries' 900-acre Hopkinton operations.

Land clearing with the help of work horses before the mechanized era and the advent of the tractor.

the Arnold Arboretum of Harvard University.

In 1923 the Mezitts acquired an eight-acre airport in Weston, where they established Weston Nurseries to grow perennials and ornamental plants. In 1944, with 75 acres already under cultivation, they purchased some 300 acres of largely abandoned hilly farmland in Hopkinton that offered promise of growing a far greater variety of nursery crops. These new fields were cleared, graded, drained, and prepared while operations in Weston continued. By the late 1940s loading and shipping docks, propagation greenhouses, and repair facilities had gradually shifted from Weston to

SHAWMUT COMMUNITY BANK

The main office of Shawmut Community Bank is at 80 Concord Street.

and uncertain credit were unable to meet urgent demands. A national banking system was passed by Congress in 1864, and within a few months 600 national banks (many converted from state banks) were in operation, among them the "new"

Today several branch offices, such as this one on Cochituate Road, offer customers convenient service.

Like a continuous golden thread, the story of Shawmut Community Bank is woven through the fabric of Framingham's financial history—linking more than 15 decades of service to the towns and villages of South Middlesex County.

Andrew Jackson was President of the United States when the Framingham Bank opened for business in September 1833. Its new building—a two-story brick structure—added much to the appearance of bustling Central Square during the heyday of stagecoach travel along the Boston-Worcester Turnpike. There were no banks in adjoining towns, and the success of the new institution is hinted at in this early record: "That Oliver Dean and Charles Merriam be a committee to take into consideration and make suitable inquiry on the subject and propriety of getting a more perfect and intricate lock to the vault. . . ." To further protect increasing funds in 1843, "the President and Cashier were chosen as a committee to procure some suitable person to sleep in the bank."

When a new form of transportation, the railroad, was proposed for Framingham, stagecoach owners in

Central Square feared competition and forced it to locate in the less-developed south end of town. The Boston line extended through Framingham to Worcester in 1834, and by 1880 there was a strong drift of business from the Centre Village to South Framingham, where three new banks had opened. In the spring of 1888 the directors reluctantly voted that "it is expedient and desirable to remove this bank to South Framingham," and removal was completed by the following September.

During the Civil War era state banks operating under different laws

Framingham National Bank, which now had authority to issue notes secured by government bonds.

In 1971 Framingham National Bank joined what was then called the National Shawmut Association, and in 1972 merged with Waltham Citizens Bank and Newton National Bank to become Community National Bank. Since 1975 it has been known as the Shawmut Community Bank. During the intervening years the institution has brought both personalized customer service and advanced banking technology to customers in the MetroWest area. Shawmut is a member of the largest shared electronic teller network in Massachusetts, and is now able to offer greater opportunities for advancement to its valued employees.

FRAMINGHAM TRUST COMPANY

By modern standards, life in 1909 was far from comfortable. But for the 12,000 residents of Framingham, it was a peaceful, progressive year. Fine homes lined tree-shaded avenues; children romped behind horse-drawn street sprinklers; and a new high school had just been completed at a cost of $150,000.

Against this background, a group of Framingham's leading business and professional men met at Ira Lewis' furniture store on May 11 to elect Enos H. Bigelow president of the Framingham Trust Company, a new bank destined to play a major role in the future growth and prosperity of its hometown.

Opening day—August 15, 1910—made front page news in *The Framingham Tribune,* one of the town's three newspapers. According to the article, "the company starts with a capital of $100,000" and "the bank is equipped with up-to-date facilities including a Brandt automatic cashier and Dalton adding machine."

As Framingham grew, so did the new bank at 36 Concord Street. By

The present Consumer Loan Center and six-story Main Office building at 5 Whittier Street, Framingham.

1911 resources had increased to more than $586,000, and despite the hard years during World War I, the bank's resources exceeded two million dollars by 1921.

Through the Roaring Twenties and the Great Depression townspeople continued to look to Framingham Trust for friendly help and advice. Larger quarters became necessary and the bank moved in the spring of 1929 to 79 Concord Street—formerly the historic Kendall Hotel. President Bigelow continued to guide the institution from opening day until his death in 1945.

During World War II most of the new employees were women, doing their share while many of the regular staff were serving overseas. Postwar prosperity brought installment lending to a new high, and Framingham Trust was proud to help local people achieve their dreams and ambitions. As new homes began to dot the landscape, additional branch offices were opened in Framingham, Ashland, Holliston, Hopkinton, Sherborn, and Sudbury.

Today Framingham Trust has close to $300 million in total assets. The bank presently has twelve full-service branches, one 24-Hour Banking Center, and a consumer loan center. It

also has fourteen 24-Hour Bankers. A wide range of financial services are offered to both consumers and businesses including various checking and investment accounts, installment loans, MasterCard, mortgages, safe deposit boxes, and trust services.

"Framingham Trust Company is proud of its past," remarks William A. Anastos, president since 1978. "Our reputation as a bank for all the people is well established, and we intend to remain ever sympathetic to the hopes and dreams of our customers throughout the MetroWest area."

The first quarters in the Nobscot Block, 36 Concord Street, Framingham.

YOUTH GUIDANCE CENTER OF THE GREATER FRAMINGHAM MENTAL HEALTH ASSOCIATION, INC.

The Youth Guidance Center of the Greater Framingham Mental Health Association, Inc., is the major children's mental health clinic for the nine-town area of South Middlesex County. The services it offers include treatment to families in which there has been child abuse or neglect; immediate intervention for teenagers and their families in crisis; services to pregnant and parenting teenagers; specialized training to prospective foster families; support to children and families experiencing problems related to incest and sexual abuse; and much more. Fees for these services are not fixed, but are based on a sliding scale depending upon income. The center also accepts payments from insurance carriers for its services.

It all began in late 1953, when the Social Action Committee at Grace Congregational Church, after a brief study, decided there was a growing need for a mental health facility to serve the Framingham area. The initial organization was formed in early 1954, and laid the groundwork for the Greater Framingham Area Mental Health Association. It was this group that saw the actual opening of the Youth Guidance Center on September 12, 1955.

For more than 30 years the Youth Guidance Center has consistently provided health-oriented, preventive, and educational programs for area children, in collaboration with the Massachusetts Departments of Mental Health, Social Services, Public Health, and participating communities.

The center today offers a wide range of child-related services. For families in the Hispanic community, a bilingual, bicultural professional staff provides on-site and outreach mental health services. A Mental Retardation Clinical Resource Team serves mentally retarded clients of all ages who are living in a variety of community settings. Parent counseling and behavior management

For over 30 years the Youth Guidance Center of the Greater Framingham Mental Health Association, Inc., has been providing health-oriented, preventive, and educational programs for the children of a nine-town area of South Middlesex County from its headquarters at 88 Lincoln Street, Framingham.

consultation are also offered to the hearing-impaired by signing therapists.

"These programs are not poured in concrete," explains executive director Stuart I. Meyers. "Our programs are continually changing and being tailored to meet the current needs of clients and agencies."

From its inception, the focus of the center has been to establish cooperative working relationships with area school systems. Today it still organizes educational programs, including conferences for professionals as well as the community.

The Youth Guidance Center has grown in all directions since its birth in 1955. But its original commitment—rapid response to the changing needs of the family—remains unchanged. "We're in a nonprofit business to serve people," says director Meyers, "and we feel that where children are concerned, only the best is good enough."

THE MIDDLESEX NEWS

Charles J. MacPherson could see the handwriting on the wall. His small weekly newspaper—*The Framingham Tribune*—had a decade of success behind it. It had grown from one small office to an entire floor, and finally moved to its own home, the Tribune Building facing Irving Square. Business was booming in South Framingham. The Para Rubber Shoe Company, a major industry, employed many residents. The town needed a daily paper, so MacPherson started the *Daily Tribune* in the autumn of 1890.

Prosperity was short-lived, and when Para Rubber closed in 1891, the *Tribune* suffered with the rest. It suspended its daily edition in 1893 for lack of advertising.

But MacPherson's dream of a daily paper for Framingham never died. On July 6, 1897, after learning that the Dennison Manufacturing Company was about to locate here, he started another daily—*The Evening News,* later known as the *Framingham News,* which survives to this day as *The Middlesex News.* Located in the basement of the Tribune Building, under a plumbing shop, it had only 300 subscribers until the advent of the Spanish-American War, when an influx of recruits for the Massachusetts Volunteer Militia made Framingham a news center, giving the fledgling daily its first impetus. In less than 10 years the *News* moved upstairs and circulation jumped fourfold. By World War I more than 5,000 copies a day rolled off the press, reaching 90 percent of the homes in Framingham.

Quarters at the Tribune Building were cramped after the war, and the paper moved to a new building at 15 Howard Street in 1928, where it remained for 37 years. Circulation increased to 14,000, and the 33 employees were again crowded. On Memorial Day weekend in 1965, the *News* moved to a spacious new lo-

The front page of the May 8, 1916, edition of the *Framingham Evening News.*

The Middlesex News *and its 86,000-square-foot, $7.3-million plant at the Framingham Industrial Park.*

cation on Cochituate Road near Shoppers World. At this point, the growth rate became phenomenal. A unique zoning concept, grouping certain communities to specific editions, helped boost circulation more than 50 percent in five years.

In 1971 the MacPherson family sold the *Framingham News* to Harte-Hanks Communications, Inc., of San Antonio, Texas. The name was changed to the *South Middlesex News,* in keeping with the regional newspaper it had become. By 1979 circulation topped 50,000 and the paper became known as *The Middlesex News* as its staff of 340 moved to the current 86,000-square-foot, $7.3-million plant at the Framingham In-

dustrial Park.

In 1983, to describe its territory in the burgeoning area between Boston and Worcester, *The Middlesex News* coined the phrase "MetroWest"—a definition that has since been adopted by industry and government in the Route 128-Route 495 belt.

In 1986, with more than 600 people working three shifts, the *News* became flagship to The News Transcript Group when parent company Harte-Hanks acquired the Century and the Transcript papers north and south of Boston.

Today The News Transcript Group represents 3 daily, 12 weekly, and 4 total market products that collectively reach 300,000 households.

O.B. HILL MOTOR TRANSPORTATION COMPANY, INC.

When fire swept through the Beverly Draw Bridge at Beverly, Massachusetts, two locomotives, eight budliners, five Pullman coaches, and two hopper freight cars were stranded on the wrong side of the river. They had to be carried around the charred bridge and put back on the track.

O.B. Hill Motor Transportation Company of Natick won the contract. The firm loaded the 125-ton locomotive and the 35-ton hopper cars on specialized trailer equipment, one of the rigs having 48 wheels, and hauled them five miles along a highway, down a busy street, and through a shopping center. A few days later the budliners and Pullman coaches followed, and within two weeks all were safely set down on the rails again.

"That job wasn't unusual for our firm," explains company president Oliver B. Hill, Sr. "Ever since we bought our first truck back in 1950, we've welcomed assignments that call for real Yankee ingenuity.

"Our indoctrination into hauling oversized equipment resulted when the Massachusetts Turnpike was under construction. We had an inquiry to transport the steel bridge beams. Labor Day weekend was spent building a pole trailer and the following Tuesday morning we were in business. That led to the building of other specialized equipment in our own shop.

"The largest commodity we have been called upon to transport was a series of 176-foot-long steel bridge girders which we moved through the city of Boston, also for the Massachusetts Turnpike extension. These were more than four times the length of a typical trailer load.

"We've been involved in such construction projects as the John Hancock Tower, Provident Institution for Savings, and the new Federal Reserve Bank in Boston," remembers Hill. "We once transported four 165-ton heat exchangers from the General Electric plant in South Portland, Maine, to a local barge-loading point for water transportation to a plant in Puerto Rico."

Joined now by his two sons, Andrew and Bryant, "O.B." has expanded into the crane and rigging business in an effort to offer customers package programs in loading and unloading, as well as storage and warehousing of heavy commodities. The company presently performs turnkey plant or machine shop relocations. "We dismantle machinery as necessary, and load it onto trailers. If warehousing of the machinery is necessary, we provide that service, then deliver and install when the new location is ready." The company performed such relocations from Maine to Texas.

In 1984 the firm outgrew its former facilities and constructed a new 13,000-square-foot combination office complex and garage. O.B. Hill Motor Transportation Company, Inc., and its affiliates are now licensed to operate east of the Mississippi River, and look forward to many more years of pioneering in oversized and overweight hauling techniques.

Above
En route with one of the hopper cars and one of the locomotives transported from the dead track north of the burned-out Beverly Draw Bridge in Beverly, Massachusetts, to a live track in downtown Danvers.

Right
With a diverse fleet of trucks, cranes, and forklifts, the firm loads and unloads warehouses and installs all types and sizes of machinery and contractors' equipment, providing a full-service operation for customers' various needs.

ALAN'S LANDSCAPING AND LAWN CARE SERVICES

Without realizing it, most residents of MetroWest have enjoyed the results of Alan's Landscaping and Lawn Care Service. The manicured lawns and shrubs at the Fountain Head apartment complex in Westboro, and new landscaping around the Teletron building in Ashland, and the design installation and maintenance off Fairway Estates in Natick are just a few examples of Alan's quality work.

The firm's gross sales now exceed $750,000 per year, and 10 to 30 employees are on the payroll, depending on the season. Alan Steiman has also formed a housing development corporation called South Street Realty Trust—based on experience he has gained since he first became interested in landscaping when he was four years old.

"My grandfather, Scotty Levitin, did lawn care work around Brookline years ago," Alan remembers. "He'd take me out on Saturday morning and let me dig holes for half a day for 25 cents. After the holes were dug, we'd fill them in again, but it was good practice. I worked with him until I was seven and had learned how to plant flowers and shrubs."

After living in Ohio for a few years, Alan's family bought a house in Framingham, and he began working around the yard. Soon neighbors began asking him to cut lawns and do minor landscaping jobs. By the age of 16 he had a lucrative business, several part-time employees, and the highest absentee rate in his high school. "But I was earning as much as my teachers," he recalls, "and I knew where I was going."

After high school, Alan attended Stockbridge College at the University of Massachusetts in Amherst to study landscaping. His mother, Barbara

Steiman, helped keep the business alive during the week, answering the phone and dispatching employees to jobs. Alan took over on weekends.

After graduation, the business started growing. "It's always been more than a job," Alan explains. "It's a way of life. We're on call 24 hours a day, just like firemen."

Alan's Landscaping and Lawn Care Services has come a long way since the day when its owner dug holes and planted shrubs. Services today include sanding and snow removal; spring clean-up; mowing; shrubbery planting and pruning; autumn clean-up; designing, installing, and maintaining swimming pools; and landscaping private homes, office buildings, restaurants, apartment complexes, and industrial parks.

Senior foreman Robert White, who has worked with Alan "since the beginning," remembers that equipment and vehicles were originally kept in

An early portent of things to come for Alan Steiman.

Framingham at 307 Water Street until 1980, when fire ravaged the property. Alan then moved to his present location—a 250-year-old farmhouse in Northboro, with a barn and ample grounds for his equipment.

"You don't pay until you're happy" has been his motto from the beginning, and so far, says Alan, "we've always been paid."

Alan's Landscaping and Lawn Care Service is prepared for any customer request, such as this sculptured snowman.

W.A. WILDE COMPANY

The W.A. Wilde Company has become one of the largest direct-mail specialists in the United States because of its customer-centered business philosophy. You sense it the moment you enter the firm's immaculate new lobby on a crisp winter morning, and catch the aroma of mulled cider warming on a wood-burning stove in the corner. You feel it as you glance into orderly office spaces on your way to the spacious plant in back. "Being good enough isn't good enough for us," explains company president Thomas H. Wilde. "There are plenty of direct-mail firms that are good enough. To succeed for five generations, you have to be demonstrably better than good. We try to cut our margin of error down to zero."

It all began in 1868, when an enterprising young Yankee named William A. Wilde opened a publishing business in Boston. Wilde specialized in nondenominational religious books that were sold to clergymen across the country. He was succeeded by first one and then a second son who continued to increase the size of the company during the second generation of family leadership.

In 1959 Alfred A. Wilde, the third-generation chief executive officer, moved the business to Natick, where he continued to publish religious books, but the once-thriving firm with offices as far away as Sydney, Australia, was being pinched by severe competition. "By 1968 it was obvious that we should jettison the publishing activity," explains Wilde. "We turned our focus to direct-mail selling instead."

The company moved to Pope Industrial Park in Holliston in 1970, and expanded from one to five separate buildings before consolidating under one roof at its Summer Street facility in 1983.

W.A. Wilde's Information Services

Division offers prospective clients a more effective and comprehensive way to approach and carry out the entire marketing/sales cycle. Through its basic lettershop data-processing services and the unique SalesBase program, W.A. Wilde gives each client a sharper yet more flexible direct marketing support system.

Today W.A. Wilde Company serves more than 300 clients, including such prestigious names as *Harvard Business Review, Oxfam America,* and *Yankee Magazine.* The Christian Science Publishing Society has contracted with Wilde to mail its periodicals to subscribers all over the world.

Thomas H. Wilde became the fourth-generation president of the firm in 1971, and has invested in state-of-the-art equipment to keep his company up to date. With more than a million dollars worth of computer hardware and software, Wilde can

Top
The company's profile may have changed dramatically since 1868, but the family resemblance has been passed down from William A. Wilde, the firm's first president, to his great-grandson, Thomas Hinckley Wilde.

Above
Cutting the grass and gardening satisfies the farmer in direct-mail entrepreneur Thomas Hinckley Wilde. He is shown in front of the W.A. Wilde Company headquarters in Holliston.

not only generate mailing lists but also monitor the mail and maintain precise inventory records. Elaborate machines label, fold, and insert computer-printed literature while 15 postage machines stamp 100,000 pieces of mail per hour.

W.A. Wilde Company offers customers personal service, on-time mailing, and professional management. "But what we're really selling," adds Wilde with a smile, "is peace of mind."

FRAMINGHAM SAVINGS BANK

The staff of Framingham Savings Bank poses with baskets of flowers from well-wishers on the opening of the bank August 17, 1929.

Promptly at 8 a.m. on June 4, 1883, the Farmers and Mechanics Savings Bank opened its doors for the first day of business. Three local boys, ages 10, 11, and 14, strolled in and made the first deposits. By the time the doors closed at the end of the day, the bank had received $2,100 in deposits.

The new institution, occupying a single room in the Liberty block of South Framingham, faced stiff competition from the two other banks in town, one of which had nearly a century of experience. The 1880s were years of growth for Framingham. Businessmen and mechanics saw the need for a savings bank in the southern area of town. Thus, Farmers and Mechanics Savings Bank was chartered on April 23, 1883.

Between the institution's first day in June 1883 and 1929, deposits increased from $2,100 to more than five million dollars. In August 1929 the bank dedicated its present home office at the corner of Park and Franklin streets.

By Farmers and Mechanics' 70th anniversary in 1953, it had opened a branch office and had assets approaching $16 million. During the next 20 years the bank became the largest thrift institution in the area, expanding to four branch offices and building assets of nearly $125 million. This explosive growth earned the institution the nickname of the "Fast Stepping Bank," and its logo of the "little man on the move" be-

came one of the most widely recognized corporate symbols around.

The bank's explosive growth also led to its name being changed to Framingham Savings Bank in 1961. "The change came because the community had outlived its identity of doing business almost exclusively with farmers and mechanics," explains former president Arthur Fitts. What has been FSB's formula for success? "We continue to provide an attitude of friendliness and helpfulness, having time for the person who needs financial help, having time for the small depositors and small borrowers."

FSB's success continued in 1974 despite talk of recession, even a depression, when the institution became one of only 17 banks in the state to show a gain in savings deposits.

While the country celebrated its 200th birthday in 1975, FSB celebrated a milestone of its own by passing $150 million in assets as well as electing a new president,

Donald R. Hughes. A scant three years later FSB passed the $200-million mark.

The bank began its 104th year in 1986 with assets surpassing the $326-million mark and with offices at 15 Park Street, 770 Water Street, 575 Worcester Road (Rt. 9), 1265 Worcester Road (Rt. 9), and 420 Franklin Street, Framingham; and at 746 Washington Street, Holliston.

FSB24/tx automated-teller machines have been installed at all bank offices, Shoppers World, on the campus of Framingham State College, and in Ashland. FSB recently joined the CASH Network, which enables its customers to use automated-teller machines at over 750 bank and supermarket locations throughout Massachusetts and New Hampshire. "Framingham Savings Bank looks forward to continuing to serve the expanded needs of our customers in the friendly and professional manner they expect and deserve," says Hughes.

Now, more than 100 years after opening its doors, Framingham Savings Bank can boast about having the largest market share in Framingham—not a bad record for a bank that began in one room with the pennies of three local boys.

The board of trustees (standing, from left): Ernest J. Chiappini; John B. Millar; Raymond F. Lawrence; F. Gerard Merser; Robert Y. Fudge, vice-president and treasurer; Charles J. Patterson; Charles D. Warner; Joseph Damigella, Jr. Seated (from left) are Sidney F. Greeley, Jr.; Romeo J. Pendolari; Donald R. Hughes, president; Victor H. Galvani, chairman of the board of trustees; Julian T. Hargraves, Jr.; and Geoffrey E. Fitts.

COAN, INC.

By the mid-1980s over 9,000 customers in thirty cities and towns within the MetroWest area were warming their homes and businesses with oil purchased from Coan, Inc. As one of the largest independent fuel oil and heating service companies in the Commonwealth, with seventy-five employees and a fleet of over fifty vehicles, the Coan commitment to the highest-quality service is the key to the firm's success—a commitment that had spanned four eventful decades.

It began in 1946 at Lincoln Square in Natick where Natick-born Francis M. Coan—an Air Force veteran returned from the war—leased a small gasoline service station. "Fran" soon established "service" as the Coan watchword: Customers who stopped for gas at the original station often found that he washed not only the outside of the car windshield but often the inside as well, an example of the extra effort that became the hallmark of this career and company.

Soon after the station opened, Fran and his brother Joseph entered the home-heating oil business. With their first delivery truck purchased in 1947, Fran drove the streets of Natick. On some days there were no customers, and sometimes there was no oil in the truck; however, it was a traveling billboard, and soon there were as many oil as gasoline customers.

A downtown Natick office was opened in the early 1950s. In a few years Fran purchased Joseph's share of the business, and by 1956 Coan Bros. had become Coan, Inc. It was a period of rapid growth for Natick and the surrounding communities as meadows and orchards gave place to thousands of new homes built to accommodate the postwar baby boom. The installation and servicing of oil heating equipment became a major element of the business, and Fran Coan, the consummate salesman,

knew that truly quality service would spell the difference between an average and an outstanding fuel oil organization.

In 1948 Fran purchased several acres of land on West Central Street in Natick, where oil storage facilities

Francis M. Coan, founder and first president.

were subsequently constructed. In 1950 his brother, John, established the Coan Transportation Company to transport oil from the Port of Boston to the Coan storage plants, which increased through the years as the firm purchased established companies in Needham, Millis, Hopkinton, and Milford. By 1978 the Coan storage facilities were comprised of four plants with a capacity of just under one million gallons of petroleum products.

The corporate headquarters, which had expanded into several downtown locations, was consolidated in 1962 into a new building on the West Central Street site, a facility that includes administration and sales offices, a display room, a completely equipped heavy vehicle maintenance

Mary E. Coan, current president.

garage, and a warehouse stocked to the roof with heating equipment and parts.

When Fran Coan leased his first station in 1946, the car he drove was a 1936 coupe owned by his new bride, the former Mary E. Walsh of Natick. From the beginning she worked with her ambitious husband in building the business. Long hours of bookkeeping and paperwork were added to her chores as mother of her first child, Kevin, who was born the same year the company was founded. A daughter, Pamela, was born in 1954.

And then in 1968, at the peak of his career, Fran Coan passed away. It was very sudden—and while Mary knew she could not fill his shoes, she was determined to keep alive the tradition of first-rate service to the Coan customers, and she stepped in as president and chairman of the board. Within a short time Natick Oil Company, located just across the street from the new Coan headquarters, merged with Coan, Inc.; and its

owner, John A. Hill, Jr., became vice-president in charge of engineering.

A new division was created within the company in 1970. A sales organization called Petroleum Engineering, it quickly grew to represent several national heating manufacturers throughout New England and eastern New York State. Kevin Coan, who sold his first oil account at the age of ten and was active in several phases of the business since the completion of his formal education, was appointed vice-president of the firm

Coan's first place of business, the original service station at Lincoln Square, Natick.

in 1976 with Petroleum Engineering his direct responsibility.

A second corporation had been established in 1975 when John Hill designed a residential heating boiler designated a few years later by the U.S. Federal Trade Commission as the most energy-efficient heating unit on the nation's market. With Hill as president Ultimate Engineering Cor-

poration began boiler manufacturing operations in a building almost adjacent to Coan headquarters, and was soon marketing the product in the northern states from coast to coast.

The development of the Ultimate boiler was indicative of the new era in the fuel oil industry triggered by the mid-East oil embargo in 1974 with the resulting petroleum shortage. A new company slogan appeared: "We Want To Sell You Less Oil." Innovative technologies were quickly adopted by Coan, and the drive was on to ensure that each customer's heating system operated as cost effectively as possible. Modern, sophisticated testing devices and highly efficient heating equipment assumed utmost importance.

Yet despite the new era of high technology and the diversification of the Coan business, the commitment to fast and efficient service to the homeowner remains the uppermost priority within the organization. Its staff has never forgotten Fran Coan's counsel that "the customer is the most important person."

A satisfied "customer" greeting the Coan oil man.

BOSTONIA BEVERAGES, INC.

Thomas H. Hoyt of Fort Fairfield, Maine, was a teenager looking for a job when a cousin in Natick, Massachusetts, came to his rescue. "There's an opening at the new Bostonia Beverage Company, right next door to my house," she wrote. Tom applied, got the position, and has never had to look for work since.

"Bostonia was only a two- or three-man operation in those days," recalls Tom's son Gary, now executive vice-president of the firm. "Dad became foreman when he was 16."

Tom Hoyt bought the company in 1938, although it was in financial trouble. He worked long hours—bottling his own formulas of the popular Bostonia beverages at night and helping to deliver them during the day, while raising three sons who are all active in the business today. Gradually his combination of good judgment and experience began to pay off, launching an era of growth and expansion that still continues.

Walter Smith, of Bostonia Beverages in 1923.

Tom Hoyt (left) and Walter Smith in front of the firm's delivery truck, circa 1925.

"In the beginning, we only bottled and sold our own soft drink, the Bostonia brand," explains Hoyt. "It came in several flavors, including orange, root beer, and lemon-lime. When Pepsi Cola first came out, the original owner didn't think it had a future. Dad felt differently, and got us a Pepsi bottling franchise in 1946."

A three-masted model schooner made entirely from Pepsi cans decorates Gary Hoyt's office today, symbolizing the company's long affiliation with the national brand. From 1975 through 1977 Bostonia Beverages was the leading distributor of Pepsi Cola in the United States—measured in plant sales per capita.

"We began bottling and distributing Schweppes soft drinks in the late 1950s," Hoyt remembers. "And of course we also sell the diet beverages now. In fact, one-third of our business today comes from diet drinks."

A visit to the sprawling Bostonia plant on Mill Street in Natick is full of surprises. Behind its modest street

frontage lie thousands of square feet of warehouse, storage, and repair facilities on a 14-acre site. Touring these buildings is like going on a geological dig, as you trace the walls and ceilings of the original facility, now almost hidden by newer walls and ceilings of cavernous additions constructed over the years as the company grew.

Although bottling has been done here since 1922, there are not bottling machines on the site today. "We moved all the bottling operations except Pepsi to a plant in Brocton in September 1981," says Hoyt, "and in 1983 we cooperated with six other Pepsi bottlers to open a plant in the town of Ayer." But space once allocated for bottling is still utilized. The "Bottle Bill," which passed the Massachusetts legislature in January 1983, gave Bostonia Beverages a new challenge: recycling.

Today the company recycles aluminum, glass, cardboard, and plastic. "We even recycle engine oil from our vehicles," adds Hoyt. "We converted an old syrup tank to hold the waste oil, and we use it to heat our warehouse."

Bostonia Beverages opposed the

Bostonia Beverages

Bottle Bill as long as possible. But when it finally became law, the firm began a policy of enthusiastic compliance. A $70,000 bailer was purchased to speed the recycling process.

Bostonia's biggest recycling challenge is not reusable plastic containers, but refillable glass bottles. These come in three sizes and two colors, and still must be sorted one at a time, by hand.

"It used to be that older folks threw away their bottles, and kids collected them for some spare change," Hoyt notices. "But today things are different. Kids are often the ones who toss the bottles out, and we've found senior citizens collecting them. It gives the older folks something to do, plus a little spending money. Times have sure changed."

Three generations of the Hoyt family have worked side by side at Bostonia Beverages. Thomas Hoyt has seen his grandson Thomas C. Hoyt become active in the firm. Donald A. Hoyt is president, Gary P.

Hoyt serves as executive vice-president and treasurer, and Richard T. Hoyt is vice-president.

With the help of 75 employees, Bostonia Beverages bottles and delivers thirst-quenching colas to 300 vending machines and countless retail stores throughout Middlesex County.

Several other flavor franchises have been added such as Lipton Tea, Hawaiian Punch, and Mott's fruit juices, to name a few, to enhance the flavor line.

Drivers Gordon Bell (left) and Howard Murtagh pose next to their delivery trucks in 1938.

KEN'S STEAK HOUSE

If Massachusetts author Horatio Alger ever wrote a rags-to-riches story about a restaurateur, he might have named the hero Ken Hanna. Assisted by his new bride, Florence, Ken opened the Lakeside Restaurant in Natick in 1935. It was a real mom-and-pop operation, with Ken tending bar while Florence prepared and served the food. "Our family lived in a small apartment upstairs," remembers son Mark. "Mom is a great cook, and Dad, well, he just loves people, and they love him too."

When Natick went "dry" in the 1930s, Ken began looking for a new location, moving temporarily to the Sandy Burr Country Club. But he felt that the undeveloped land on the Worcester Turnpike near Dick Wyman's nursery would eventually become valuable, and in 1941 he bought a chunk of it—John McHale's diner—now the site of Ken's Steak House.

"As a young man, Dad was pretty well known around town," recalls Mark. "He was captain of the Natick High School football team, and in Natick, that's almost as important as being mayor. He had a warm spot in his heart for students, and many from Babson and Wellesley College were among our early customers. They followed us to the new location on Route 9, where we also served lots of GIs returning to Cushing Hospital during the war and many never paid a check."

After World War II a large supper club named The Meadows was built just down the road from Ken's. Folks predicted trouble for the little restaurant, especially when bandleader Vaughn Monroe took personal ownership of The Meadows. But Ken was undaunted. "We'll do even better than before," he predicted, and he

was right. "The Meadows was a great place to dance," explains Mark, "but the kitchen was never very good. Folks would come here for dinner, and then go there to dance. Our business actually improved after The Meadows opened."

Each dish on the menu at Ken's Steak House is prepared to order, and one of the key ingredients is time. Among those who've waited gladly for extra-tender filet mignon or baked stuffed Alaskan crab legs are the Kennedys (Jack, Bobby, and Ted), Winston Churchill's daughter, Sarah, Perry Como, Diana Ross, Louis Rukeyser, and Robert Goulet, who is "crazy about our clam chowder." When Wayne Newton came looking for a table one evening, Ken greeted him personally. "How's your brother Fig?" he asked with a grin, cementing another friendship with

his familiar wit, warmth, and corn.

As recently as 1960 Ken's Steak House had bare wood floors, no tablecloths, and stainless steel cutlery. "Customers were attracted by our food, not our decor," Mark says with a laugh. "But as the area began to prosper, we decided to upgrade each of the dining rooms, and folks loved it." In 1963 we opened Café Five—an upscale version of Ken's with its own kitchen and menu. It costs a bit more, but it's always been crowded."

Ken Hanna is modest about his achievements. He says he was "just trying to make a living." But Ken's Steak House, whose 50-year reputation has never faded, helped put Framingham on the map.

Ken's Steak House, 95 Worcester Road, Framingham.

The Back Room, one of the restaurant's older dining rooms, was built in 1957.

FAIR & YEAGER INSURANCE AGENCY INC.

"The hurricane of 1985 may not have been an official 'hurricane' according to historic standards, but it sure kept us busy!" remembers Arthur Fair, Jr., president of the Fair & Yeager Insurance Agency in downtown Natick. "We had two emergency phone lines open, and worked by flashlight until the power came back on. There was a mountain of claims on this table, but Joan Lehmann came in on Saturday and worked right through to the bottom of the pile. She's one of the best claims managers in the business."

The company has a history of service stretching all the way back to 1898. A special "trade edition" of *The Natick Review* that year described Frank E. Yeager as "a young man, being only 25 years of age, but he has already made a place for himself among the insurance agencies of the town and Boston." In 1914 high school senior Arthur B. Fair went to work for Frank on a part-time basis. After graduation from Natick High School, he became a full-time associate, and by 1924 a partnership was formed under the name of F.E. Yeager & Company.

In 1936 Frank Yeager's son, John, joined the business, and 10 years later the Fair & Yeager partnership was established with Arthur B. Fair, Sr., and John F. Yeager.

"I first got into the business in 1952," explains Arthur Fair, Jr. "My brother, Bob, and I worked together with Dad for 20 years, before his 'official' retirement in 1972. But he came in part time long after that. In fact, he was still working a four-day week when my son Artie came on board in 1979. There were *three* Arthur Fairs on the payroll for a while!"

"My father knew Natick as a town much smaller than today," says Arthur, "and he participated in civic affairs. For more than 25 years he was a trustee of the Leonard Morse

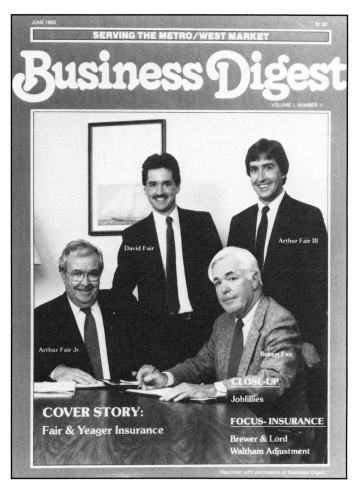

Fair & Yeager Insurance Agency Inc. was written up in the June 1985 issue of Business Digest, with members of the Fair family featured on the cover. Courtesy, Thomas Sawyer, Business Digest

Hospital. He was president of the Natick Five Cents Savings Bank (now Middlesex Savings Bank) from 1962 until 1968.

In the autumn of 1977 the agency became known as Fair & Yeager Insurance Agency Inc., with Arthur as president and his brother, Robert, as treasurer.

"Servicing the loss or claim is still the most important part of our business," explains Arthur. "Computerization and package policies have changed the face of the insurance industry, but service is still the bottom line."

The Fair & Yeager Insurance Agency building at 10 Main Street in downtown Natick.

Fair & Yeager approaches its 90th birthday with twin goals: to keep pace with industry changes and to keep faith with its customers. "Folks deserve to know," explains Arthur, "that when they walk through our door they're going to get a fair deal."

DENNISON MANUFACTURING COMPANY

"Dennison? Sure, I've heard of them. They own those old brick buildings down by the railroad tracks on Howard Street. They make paper products and shipping cartons, don't they?"

Right, but that's only the tip of the iceberg. Dennison today is one of the world's largest suppliers of identification products and systems, ranging from tags, tickets, and labels to sophisticated systems that print and attach them. Dennison coding systems provide the information required for identification and shelf-life monitoring of many consumer products. The firm's bar-code tags for airline luggage allow lasers to read destination tags and send bags to the proper gate. Dennison's "Swiftach" system of plastic sewing fasteners is used by many apparel manufacturers to attach price tags and other tickets to their products. Designers rely on Dennison to carry out their ideas in can and bottle decoration through pressure-sensitive labels, heat-transfer decorations for plastic containers, screen printing equipment, and computerized color matching.

Computer supplies and related products are also important parts of Dennison's product lines. These include flexible disks, digital cassettes, microcomputer and word-processing ribbons, computer tape cleaners and testers, print wheels, electrosensitive paper, and even ergonomic work station furniture.

Needless to say, the firm is still unmatched in marketing a highly diverse stationery line—binders, modular filing systems, felt-tip markers, pressure-sensitive labels, inked stamp pads, and many other items. The company improves, upgrades, and adds several hundred products each year for use in the home, office, and school.

Dennison Manufacturing Company is a *Fortune* 500 business with more than 8,000 employees worldwide. But its roots go back to 1844—to the small antebellum village of Brunswick, Maine, where Colonel Andrew Dennison worked at a cobbler's bench. His son Aaron, a jeweler in Boston, felt that his father could make better jewelry boxes than those being imported from England. So Colonel Dennison diversified, and began to manufacture the first paper boxes made in the United States. Both sons helped to sell the boxes and purchase the needed cardboard. The colonel's daughters cut out the boxes on the cobbler's bench and put them together. While son Eliphalet Dennison concentrated on guiding the family business, his older brother, Aaron, became one of the founders of the famous Waltham Watch Company.

In 1863 industries throughout the North were gearing up to ship vast quantities of supplies to Union soldiers fighting on Civil War battle-

Many well-known food marketers call on Dennison metallized papers to enhance labels and other product identifiers.

The System 8000™ on-line ticket printer will provide either bar code or OCR printing and facilitate retrieval and processing of data.

fields. That year Dennison Manufacturing Company developed and secured a patent on a paper washer that reinforced the hole on a shipping tag. For the life of that patent, the firm enjoyed a virtual monopoly of the shipping tag business.

By 1877 Dennison was vigorously advertising not only patent shipping tags, but also merchandise tags, gummed labels, tissue papers, a copying pad, and related products. The company began manufacturing the first decorative crepe paper made in the United States in 1892. During the next ten years Christmas seals and tags were marketed, giving rise to the multimillion-dollar gift-wrapping industry. For three-quarters of a century Dennison was a household name in the field of gift-wrapping papers, but profits eventually began to shrink because of the long lead time required for design, testing, printing, and marketing. Dennison closed its Holiday Division in 1967.

Although some production continued in Brunswick, Maine, until near the end of the nineteenth century, Dennison moved its headquarters to Framingham in 1898, occupying a

The front entrance to the Framingham plant of Dennison Manufacturing Company.

complex of brick buildings on Howard Street that formerly housed the defunct Para Rubber Shoe Company. Almost 1,000 people had lost their jobs when the rubber works closed, and business in Framingham suffered badly. Dennison's decision to locate at the empty plant was applauded by villagers, who rightly predicted that it would soon become one of the area's major employers.

Although its corporate headquarters remains in Framingham, Dennison now has subsidiaries in Canada, England, Wales, Mexico, Australia, France, Denmark, Holland, and Switzerland. There are 25 manufacturing facilities in the United States and 18 more in foreign countries. The company maintains over 100 sales offices worldwide.

In the mid-1960s Dennison was thought of as the "Xerox of Framingham" after the introduction of its "Standard Copier." It was the first copier to offer the convenience of roll-feed for its paper and employed a coated paper made by Dennison. This copier was widely used until the advent of xerographic "plain paper" technology changed the market. Keen competition spurred Dennison into several years of research, which resulted in a new method of electronic printing using ions, which are electrically charged. In 1981 Dennison formed a 50-50 partnership with Canada Development Corporation (CDC) to develop and market a high-speed, computer-controlled ion printer. The new venture was named Delphax Systems, and its current ma-

Swiftach® System 1000™ attaches tags to garments using a continuous roll of 1,000 fasteners.

chines can print up to 90 pages a minute. Xerox Corporation has since purchased from CDC its share in the venture and is now Delphax's largest customer as well.

Looking to the future, Dennison joined a group of scientists in the Boston area in 1981 to form Biological Technology Corporation, which later became known as Hygeia Sciences. Hygeia's purpose was to develop inexpensive, easy-to-use medical tests based on the new "monoclonal antibody" technology. Its first success came in 1983, when a worldwide pharmaceutical firm agreed to distribute its innovative pregnancy-detection kit to doctors and clinical laboratories. Under a later agreement, a worldwide consumer products firm, Tambrands, is distributing a pregnancy test and an ovulation test over the counter for use in the home.

From the humble start and efforts of a Maine cobbler, Andrew Dennison's company has grown into the nation's most diversified paper converter and has developed a host of new products and technologies.

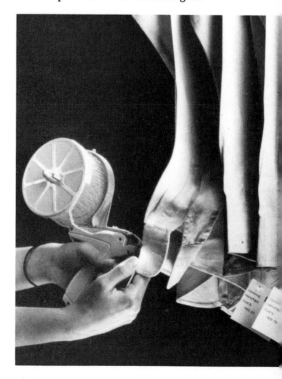

GENERAL MOTORS CORP./FRAMINGHAM

When the United States entered World War II after the bombing of Pearl Harbor, auto production in this country ground to a halt. Automotive plants converted to war production, turning out tanks, planes, and other combat vehicles. By the end of the war everyone's car was at least five years old, and even spare parts were hard to find.

Recognizing the pent-up demand for new cars that would exist after the war, General Motors prepared to build three nearly identical new manufacturing facilities. The first two were in Wilmington, Delaware, and Atlanta, Georgia. To meet the needs of customers in the Northeast, a 176-

building was constructed with steel framing and brick sidewalls. Insulation to hold back the sun's heat, combined with an extensive ventilating system, provided an even temperature throughout the plant.

Construction was completed in late 1947—a stormy winter when one blizzard followed another across the frosty New England landscape. More than 80 inches of snow had already been counted when the first two cars rolled off the production lines in Framingham—an Oldsmobile followed by a Pontiac. It was Thursday, February 26, 1948. According to tradition, the new vehicles were sent to the two oldest dealerships in New England.

The plant was described as an assembly unit, as contrasted with a fabricating plant. The thousands of different parts, metal stampings, and motors needed for Buicks, Oldsmobiles, and Pontiacs were shipped in from Michigan, Ohio, Indiana, Pennsylvania, and New Jersey. At Framingham they were assembled into automobiles—each customized to meet the special requirements of an individual buyer somewhere in New England.

To get all the correct parts to the right place at the exact moment required for assembly as the car moves along the line, an extremely intricate split-second timing schedule was essential. It was accomplished by a network of teletype machines that carried scheduling messages to many parts of the plant where parts or sub-assembly lines originated. Each part had to come out in its proper sequence and converge at the assembly

An aerial view taken September 1984 of the Framingham plant of General Motors Corporation on Western Avenue.

acre site was chosen at the crossroads of New England—Framingham, Massachusetts.

Japan formally surrendered to the Allies on September 2, 1945. Less than three months later, on November 27, ground was broken for the new Framingham plant. It would originally consist of three main structures—a manufacturing building, an administration building, and a powerhouse.

To cover more than 20 acres under one flat roof, the manufacturing

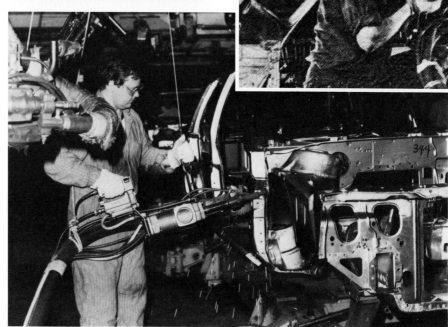

line with such mathematical accuracy that there was no chance of a green Buick fender arriving for assembly on a blue Pontiac.

At many assembly plants at that time, workers who performed operations on the underside of the cars stood in pits beneath the production line. The General Motors plant in Framingham adopted a "new and novel" assembly method—suspending the chassis assembly line in the air—permitting employees to attach parts while standing in a normal position.

When the Framingham plant opened in 1948, it was among the best equipped and most modern of more than 100 General Motors manufacturing units. Employee convenience and comfort were stressed in both planning and final layout of the plant. Although only 600 workers were on the payroll when the first car was completed, a larger staff was anticipated in the near future and two

Paint spraying in a booth of the paint department.

A spot welding operation in the body shop in the early days of the Framingham Plant and today.

hard-surfaced parking lots big enough to accommodate 1,100 employee cars were built. Large locker rooms were provided, and each worker was assigned his own locker. Well-supplied washrooms were equipped with modern circular sprays. Showers were available, and refrigerated drinking

fountains were spaced generously throughout the plant.

The medical department—staffed during all hours of plant operation—provided a general treatment room, surgery facilities, an eye room, wards for both men and women, physical therapy and X-ray equipment, ultraviolet, and infrared lamps, and short-wave diathermy. Each new employee received a thorough examination to help determine proper job placement. Employee blood types were kept on file for use in any plant or neighborhood emergency.

A gigantic cafeteria seated 700 persons simultaneously, and accommodated them in a minimum of time by means of three stainless steel serving counters. The kitchen was equipped with state-of-the art cooking facilities.

General lighting throughout the plant was provided by mercury vapor tubes, supplemented by fluorescent lighting to illuminate specific work areas where high intensity was required. The mercury vapor lighting gave more piercing illumination, which minimized eye strain and contributed to safety. Altogether, there were more than 10 miles of fluores-

cent and mercury vapor tubes in the plant.

Fresh air was poured into the manufacturing area at the rate of 1.34 million cubic feet per minute. Nearly a million feet per minute were used in the paint spraying booths, where a new water- and air-ventilating system using the down-draft principle made it possible for employees to work without the respiratory devices usually necessary in paint shops at that time.

The power plant had sufficient steam-generating capacity to heat over 2,000 ordinary homes when the outside temperature was zero. Its three giant boilers had a potenial of 4.5 million pounds of steam per day, and were heated by a very heavy industrial-grade oil that was stored in a 640,000-gallon tank.

Electricity came into the plant at 13,800 volts and was transformed as required for lights and power operations. Daily consumption of electricity when the plant opened was sufficient for a community of 25,000 persons. (The population of Framingham at the time was 25,502.)

Framingham has sometimes been called the Hub of New England, because of its central location and access to highway and railroad "trade routes" in many directions. When the General Motors plant opened, five railroad spurs served the plant area. Two of them entered the manufacturing building—each delivering raw materials as near as possible to the area where they would be used in production. The other three spurs were for the powerhouse, for delivery of automobile frames, and for outgoing car shipments. In addition, there was a truck well big enough for four large tractor-trailers to be unloaded at the same time.

Today the original "20 acres under one roof" have grown to 44 acres. The original 10 miles of fluorescent lighting fixtures have stretched to 12 miles, and there are more than nine miles of conveyors in the plant.

In 1981 the plant underwent a major renovation, which included an extension to the body shop section, the addition of 16 welding robots designed for precision welding, and a modernizaton of equipment for the new front-wheel-drive cars now being manufactured in Framingham.

When operations first began at the Framingham plant, it was the newest of seven existing plants in the Buick-Oldsmobile-Pontiac (B-O-P) Assembly Division. General Motors found it advisable to make adjustments in its operating facilities in order to meet the mounting demand for Chevrolets in the New England area in 1959. At that time the Framingham plant was transferred from the B-O-P Division and operated under the dual management of the Fisher Body and Chevrolet Motor divisions.

In the early 1960s an expanding population and a stable economy increased the demand for new cars beyond the capacity of most plants. It became necessary for many plants to inaugurate a second production shift. Framingham was one of the plants selected for a two-shift operation, which began on February 17, 1964.

The roll test operation—a functional check of transmission, engine, and speedometer.

Final assembly—the finished product coming off the assembly line.

Four years later, in the spring of 1968, the Framingham plant rejoined its original division, which by then had been renamed the GM Assembly Division. Ever since then, intermediate-style Buick, Oldsmobile, and Pontiac automobiles have been assembled on the site.

A slumping economy cut deeply into automobile sales in early 1974. At that time the plant in Framingham was returned to one production shift. It continued single-shift operations until October 12, 1976, when increased auto sales permitted resumption of the second shift.

Hard times hit the General Motors Plant in Framingham in the early 1980s, when a serious economic recession threatened auto manufacturers throughout the United States. Sales dipped so low that production halted in October 1982 and the plant—which had employed nearly 4,000 workers—was closed.

Only a handful of key employees remained to provide essential services, while thousands applied for unemployment compensation and hoped that Christmas would bring an economic upturn. It was not encouraging to learn that General Motors had also closed two other plants in California—both permanently.

By the following spring auto sales began picking up, and on March 7 the Framingham plant restarted one production shift. The second shift resumed operation on December 12, just two weeks before Christmas, giving Framingham the one gift it most wanted and needed.

In July 1984 the General Motors Corporation reorganized its North American operations and the Framingham plant was assigned to the new Chevrolet-Pontiac-GM of Canada Group (CPC). The plant now manufactures front-wheel-drive automobiles, Chevrolet Celebrity, and Oldsmobile Ciera.

Over 40 years have passed since the day ground was first broken for the General Motors plant in Framingham. Only a few old-timers remember that cold November evening—so soon after the end of the war—when more than 700 people attended a "Welcome to Framingham" dinner in Nevins Auditorium, sponsored by the Chamber of Commerce. Plant manager Clare Swayze and his staff were there, plus a long list of GM officials from Detroit and New York. U.S. Ambassador Joseph P. Kennedy, father of former President

John F. Kennedy, was one of the principal speakers. Many predicted that the General Motors plant would someday become the largest employer in Framingham—and they were right. Today plant employees live in 226 towns and cities in five states, and some drive as many as 65 miles to work.

Current plant manager Frank Bellafato looks back with pride, and forward with confidence. "Framingham had a history of auto manufacturing long before we arrived," he recalls. "Around the turn of the century, an electric car was developed at the Waverly Bicycle factory, near where the Dennison Manufacturing Company is located today. In the early 1920s Richard Long manufactured the Bay State automobile in Framingham. You might say we inherited a 'long tradition' of quality coachmanship. But many feel that our opening marked a turning point for the town. Since our arrival as the only auto-manufacturing plant in New England, many industries have been attracted to the area and Framingham still hasn't stopped growing."

THE FAFARD COMPANIES

"Condominiums are as American as apple pie," insists Howard Fafard, and more than 1,000 families who now own his condos seem to agree. His first project—five homes in Milford—brought orders for 10 more, and steady growth over the next 20 years puts current sales at about $60 million annually.

Fafard, who lives in Framingham, grew up during the 1950s housing boom when developers covered meadows, orchards, and at least one golf course with single-family houses. "Those slab ranches were ideal starter homes" remembers Fafard, "before real estate prices started skyrocketing. Today condominiums are the affordable answer for young professionals, provided construction is both solid and imaginative."

As a full-service real estate firm, The Fafard Companies owns its own land-development equipment. Madlyn Fafard, who is a partner with her husband, explains what this means. "We're able to take a piece of undeveloped land, design a project, secure the necessary permits, do the engineering and site work, pour the foundations, erect the buildings, landscape the grounds, coordinate interior colors and carpeting, market the space, and turn over the keys to the new owners." This approach results in uniformly high quality and lower costs.

Fafard's first planned unit development is Ledgemere Country, located in Ashland. When finished, it will include 700 town house condominiums, 60 single-family homes, 230,000 square feet of shopping space, and between 200,000 and 300,000 square feet of industrial space on 512 acres.

A drive through Ledgemere reveals

Heavy on-site equipment used by The Fafard Companies in its home-building, commercial, and industrial projects.

Fafard's philosophy of protecting the natural environment. Buildings are sited to conform to existing land formations. Exteriors walls are wooden, stained in one of 10 earth tones to blend peacefully with their surroundings. According to Madlyn Fafard, "overall harmony" is essential in this type of low-rise, multifamily housing.

The Fafard Companies is also opening a second Ledgemere Country in Salem, with 600 town houses, a shopping center, and an industrial park. In addition, the firm has done a historic renovation of the old high school in Medford (now known as The Schoolhouse)—converting it into 111 condominium units. Treetop Park, a 64-unit condominium complex in Westboro, is now com-

plete, as well as a modern plant in Marlboro, where Ken's Salad Dressing is made.

The firm's commercial ventures include Westborough's Westmeadow Plaza, Bass River Research Center in Beverly, the Sudbury Inn Marketplace, Natick Crossings, Quarry Square in Milford, and Townline Plaza in Ashland.

"We have around 300 people on our payroll," says Howard Fafard, and we're all committed to the same philosophy—building affordable housing for middle America."

These condominiums are typical of those built by The Fafard Companies.

HANSEN ELECTRIC SUPPLY, INC.

Flip a light switch at the Natick Hilton, or Jordan's in Shoppers World, or Framingham Union Hospital—even at Bowditch Field—and you'll probably be using equipment supplied by Hansen Electrical Supply on Waverly Street in Framingham. "Today our 3,500-square-foot lighting salon is one of the largest in New England," explains owner Wayne Hansen, "but when we started out, my office had a dirt floor."

Hansen first entered the business in the 1950s as a truck driver with Thomas F. Kearns Electrical Supply Company in Boston. Five years later he was chosen to manage the small branch store in Framingham, and within a year his efforts began to show success. At that time owner Norman Baxter died, and Wayne (his son-in-law) was given the opportunity to buy the Framingham branch. With the help of his wife, Barbara, and a cadre of loyal employees, Hansen has enjoyed an annual sales increase for the past 25 years, even during the 1981-1982 recession.

"Our first store was 1,500 square feet. Today our new warehouse alone covers 30,000 square feet," says Hansen, "and we expect more growth in the future."

Barbara Hansen is familiar to many as the author of "Light Up Your Life" advertisements in the *Middlesex News*, where she offers interesting and useful decorating tips. "She's been great," remembers Wayne, "putting up with my long hours while we raised five children." Two of the Hansens' sons and two sons-in-law are now active in the business.

The housing construction boom in Framingham and Natick was already under way when Hansen Electrical Supply was incorporated in 1960. Some subdivisions were nearly 10 years old, and original owners with growing children were getting crowded. "That's where we came in," recalls Hansen. "Ordinary folks converting garages into family rooms, or putting on an extra bedroom, came to depend on our competitive prices and helpful service. Quite a few of these new customers came back with bigger orders when they were ready to build their next home. We've had repeat business like this from as far away as Hawaii."

Impressive as it is, the storefront showroom only brings in about 10 percent of Hansen's business. The company is primarily a wholesale electrical supplier, and it has become experienced in the intricacies of sophisticated industrial installations. According to one contractor, "Whenever I have an electrical problem, and they are getting more numerous and complicated every day, I can always turn to Hansen and find the help I need." Manufacturers echo this sentiment, adding that Hansen is "unfailing in its business commitments."

Wayne Hansen is active in community affairs, serving as corporator for Framingham Union Hospital and the Framingham Savings Bank, chairman of the Millis Board of Appeals, treasurer and director of the Nantucket Angler's Club, member of the Boston Athletic Association, 32nd-degree Mason/Aleppo Temple, past deputy district governor of the Framingham Lions Club, member of the United States Power Squadrons, past governor and chairman of the Lighting Committee for the National Association of Electrical Distributors in the United States, and member of the American Legion.

Hansen Electric Supply, Inc.'s, new home, at 64 Waverly Street on Route 135 in Framingham, contains 30,000 square feet of scientifically designed electrical distribution facilities.

Wayne Hansen (center), owner of Hansen Electric Supply, Inc., is flanked by Bernie Coffey (left) and David McGaughey in this 1962 photo. Both employees are still with Hansen in 1986.

HARGRAVES, KARB, WILCOX & GALVANI

A successful lawyer who never went to college? That's what happened to the late Fred Hilton, whose Framingham law firm is known today as Hargraves, Karb, Wilcox & Galvani.

Fred Hilton graduated from Framingham Academy and High School in 1899. At that time the two organizations granted a combined degree. For financial reasons, he decided to skip college and applied directly to Boston University Law School, where he is credited with being the last student who was ever accepted without a college degree.

Hilton graduated from law school in 1903, and began his practice in Boston. He served as a state representative, a state senator, and later as town moderator. As late as 1917 he shared law offices at 99 State Street with John M. Merriam, who remained long after Fred Hilton moved his practice to Framingham, his hometown.

Fred Hilton had been active in Framingham even before moving his practice there. He became director of the Framingham Cooperative Bank in 1907, vice-president in 1938, and president in 1945. He was also an early director of the Framingham Board of Trade and was active in Rotary and in the bond drives of World War I. He also developed Brewster Road and was responsible for building homes there.

During World War II, Hilton formed a partnership with Boston trial lawyer (and Framingham native) Julian Hargraves. The firm of Hilton and Hargraves occupied offices at 24 Union Avenue, in the Hemenway Block. In 1949 Richard Karb became an associate, but was temporarily called away to serve with the Marine Corps in the Korean Conflict. Francis Wilcox, still green from law school, agreed to join the firm during Karb's absence. But he remained after Karb's return, and in 1952 the partnership of Hargraves, Karb & Wilcox hung out its shingle. The addition of Victor Galvani a few years later gave rise to the present firm name.

During the ensuing decades other attorneys joined the ranks as partners, including Edward Mahan and James Sweeney, who came on board together in the mid-1960s. Sweeney left the firm several years ago to accept appointment to the bench as a justice of the Middlesex County Probate Court. The most recent additions to the partnership roster were Paul Galvani, son of Victor Galvani, and William Mayer.

The close ties between the firm and the Framingham community it serves is reflected by the fact that, with one exception, all of the firm partners, both past and present, were or are Framingham natives.

The legal needs of Framingham have changed dramatically since the days when Fred Hilton used to walk to work from his home on Brewster Road. The firm of Hargraves, Karb, Wilcox & Galvani has kept pace with these changes to the point where the services it presently offers are on a par with those formerly provided only by the old-line law firms of major cities such as Boston.

R.H. LONG MOTOR SALES COMPANY

The R.H. Long Company manufactured about 4,000 Bay State automobiles between 1922 and 1925. The car came in various styles including coupe, sedan, and roadster. The aluminum bodies were manufactured in Framingham and the cars were also assembled there. The well-built body of the Bay State featured a southern ash wooden frame with aluminum sheet metal and fine coach work, including high quality broadcloth upholstery. Engines included either a Continental six-cylinder or a Lycoming straight eight-cylinder.

Successor to the R.H. Long Company was the R.H. Long Motor Sales Company, also founded by R.H. Long. In 1927 it became a franchised Cadillac dealership. Shortly afterward it was also franchised to sell Pontiacs and GMC trucks.

The Long dealership today is a full-service dealership, including leasing. It has nearly 100 employees, and is located at the corner of Waverly and Mellon streets, and also across the street at 613 Waverly Street.

It has received many awards, including *Time* magazine's Quality Dealer Award. For several years it has been the only dealership in New England enjoying Master Dealer status for both Cadillac and Pontiac. Current president Charles F. Long has twice served on the General Motors President's Dealer Advisory Committee.

Today R.H. Long's sales volume in cars and trucks is one of the highest in New England.

This 1925 Bay State Roadster was restored by the Long dealership in 1975 and ran like new, as did its original Waltham clock.

COMFORT AIR SYSTEMS

The next time you step into the Saxonville Public Library on a scorching summer afternoon and breathe a sigh of relief as you feel the refreshing air conditioning, remember Bob Kinz and Comfort Air Systems.

Robert Kinz graduated from Northeastern University as a mechanical engineer. He entered the U.S. Army as a second lieutenant assigned to the post of engineers as assistant to the chief of utilities for the headquarters of the Corps of Engineers at Fort Belvoir, Virginia. It was here that he developed an interest in air conditioning.

Upon discharge, he went to work for the Trane Company, a leading manufacturer of heating and air conditioning equipment. After six months of training, he was assigned to the Boston sales office as sales engineer. Four years later, after watching Trane assist one of its dealers to begin his own business, he resigned from the company hoping it would offer him the same financial backing, which it did. With its $25,000 guarantee, he went to the Framingham Trust Company and obtained a loan.

In August 1968 Kinz opened the doors of his new business as its only employee. The original plant, located at 18 South Street in Framingham, covered about 1,500 square feet.

After being in business only three months, he obtained the first big order—designing and installing a heating and air conditioning system for a building in Acton, for $27,000. By the end of the first year there were three employees including the owner, and two trucks. Eighteen years later there are about 100 employees, with 50 trucks and 14 cars.

By 1974 Comfort Air Systems had outgrown its tiny facility on South Street. The owner built an 11,000-square-foot building at 95 Eames Street. Fortunately, he also purchased three additional acres of land at the rear of the building. In 1976 one more acre was added. By 1984 expansion was necessary once again, and construction began on a 43,000-square-foot plant. At this time the company also made a major purchase of sheet-metal equipment—a coil line and cybermation machine.

In 1969 Dick Bertrand, presently the vice-president and outside field supervisor, joined Comfort Air Systems. Three years later John N. Celona, sales manager and general manager of the New Hampshire branch since January 1986, joined the firm and in 1974 Glenn G.

A helicopter delivers a rigging of heating and air conditioning equipment onto the roof of a large commercial building.

Hodson, currently vice-president and operations manager, joined the management team.

Although Comfort Air Systems was always involved in the design, installation, and servicing of heating and air conditioning equipment, it was not until 1981 that the firm es-

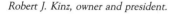

Robert J. Kinz, owner and president.

A computer operated Cybermation machine cuts out fittings for sheet-metal duct systems.

tablished a separate service company—Comfort Air Systems Services, Inc.—to provide maintenance for its own installations and to seek out service contracts for office buildings, commercial sites, manufacturing plants, and private residences.

In 1972 Comfort Air Systems became one of the first heating and air conditioning companies to rig air conditioning equipment on a roof using a helicopter, remembers president Kinz. "But our most interesting assignments usually involve energy conservation.

"In 1976 we designed a sophisticated system at the Babson College Recreational Arena. In that case we used the heat rejected from diesel generators at the arena to heat the locker rooms and offices.

"In 1979 we designed an elaborate heating and air conditioning system for an office building in Burlington. We used solar collectors on the roof and a groundwater source heat pump.

"In 1982 we designed a heat reclamation system for the Wachusetts Ski Lodge, using the heat rejected from the snow-making compressors to warm the lodge itself."

Comfort Air Systems, located at 95 Eames Street, occupied an additional 43,000 square feet which had been added to the facility in October 1984.

Besides designing and installing standard heating and air conditioning systems for office and commercial buildings, Comfort Air Systems has also engineered clean rooms and other sophisticated applications. Today the company is using a computer to project energy costs, estimate sheet-metal systems and piping systems, and to support engineering. A computer is also used in conjunction with the firm's cybermation machine—enabling it to cut fittings by

machine in five or six minutes instead of as long as 45 minutes. "Our cybermation machine is one of the first to be used in the MetroWest area," explains Kinz.

Because Comfort Air Systems does such a large amount of business, it is able to purchase many sheet-metal materials and pipe fittings as well as refrigeration parts from local Framingham distributors—increasing the firm's sales volume substantially.

"The key to our business," explains Kinz, "is people. Half of the employees who worked for me back in the early 1970s are still on board. Most of our business is within a 50-mile radius of Boston, but we have had clients in several other New England states. We're prepared to tackle any air conditioning or heating need—no matter how complicated—from the operating rooms at Framingham Union Hospital to the computer room at Framingham State College. We've even installed heating and ventilation equipment for three barns at Macomber Farm."

Coil lines used to fabricate straight runs of duct are inspected by owner and president Robert J. Kinz (right) and vice-president in charge of field operations Richard Bertrand.

CONSOLIDATED GROUP, INC.

Most of the companies making the American economy grow and prosper today are small; indeed, the majority of firms doing business in this country employ fewer than 100 people.

The owners of these small businesses—the companies that are the true foundation of our economy—are faced with the problem of offering compensation and benefits that will attract and keep the best employees.

Since the spring of 1971 Consolidated Group has been forging a link between these small businesses and major, nationally known insurance carriers—a link that enables small employers to offer life, medical, disability, and dental benefits at reasonable rates.

By creating a "multiple employer trust," Consolidated Group "groups the small groups," spreading the risk over the ensuing larger body, thus keeping costs and premiums reasonable and affordable.

Consolidated Group offered its first small group insurance plans in New England and, as the business grew, gradually expanded both its territory and the kinds of benefit plans it offered. Today Consolidated Group benefit plans are available nationwide, and thousands of small companies now request insurance through the firm each month.

As marketers and administrators of these small group plans, Consolidated Group, from its headquarters in Framingham, provides such services as underwriting, marketing support, premium billing, claims payment, customer service, and administration. The company markets its products exclusively through independent insurance agents and, in addition to its national headquarters, now serves them through more than 20 regional offices throughout the country.

Consolidated Group began with one small office in Natick, but by 1981 its growth had it "bursting at its seams," with staff at four locations in the MetroWest area. It was then that the firm purchased the former Astra Pharmaceutical Building in Framingham and renovated it, adding two floors of office space. Now more than 300 Consolidated Group people make their business home there.

Thriving Consolidated Group has been among the 500 fastest-growing privately held companies in the United States, as determined by *Inc.* magazine, in 1984 and 1985.

In response to the steep rise in health care costs, innovative, alternative health care delivery systems, including health maintenance organizations and preferred provider health plans, are gaining increasing importance. As they do, Consolidated Group is there, continuing to offer small groups the finest in health care benefit options.

Consolidated Group's headquarters in Framingham.

FITTS INSURANCE AGENCY, INC.

The Fitts Insurance Agency has been serving the Framingham area from its 40 Union Avenue location since the 1940s.

Arthur M. Fitts, Jr., founder and chairman of Fitts Insurance Agency, established the company in 1932 because "I wanted to work for myself." His father and uncle, Arthur and George Fitts, had owned a fish market in Framingham for many years—eventually constructing the Fitts Building on Concord Street. "The market was sold," he recalls, "and I had worked for several other local employers, including R.H. Long, before starting a business of my own.

Helped by one part-time employee, Fitts opened his agency on Irving Street, later expanding into larger quarters at 20 Union Avenue. "We moved to our present location at 40 Union Avenue in the early 1940s," says the entrepreneur, "and we haven't got much surplus space here anymore."

Fitts Insurance has always specialized in service—meeting the needs of Framingham residents for more than

half a century. "The days of hand billing are long gone," explains the founder, "replaced by our modern computers. But customers have never been mere numbers to us. We are a family company, and still try to be personally acquainted with all our clients." Over the years the firm has developed into the largest insurance agency in Framingham, proving the worth of its person-to-person business style.

The organization sells a wide range of commercial insurance. It offers special programs for retail stores, condominium associations, restaurants, contractors, oil jobbers, manufacturers, bakers, and many others. In addition, optometrists, opticians, veterinarians, and funeral directors can obtain needed coverage through poli-

cies offered by Fitts Insurance.

The firm also has a Personal Lines Department, which handles home, auto, and all other personal coverages. "Special credit discounts and check-writing authority for prompt settlement of claims are among the benefits of doing business with us," notes Geoffrey E. Fitts, company president.

To round out its list of services, the agency has a Financial Services Department. George Hulme, vice-president and treasurer, explains that this department specializes in both personal and group insurance needs—including life, accident, health, dental, disability, Keogh, pensions, and IRAs.

Owned and operated by a family whose roots run deep in the history of Framingham, Fitts Insurance Agency, Inc., has epitomized courteous service and professionalism for over 50 years.

PERFORMING ARTS CENTER OF METROWEST

The mission of the Performing Arts Center of MetroWest (PAC) is to sponsor workshops, lessons, and performances in music, dance, and theater. It includes a nonprofit school that is an accredited member of the National Guild of Schools for the Performing Arts. PAC teachers are notable for their excellent credentials.

PAC is considered the founder of community theater in Framingham. Its first production, "Guys and Dolls," was staged in 1983, and since then PAC members have been instrumental in developing other theatrical production groups.

Formed in 1982, PAC originally concentrated on supporting a community school that offered private lessons in all musical instruments and voice, and a variety of dance and dramatic training. Then, as now, students ranged from beginners to those desiring to perform professionally, and included all age groups.

PAC was located in downtown Framingham at the Civic League until October 11, 1985, when it opened an office at Framingham State College. Many members of the Performing Arts Center also were active in a campaign to save the Civil League, which had been scheduled to be disbanded.

With an office at the D. Justin McCarthy College Center, the Performing Arts Center and Framingham State College entered a new collaborative relationship. College president Paul Weller welcomed this symbol of his efforts to work with the local community in developing cultural opportunities for area residents.

"We had already collaborated successfully with the college on special programs," explains former PAC president Valerie Knotts. "In 1985

PAC and the college Student Union activities board co-sponsored a ballet series to sellout audiences. Programs by the Boston Ballet and the Connecticut Ballet filled the 800-seat Dwight Auditorium, largest in the area. We're also assisting the college to refurbish the auditorium through fund-raising activities."

The Performing Arts Center now serves a broader population with satellite programs at local schools and agencies, including Massachusetts Bay Community College in Wellesley and the Cushing Hospital in Framingham. Funding from the Framingham Arts Lottery Council has enabled PAC to establish such outreach programs. A "special needs" grant has also brought arts entertainment to the elderly and handicapped residents of Framingham.

"A source of enrichment for individuals and the community. . . ." That's how members describe the

Performing Arts Center. During the past five years increasing numbers of students and sellout audiences have come to appreciate this resource for instruction and performance of music, dance, and drama.

A young dancer practices her skills at the bar.

The Performing Arts Center's quality teachers and eager students promote a creative learning environment for area residents.

FRAMINGHAM PEST CONTROL, INC.

Edward Honen founded Framingham Pest Control, Inc., in 1943.

Thomas Gibbons, Sr., son-in-law of the founder, operated the business until his death in 1983.

"Not everyone remembers," comments Tom Gibbons, Jr., owner of Framingham Pest Control, Inc., "but there used to be a pond out in front of The Meadows, Vaughn Monroe's supper club on Worcester Road. My Dad and I both knew Vaughn, and one day he called us with a problem. It wasn't termites. It was raccoons! They were around the pond at night, and evidently bothered the customers. It was the most unusual pest-control call we ever received."

Framingham Pest Control, Inc., was started—almost by accident—in 1943. Edward Honen was running a "help wanted" bureau in an office near the Arcade during World War II. A pest-control firm near Worcester asked Ed to act as its answering service for this area, and he agreed. But he soon discovered that his employers were not following through on the arrangements he made for them on the phone. Customers be-

gan to complain, and Ed decided to do the job himself. With the help of his wife, Alma, he operated the business successfully from his home in Ashland.

When Ed passed away in the early 1950s, Alma tried to continue the family business but found it too much for one woman. Her son-in-law, 43-year-old Tom Gibbons, Sr., was in the insurance business but longed to be self-employed, and Alma sold the pest-control business to him. It was in an embryonic state—netting only $2,000 to $3,000 each year.

Tom Sr. ran the business from Alma's home for a year or so, and then in 1955 moved to 357 Worcester Road, where it has been a familiar landmark for over 30 years.

Tom Gibbons, Jr., grew up with the business, and after finishing school decided to join his father for a few years. Later he moved to Walpole and established his own business, Walpole Pest Control, Inc. Tom Sr. continued to operate Framingham Pest Control until his death in 1983.

"It was his life," remembers his son, who now owns both the Walpole and Framingham firms. "Even though Dad was legally blind during the last few years, he kept the business going." Much of the credit for this goes to his faithful secretary, Josephine Sanborn, who has been with the company for more than 30 years.

Today Tom Jr.'s son is working at the Walpole firm—the fourth generation of the family to be on the company payroll.

"There's more to pest control than just pesticide," explains Tom Gibbons, Jr. "We offer an integrated pest-management program that involves not only pesticide, but also structural changes when needed and housekeeping improvements attuned to the environment. Our aim is to protect our clients' homes from pest infestation, with minimal governmental impact."

THE CAHNERS COMPANIES, INC.

The Cahners Companies, Inc., one of the largest development and management companies in the South Middlesex area, presently owns nearly two blocks of office and retail property as well as over four acres of parking in the downtown Framingham central business district. In the early 1980s president Robert M. Cahners recognized the potential of the area as an exciting and viable business center. As a specialist in the tasteful renovation of older commercial properties, he was intrigued with the architectural character of the turn-of-the-century structures. He envisioned restoring the original character of each building.

To accomplish this goal, the company instituted a two-phase plan.

Phase I involves the acquisition of major, well-located properties with suitable parking facilities. Phase II is an extensive program to promote downtown Framingham as a vibrant business area.

Under Phase I, in 1982 Cahners acquired a three-building parcel on the east side of Concord Street—the Prindiville, Arcade, and Mullaney buildings. The purchase included nearly three acres of paved parking—the largest in the downtown area. Because of its central location, the parcel assured adequate parking for future Cahners acquisitions. The first row of structures was extended with

Above
Robert M. Cahners, president of The Cahners Companies, Inc.

Below
The Amsden Building, in addition to its renovated shops and offices, boasts a former third-floor bowling alley completely refurbished into office space. Photo by Gregg Shupe

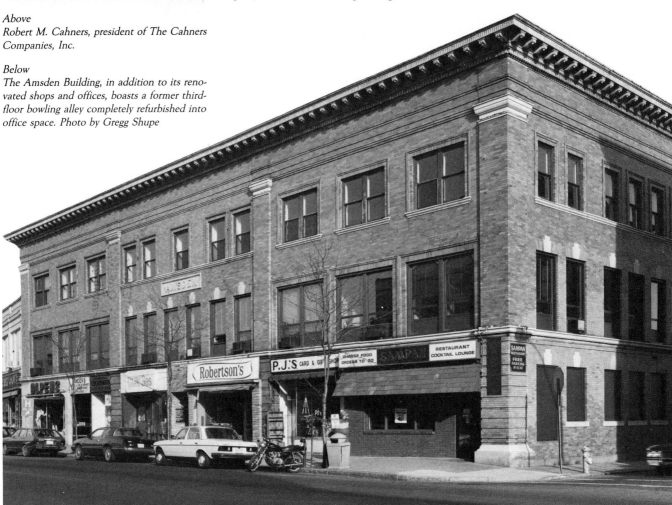

The Kendall Building, located in the heart of downtown Framingham, has undergone complete restoration. Originally built as a grand hotel at the turn of the century, the property offers over 50,000 square feet of office and retail space. Photo by Gregg Shupe

the purchase of the neighboring Amsden Building in 1984.

In 1985 the company completed the assembly of its two downtown blocks by procuring a historic landmark—the Kendall Building. Opening as the Kendall Hotel on April 25, 1899, it became one of the grandest in New England, boasting such luxuries as hot and cold running water, in-suite baths, gas and electric service, steam heat, an elevator, a barber shop, a billiard room and bowling alley in the basement, and public and private dining rooms. Under the management of the Ensworth family between 1922 and 1945, the hotel was one of the best known in the area. Rotary and Kiwanis met there regularly, and the Boston Redskins (now the Washington Redskins) were quartered at the hotel while they trained at Bowditch Field. Most recently, the Kendall Building was headquarters for the Framingham Trust Company, and now serves as the main offices of The Cahners

Companies. In renovating the property, Cahners has insisted that the magnificent original woodwork and ceiling detail on the first floor be preserved by current and future tenants.

Upgrading of the properties has been controlled to accommodate the overwhelming demand in the downtown area for moderately priced, comfortable space rather than expensive luxurious offices and retail quarters. A general exterior facelift is currently in progress under a master plan to improve the overall appearance of the central business district.

"These downtown buildings are solidly built," explains Cahners, "and we want to keep them in good condition by careful management and gradual renovation. However, we try to avoid extensive renovations that could cause gentrification, forcing smaller business people to look elsewhere for reasonable rents."

Under the Phase II promotional program, the firm will devote its advertising and publicity to promoting downtown as an important commercial area rather than concentrating on specific buildings or space avail-

A spacious street-level computer showroom is beautifully housed amid fine detailing from another era. Photo by Gregg Shupe

ability. Within a five-block area there are 61 business and financial service companies, 60 legal and accounting firms, 77 retail stores, 25 restaurants, and 45 personal service companies. With such an excellent basis for further growth, along with conveniently located buildings at moderate rents, Cahners feels businesses of all sizes can take advantage of the MetroWest economic boom by locating in downtown Framingham.

Robert M. Cahners, who received his undergraduate degree at Dartmouth College and attended Harvard Business School, brings to the area extensive experience in property development and management. Before founding The Cahners Companies, the 44-year-old president was executive vice-president, treasurer, and director of Hunneman Investment Management Corporation. At Hunneman, he was responsible for the administration of the company's portfolio of 50 managed properties. He also had overall management responsibility for Hunneman's commercial property acquisition program.

Before joining Hunneman, Cahners served as associate director of property management at The Beal Companies, a major property owner in the greater Boston area. At Beal he handled the leasing and management operation of a substantial downtown office building portfolio.

MULLEN LUMBER COMPANY

Sudbury, Massachusetts, was a quiet country village in 1955 when 50-year-old Thomas J. Mullen built his first lumberyard on Union Avenue—near the Boston Post Road. After years spent working for other lumber companies, he'd started his own business three years earlier. From his home in Waltham, he began as a lumber broker. His wife, Winifred, already busy raising five children, answered the phone and took the orders, while Tom's only paid employee, Ronald Ham, delivered orders in the firm's single truck.

"Those were modest beginnings," remembers Burton Mullen, son of the founder and now president of Mullen Lumber Company. "But Dad had a knack for seeing beyond the horizon. That's one reason he located the lumberyard here at the junction of the B&M and New Haven railroad lines. He expected the business to grow far beyond Sudbury, and it has."

Helen Bacon remembers the early days clearly. "Sudbury had a population of 4,500—and one general store—when Mullen Lumber Company first opened. Ron Ham, now vice-president of the firm, was the only employee and I heard that Mr. Mullen needed a secretary." Helen took the job, and has kept the front office humming ever since. "We've had three decades of jokes about Ham and Bacon," she says. "There's no need to mention it in the article."

Thomas Mullen sold the business to his son in 1975, after Burt had been on the payroll for 15 years. But the elder Mullen remained actively involved with the company until his death in 1985.

"I started out selling in Boston," recalls Burt Mullen. "The 1960s were years of downtown revitalization, and we were deeply involved in it. Major clients included the Prudential Center, Government Center, and the new City Hall." Mullen Lumber

Company has also left its mark of quality on Sullivan Stadium and the new Copley Place.

"Most of our deliveries are within a 50-mile radius of Sudbury," Mullen explains. "But we've also served customers on Cape Cod and Nantucket. In fact, we once provided lumber for a complex of 250 apartments in Richmond, Virginia."

Today, with 45 employees and 12 vehicles, Mullen Lumber Company looks back on almost a third of a century of steadily increasing sales.

"We've sold thousands and thousands of housing units over the years," reflects Burt Mullen. "Our past speaks for itself. Today we're looking forward to another 30 years of successful service to the Metro-West community, and beyond."

Mullen Lumber Company began operations in 1955, when this photo was taken. Sudbury was a quiet country village with a population of 4,500 and one general store.

BROSSI BROTHERS

William Brossi was born in Bardi, a small mountain village in the province of Parma, Italy. When he was eight years old his parents removed him from school to help on the family farm. At the age of 14 he was sent to England to work, returning to Italy four years later to serve in World War I. William immigrated to the United States when he was just 24 years old.

The Brossi Brothers, as teenagers, shoveling sand and stone into their father's single-cylinder magnetic concrete mixer with an over-sized flywheel.

Four years after passing through customs at Ellis Island, with only a second-grade education, he started a business in Wellesley, Massachusetts, as a general contractor. In those early days William's only vehicle was a bicycle, and he carried his tools strapped on his back.

In Wellesley he met his future bride, Jennie Mortarelli, who coincidentally was born in Villa Zani, a tiny village in the valley on the other side of the mountain range from Bardi, William's hometown. They were wed at the beginning of the Depression, and began working together in pursuit of the American Dream. During the Depression years they tried to find work for as many fellow

Joseph and David Brossi in front of their Old Path Village Plaza, built alongside historic Old Connecticut Path.

immigrants as possible.

Besides doing the books for her husband, canning produce from their garden, and working outside the home, Jennie gave birth to three children—Joseph, David, and Theresa. Joe and David recall that the "basic training" their Dad put them through as teenagers was tougher than infantry training in the Army! They mixed mortar and concrete by hand, carrying the hod up the never-ending oak ladder to supply their father—who seemed to devour both bricks and mortar immediately.

After military service the brothers agreed to continue and expand their father's business. With a total of $4,500, they used $500 as down payment on a truck and $3,000 to buy their first house lot. Surveying was originally done by John Ciarcia, a classmate of David's at Wentworth Institute, who later married Theresa Brossi.

Much of the credit for surviving those early years goes to their beloved mother, who passed away in 1982. She provided constant encouragement and a good dose of wisdom and cheerfulness. The brothers would joke with their mother that, with her sincerity and warmth, she sold more homes over the phone than all the other sales people combined.

Over the years the Brossi Brothers have seen Framingham change from a farming community to the bustling hub of the MetroWest area. They are proud of the structures they have added to the community. Each project—from a single home to a shopping center—is carefully nurtured and supervised from design to occupancy.

Today Brossi Brothers has a full spectrum of real estate holdings, all of which the firm designed and built and now meticulously manages. Its unusual attention to detail is expressed at Old Path Village, which the company built adjacent to Old Connecticut Path in Framingham. Realizing that the area was rich in history, the brothers researched its past and erected a bronze historic marker on the site. Retail and office space was built incorporating pitched roofs, brick sidewalks, chimneys, and post lanterns originally designed by Paul Revere and used on Beacon Hill in Boston.

With tradition rooted in the past and a strong commitment to the future, Brossi Brothers is a proud partner in progress.

SHERIDAN, GARRAHAN & LANDER

Sheridan, Garrahan & Lander was founded a half-century ago by Carl A. Sheridan, now retired from the firm. Sheridan, a graduate of Suffolk University School of Law and holder of an honorary doctorate in public administration, is a former moderator of the town of Framingham and chairman of its finance committee. He has served the Commonwealth of

John P. Garrahan, Esquire.

Massachusetts in many elective and appointive capacities, including state representative and governor's councillor and commissioner of administration and finance. Other original partners in the firm have become presiding justices in various courts of the Commonwealth.

Sheridan, Garrahan & Lander is a comprehensive law firm in the traditional sense, with an added dimension of sensitivity and responsibilities to its clients that goes beyond narrow

legal confines. The firm is prepared to counsel and advise on a wide range of business management, real estate, community planning and zoning, taxation, estate planning, health care, and similar subjects.

New areas of law are constantly developing. Applications of existing law are steadily expanding, and many of these relate to business, planning, zoning, and health spheres. To carry out what it perceives to be the full range of its responsibilities to business, health care, and individual clients, Sheridan, Garrahan & Lander continuously monitors and evaluates the effect of these changing legal circumstances.

By encouraging internal specialization, the firm enables several attorneys to serve the varied needs of each client, thus allowing the client to develop rapport and confidence in a broader segment.

Over the years Sheridan, Garrahan & Lander has expanded steadily. Today the firm includes 17 attorneys who represent a broad range of educational and professional backgrounds, and a total staff of more than 35 people. Further growth is anticipated, and the firm is carefully planning further expansion in order to continue offering clients a wide range of legal services, with specialization in litigation, banking, probate, health care, domestic relations, tax law, business practices, real estate planning, and zoning.

Sheridan, Garrahan & Lander is deeply rooted in the South Middlesex, western Norfolk, and eastern Worcester County areas of the Commonwealth. Its members are graduates of Harvard Law School; Boston College Law School; New England School of Law; and Boston University, Northeastern University, and Suffolk schools of law. Undergraduate studies were pursued at colleges and universities ranging from the University of Dublin (Ireland) to

Jay J. Lander, Esquire.

Harvard, Bates, Brandeis, Boston College, and Holy Cross.

In addition to being officers of the courts, lawyers—by the very nature of their calling—have special obligations to be good citizens and community leaders. Sheridan, Garrahan & Lander actively encourages its members and associates to participate extensively in a well-rounded program of community affairs. Since the firm's inception in 1936, members have been engaged in a wide range of civic and philanthropic activities, supporting charitable, cultural, and religious organizations. Members have served their communities as moderators; selectmen; state representatives and senators; and presidents and members of the boards of local hospitals, the United Way, the YMCA, Catholic charities, Juvenile Diabetes Foundation, and other philanthropic organizations.

The firm also takes part in bar activities, not merely as members but as active contributors to committees and working groups. Various members of the firm have filled top positions, including the presidency of the South Middlesex Bar Association. In addition, members have written, lectured, or taught courses on taxation, real estate law, health law, commercial law, legal economics, and other legal topics.

John P. Garrahan, senior partner, remembers the impact the firm's policy of civic responsibility has had on Framingham. "Carl Sheridan was State Commissioner of Administration and Finance under Governor Herter when the Massachusetts Turnpike was being constructed. He

was instrumental in securing two exits from Framingham, because he recognized the significance of its location as the hub of MetroWest."

Sheridan, Garrahan & Lander has acted as legal advisor to the Framingham Union Hospital as it grew from a cottage hospital to a major center. The firm also was instrumental in the planning and zoning of the Framingham Industrial Park, and is today representing Shoppers World as this "grandfather of regional shopping centers" prepares to expand and accommodate the increased requirements of a growing MetroWest community.

As always, the firm emphasizes sound business management in the conduct of its law practice. To that end, it has created an efficient busi-

ness infrastructure in its offices, including computerized systems for word processing, and real estate transactions. Paralegals are used extensively to further minimize the cost of legal services.

This painting by Peg Crane surrounds the town seal of Framingham and the Revolutionary Minute Man statue that stands in Buckminster Square with the historic buildings of Framingham. From the upper right, clockwise, Horace Mann Hall, one of the first dormitories built at the Framingham State Teachers College; New Framingham Public Library; Danforth Museum and School and headquarters of the Callahan Senior Citizens' Center; Framingham Memorial Building, home of the Framingham town offices; Village Hall on the Framingham Centre Common; First Baptist Church, a Christopher Wren design; and Pike Haven House, the second-oldest home in Framingham.

TOM AND JOAN CUDDY REAL ESTATE

Tom and Joan Cuddy are "star" real estate agents in more than one way. During the years when the Chateau de Ville brought Hollywood-style entertainment to Framingham, Cuddy Real Estate was often asked to provide suitable homes for well-known performers. "Johnny Carson insisted on a six-bedroom house, with a tennis court and in-ground pool," recalls Tom Cuddy. "He wanted a TV in each bedroom, and a set of drums for his own amusement. It was a hard package to put together on a temporary basis, but we did it."

The corporate headquarters of Cuddy Real Estate at 310 Union Avenue, Framingham.

Joan and Tom Cuddy

Joan Cuddy, his wife and business partner, became a star in her own right when she first entered the real estate business in 1965. "I'm from Naples, Italy," she explains, "and Italian women have a traditional role—stay home and take care of the family. So I never held a job until my oldest son was in high school. After earning my license as a real estate broker, I tried to find work with various agencies, but nobody wanted to hire a woman! Finally an agency owned by a friend of the family gave me a chance, and I stayed there for some time. I worked night and day, and proved that a woman can be a first-rate real estate broker. Today

some of the finest brokers in the business are women."

Husband Tom had a business too—T.J. Cuddy Construction Company—however, he decided to expand his practical experiences in this field and follow in his wife's footsteps as a real estate broker. Since then he has earned the title "Certified Residential Broker," awarded by the National Association of Realtors.

"We do specialize in many areas of real estate," says Tom, "but about 90 percent of our business involves private homes." The agency has grown steadily over the past 20 years: Today it has more than 100 realtor associates. "We're bigger now," adds Joan, "with offices in Westboro, Ashland, and Holden, as well as Framingham, but we're still a family-run operation, and we think of our staff as family."

Cuddy Real Estate has long been on the cutting edge of industry progress. Tom Cuddy III, general manager and vice-president of the company, recalls that his parents helped bring MetroWest real estate "out of the

dark ages.

"Cuddy pioneered the use of logos, sophisticated marketing techniques, cooperation among brokers, and the concept of multi-office locations," he relates. "And my father was promoting the sale of condominiums long before they became popular." In fact, Cuddy Real Estate marketed one of the first new condominium developments in MetroWest—Apple Tree Hill in Hopkinton.

Today the firm leads the local industry in another new concept called zero lot zoning. "These are individually owned homes with very little land around them," says Tom Cuddy. "They're not condominiums, but well-designed detached town-homes." Zero lot zoning properties successfully marketed by Cuddy Real Estate are located on Grove Street and Maynard Road in Framingham, and are known as Danforth Village and Maynard Close.

PYNE SAND & STONE COMPANY

There's at least one couple in Hopkinton who'll never forget the Blizzard of 1978. They were expecting a baby when the heavy blanket of white fell, blocking their country road and trapping their car in the garage. "I waited all night," remembers the husband, "and at 2:30 in the morning I heard a noise and saw lights coming up the road." He ran outside to stop the plow, operated by Pyne Sand & Stone Company, and told the driver his plight. It only took a few minutes extra to plow out the driveway, and the baby was born at the right time and place.

Joseph V. Pyne and his wife, Margaret, would have been proud. That was the kind of good-neighbor policy they adopted when they started the company in the late 1940s. Joe had experience as an all-around handyman when he bought his first dump truck to do general contracting. Margaret handled the books and phone—while raising four children—from their family home on Main Street in Hopkinton.

Joe is remembered not only as a square-dealing businessman, but also as a civic leader involved with many town committees. Joining the Hopkinton Volunteer Fire Company at an early age, he soon became its chief—a responsibility he shouldered with pride until his untimely death in 1964.

Under Joe's direction, Pyne Sand & Stone outgrew its office space in the family dining room, and moved to its present location on Fruit Street. "When Dad passed away, my brother Joe and I kept the company going, with the help of Dad's foreman, Dick Stewart," remembers Jim Pyne, who was only 22 years old at the time and "definitely not interested in management." In those days the firm divided its interest between selling "materials" —sand for ice control and stone for drainage and septic work—and building subdivision roadways in Hop-

Joseph V. Pyne (above) and wife, Margaret (above right), founded the Pyne Sand & Stone Company in the late 1940s. Joe ran the business while Margaret handled the books and telephone from their family home.

kinton and Milford. "Dad had been doing a lot of labor-intensive projects between 1950 and 1964," explains Jim, "like water main and drain installations. But we found an increasing demand for high-quality materials, so we gradually phased out the construction side of the business."

Focusing on the growing need for materials, the partners built a new processing plant in 1973, which separates ordinary fill into sand and stone. "We did the wrench turning on that job ourselves," recalls Jim with a smile. "The new plant boosted our production from 75 to 200 tons

per hour, and we still can't keep up with demand."

Today Pyne Sand & Stone occupies more than 100 acres on Fruit Street, and operates 30 vehicles. The small office building, constructed in 1971, is overcrowded and slated for expansion. After 10 years with the firm, Joe Jr. has sold his interest to brother Jim and partner Dick Stewart, who are now co-owners.

"Hopkinton is growing now," explains Jim, "but you still have to be a good neighbor to have a good business. We've tried to honor Dad's reputation as a fair dealer. Every ton we sell weighs 2,000 pounds."

MARCONI'S RESTAURANT

Marconi's is more than a restaurant. It is a tribute to the Rotelli family members, who have proved over four generations that hard work, courage, and kindness are still the ingredients of true success.

When Peter and Louise Rotelli were married in a small Italian village in 1920, they didn't wait for opportunity to knock. Within three months Peter brought his bride to the United States, and settled in New York City. "We had nothing then," Louise remembers, "but we worked day and night." She made pennies a day as a seamstress, while Peter (who had been a cook in the Italian Army) became a chef at the Hotel McAlpen.

In 1932 they moved to Framingham. In the pit of the Depression, Peter worked odd jobs in construction while Louise sewed and took care of their two children, Marco and Rita. After five years they had saved enough to buy a five-room house on Route 126 near the Framingham-Ashland town line. "We lived upstairs," Louise explains, "while Peter converted the first floor into a restaurant. We called it Marconi's, after our son, Marco."

"Beer was a dime, and pizza cost a quarter," Marco recalls. "Steamers? They were free for the asking!" Although he was only 10 years old, Marco was already active in the family business, unaware that his penchant for hard work would eventually turn tragedy into triumph for the little restaurant.

Marconi's was just about to celebrate 20 years of steady growth when—in a few short hours—it was completely destroyed by fire. "Our entire family was distraught," Louise remembers, "especially Peter. He was so depressed that he left everything behind and drove down to Florida.

The original Marconi family home and restaurant in 1937.

Imagine, a lifetime of work up in smoke!" Marco followed his dad to Daytona and, sitting beside him on a sunny beach, offered to help rebuild his shattered dream. Within a year after their return, a new concrete structure had risen from the ashes, and Marconi's reopened for business. Peter Rotelli, who lived to see his new restaurant prosper, died in 1956. Marco continued in his father's spirit of perseverance, working 70 to 80 hours each week—supported by his wife, Lena, his sister, Rita, and his mother, Louise.

"Our whole family has worked to make the restaurant a success," says Louise with a smile. Marco's daughter, Linda; Rita's four children, Gloria, Cindy, Peter, and Karen; and her husband, Kevin, have taken orders over the telephone, helped with pizzas, or hostessed. Linda's husband, Bruce, who studied nuclear physics in college, has been manager for the past 10 years. "I switch from splitting atoms to splitting meatballs," he jokes. Their nine-year-old daughter, Kim, already has experience with the dishwasher, although her specialty is public relations.

"It's been 50 years since we served our first pizza," Louise remembers. Today the restaurant seats 275 guests, serving 5,000 to 6,000 meals each week. Customers from Brookline to Rhode Island willingly wait in line for Marconi's famous Italian dinners, but also for an opportunity to chat with Louise Rotelli and her children and grandchildren—a family whose achievements make everyone feel a little richer.

Louise and Peter Rotelli, originators of Marconi's, which was named for their son, Marco. Photo was taken in 1937.

WHITE HARDWARE COMPANY, INC.

Harry E. White wasn't afraid to take chances. After 25 years with St. George's Hardware, he and partner George Gipps started their own company—Framingham Hardware—in the Odd Fellows Block on Hollis Street in 1924. When the stock market crashed in 1929 and George wanted to sell out, Harry bought the business and put up his now-familiar sign—White Hardware.

Depression-era business was slow, but Harry developed close links with Framingham Cooperative Bank. As the bank's collection of repossessed houses increased, it turned to Harry for the hardware needed to maintain the properties.

At the same time, Harry looked for ways to economize. Rent was going up in the Odd Fellows Block, and in 1932 Frank Scott, who owned the neighboring Eames Block, wanted to replace his billiard hall with a more respectable tenant. So White Hardware moved into 36 Hollis Street, later expanding into 30 Hollis Street, and by the end of the war Harry had obtained a loan from Framingham Cooperative Bank to buy the entire building.

Harry's sons, Don and Fred, both grew up in the hardware business, and entered it full time when they finished school. During the war Harry wrote to Don, who was stationed in England, about the store. "Your mother is doing a whale of a job as a clerk and I think she could run the business. You almost have to knock her out to make her give up."

When their father passed away in 1954, Don and Fred became co-owners, continuing the firm's reputation as "a real hardware store." In 1959 Don was honored by appointment to the board of directors of the New England Hardware Association. Seven years later he was elected president, after serving ably as clerk and vice-president.

Fred White sold his interest in the

By the late 1930s, when this photograph was taken, White Hardware occupied this building at 36 Hollis Street.

firm to Don in 1967, who joined the True Value affiliation in 1971. Like his father, Don was willing to take risks, and in 1974 he moved the company from its 45-year home at Irving Square to its present location at 428 Franklin Street, doubling his floor space to 12,000 square feet. Don's wife, Betty, joined the firm in 1965, and worked until 1977 when Don became ill.

Don's son, Robert, took over management of the company in 1978, when his father died. His sister, Marjorie, joined the firm two years

Today White's, a True Value hardware store, is located in this 12,000-square-foot facility at 428 Franklin Street.

later to run the billing office. In 1984, as business increased, the inside retail area was remodeled and enlarged.

"Sales have more than doubled in the past five years," Bob explains. "We've come a long way with our policy of putting people first. As my dad once said, 'They're not just another sale to us; they're customers.' We expect to achieve two million dollars in sales during 1986—but we still provide all the service you look for in 'a real hardware store.'"

STREHLKE CORPORATION

The Strehlke Corporation is a Framingham organization that develops, constructs, owns, and manages more than 450,000 square feet of office and industrial properties in the MetroWest area.

Jointly owned by brothers Albert and Richard Strehlke, it traces its roots back to the early 1960s, when the Strehlkes began looking for a larger site for their family business—Colonial Floors—still located on Waverly Street in downtown Framingham. They purchased the old Natick Ice House—which had already been converted into a foundry—intending to renovate and occupy it. After converting it into a multitenant office complex, they decided to lease the space instead of occupying it. Known as the Natick Office Park, this initial Strehlke project became the first suburban office building of its kind in Natick.

While Albert maintained the prosperity of the original family firm—Colonial Floors—Richard Strehlke began building a strong team of experienced professionals whose suc-

cessful development projects have contributed to the growth of Metro-West. Today the firm's capabilities encompass the full range of development skills. Strehlke's successful development record has established close relationships and an excellent reputation with local and regional lending institutions, resulting in innovative and practical financing programs.

Strehlke Corporation is thoroughly familiar with all aspects of the construction process. Its in-house construction specialists continuously negotiate favorable contract prices and implement strong financial controls throughout the building process.

The firm also maintains long associations with experienced architectural firms and understands the important challenge of blending an

Framingham Executive Park, developed and managed by the Strehlke Corporation, offers finest-quality executive office space available for tenant growth and needs.

attractive, efficient structure with the financial realities imposed by the marketplace.

Strehlke Corporation is a successful landlord, using both in-house staff and outside brokerage specialists to introduce and show its buildings and negotiate equitable long-term leases. With more than 100 tenants, the firm takes pride in a fine management staff that handles countless details from bookkeeping to daily maintenance.

Successful development projects undertaken by Strehlke include Framingham Executive Park, a four-building office complex on Speen Street near Old Connecticut Path; Natick Office Park, being modernized again, 22 years after its original conversion from a foundry; the ultramodern Consolidated Group building at the Framingham/Southboro line; the Lincoln Medical Center adjacent to Framingham Union Hospital; and the Jonathan Maynard Office Center, formerly the Jonathan Maynard School on the green at Framingham Center.

THE FLATLEY COMPANY

"Service to the community" has been the operational philosophy of The Flatley Company ever since its founding in 1959. "Fulfillment of community needs is the only logical approach to real estate development," explains Tom Flatley. "We avoid the 'build at any cost' attitude, integrating sound business practice with the cooperation of local governments to form a finished product that best satisfies the social, environmental, and economic requirements of the communities we serve.

With more than a quarter-century of success behind it, The Flatley Company has emerged as a leader in New England real estate development, including residential development and management and commercial and industrial construction, ownership, and management. The Flatley Company also owns and operates the Sheraton Tara Hotels and Mayo Health facilities, which consist of five award-winning nursing homes in eastern Massachusetts.

Residents of south Middlesex County are acquainted with four Flatley Company landmarks—the Sheraton Tara Hotel and adjacent Framingham Office Park, the Kathleen Daniel Health Care Center, and Bayberry Hill Estates.

Marking its first year of operation in 1972 with an award for design excellence from the Sheraton Corporation, the Sheraton Tara Hotel in Framingham is now familiar to travelers along the Massachusetts Turnpike. The original "castle" has been expanded from 200 to 375 rooms, increasing at the same time the restaurant and ballroom facilities that helped the hotel to earn a "Four Diamond" rating from the American Automobile Association, the highest mark given in AAA's annual Tour Book.

Adjacent to the Sheraton Tara Hotel, The Flatley Company has constructed two office buildings—the Framingham Office Park. Built about 10 years ago, each consists of 56,000 square feet of office space. Major tenants include Dunn & Bradstreet, Apollo Computer Corporation, and Yankee Atomic.

The Kathleen Daniel Health Care Center was the third skilled nursing facility in The Flatley Company's health care division. Since first opening its doors in 1969 with 24 beds, Kathleen Daniel has provided a warm and safe environment for residents unable to care for themselves.

Bayberry Hill Estates, located on Route 9 opposite Shoppers World, has given new meaning to the phrase "luxury apartment living" since its construction in the early 1970s. Its hilltop location, visible for several miles, gives residents a commanding view of the neighborhood and an occasional glimpse of the skyscrapers in downtown Boston. After seeing the Olympic-size swimming pool, elevated tennis courts, indoor squash courts, saunas, game room, and health and fitness center with Nautilus lifecycles and free weights, one visitor remarked, "Do people actually *live here?* It feels like a vacation paradise!"

Beginning with one residential property in 1959, The Flatley Company today includes over 6,000 residential units, six health care facilities, four Sheraton Tara Hotels with two under construction, and more than five million square feet of commercial and industrial space.

Bayberry Hill Estates has given new meaning to the phrase "luxury apartment living" since its construction in the early 1970s. Photo by Gorchev and Gorchev

The original architect's rendering of the Framingham Office Park before construction.

THE FLATLEY COMPANY

UNITED BUILDERS SUPPLY COMPANY, INC.

Bermuda hotels are famous for their charm and hospitality. But who do they call if construction supplies are urgently needed? When fire struck the Holiday Inn near St. Georges a few years ago, destroying several rooms, the manager never even blinked. He called United Builders Supply Company in Framingham, Massachusetts.

"We carted the Sheetrock down to Logan Airport," remembers company president Joe D. Seifer, "but it was too bulky for them to handle. We had to truck it all the way to New York City, where the large cargo planes land. It was expensive, but we've worked with so many Holiday Inns that they called us automatically."

Most United Builders Supply customers are located within a 50-mile radius of Framingham, where the firm's offices and 25,000-square-foot warehouses are located on three acres of land fronting on Waverly Street.

"We have between 36 and 40 full-time employees today," explains Joe Seifer, "but in the beginning we had only two." That was in 1952, when Interstate Building Wrecking occupied the site. "I bought that company for $3,000," recalls Joe, "and we continued to rent the land for $55 per month."

For Joe and his wife, Blanche, it was a family affair. Changing the name to United Builders Supply, they began selling masonry supplies—bricks and blocks—buying them from wholesalers and delivering them to customers in Framingham.

"Big construction companies like Campanelli and Cerel were steady customers," says Joe. "There was a building boom in Framingham in the early 1950s. Subdivisions like Pine-

United Builders Supply Company, Inc., services a 50-square-mile area around Framingham from this 40 Waverly Street location.

Part of the 1979 fleet of company vehicles.

field and Cherryfield were being built and we supplied brick for a lot of chimneys."

By 1959 the firm was ready to expand, and became a full-service lumberyard. Joe had purchased the property and buildings, including an adjoining house where he lived with Blanche and their children for five years.

"Blanche was our original book-keeper," he remembers, "and she often worked late into the night, sitting at the dining room table. We didn't even own a forklift truck in those days, and after work we'd go down to the railroad siding, identify the box-cars that contained our goods, and unload them by hand."

By the early 1970s United Builders had a well-established reputation, and Joe Seifer decided to "specialize." He discontinued the lumber service and focused on drywall. Framingham was experiencing a second building boom, but instead of single dwellings, apartment houses were in demand. New projects included the Waterview Apartments, with 1,000 units, and a new Holiday Inn hotel.

"We've provided Sheetrock for Natick Mall," Joe adds, "as well as Shoppers World. We furnished steel reinforcement needed to support the familiar dome at the Jordan Marsh Store. Like any other steel structure, that dome contracts and expands with changes in temperature, and it had to be fitted carefully."

United Builders Supply Company has also supplied drywall and associated products for Boston skyscrapers, including Sixty State Street and Harbor Towers. The firm will be closely involved in the current renovation of Hynes Auditorium at the Prudential Center. But why would major accounts like these turn to a supplier in Framingham? Joe Seifer explains.

"Only 25 percent of our business today involves private housing. The rest is commercial building work, and we are best qualified to deliver the large quantities of drywall these major projects require.

"A single four- by 12-foot sheet of drywall (one-half-inch thick) weighs 96 pounds. Multiply that by the

United Builders began selling masonry supplies but today specializes in drywall and steel products.

number of sheets needed to do the interior of an office tower or auditorium, and you've got a heavy load. Back in 1965 we bought the first 'boom truck' in MetroWest for $15,000. It could lift a load of drywall 21 feet high. Today we own a fleet of eight such vehicles, including two of the highest in New England. Our newest one, which carried a $200,000 price tag, can hoist that heavy Sheetrock 80 feet in the air. Not only do we have the inventory needed on big projects, but we also have the capacity to deliver, which is equally important."

A third of a century later, United Builders Supply is still a family affair. Joe Seifer's daughter, Donna, wears two hats—office manager and credit manager. His son, Alan, manages newly organized real estate development and building activities, while son-in-law Alan Walis serves as operations manager.

Relaxed and confident, Joe looks forward to continued growth in the coming years. "The high-tech building boom is having a major impact on New England," he observes, "and MetroWest hasn't stopped growing yet."

SILTON GLASS COMPANY, INC.

Founded in 1932 by Charles L. Silton, Silton Glass Company has been in business continuously for 54 years. Still located at the original site, 612 Waverly Street (Route 135), it is also located on the Boston Marathon route, approximately five miles from the start. Originally established as a used auto parts business, Silton Glass also replaced broken car windows. At that time a Model T windshield cost two dollars—one dollar for the glass and one dollar for the labor. Today that same windshield would cost $47.50—$7.50 for the glass and $40 for the labor.

In 1956 Silton Glass was incorporated under Massachusetts charter, and as late as 1959 auto parts still constituted the bulk of the business.

Present owner George Tanguay began working for the firm in 1959, and upon Silton's retirement in 1969 purchased the glass portion of the business. Within the next two years the used auto parts portion was totally phased out.

Commercial glass was introduced at Silton Glass in 1964. It is a wholesale distributor for Chrysler Corporation glass and performs glass replacement work on any domestic or foreign vehicles. Tanguay is Chrysler Corporation's eastern regional glass manager. Silton Glass Company replaces all broken glass on Chrysler vehicles that arrive damaged by train to the railyard in Westboro.

Area residents have come to depend on Silton Glass for quality glass table tops, shower and tub enclosures, storm windows and doors, custom-designed mirrors, glass shelving, and even commercial storefronts. In 1984 the company built its first greenhouse. Twenty-four-hour emergency service is also offered.

Silton Glass' original building was 480 square feet. With renovations in 1968, 1976, and 1982, it has expanded to its present size of 7,800 square feet.

In 1979 George Tanguay and George Jr., both serious tennis players, encountered problems getting their tennis racquets restrung, and decided to try it themselves. The hobby soon turned into a business. Today Silton Tennis (USRSA Certified) restrings over 1,000 racquets per year, and sells and services PRINZE and YONEX racquets and apparel.

Silton's consistent growth can be attributed largely to the fact that it is a family-owned and -operated business with an emphasis on high-quality products and excellent follow-up service.

Founded in 1932, the Silton Glass Company is still at the original site, 612 Waverly Street.

HAYDEN WOOD INSURANCE AGENCY

Lieutenant Commander Hayden Wood wanted to establish his own business. After serving on a commodore's staff during World War II, he and his wife returned to Framingham, Massachusetts—looking for a town that felt like home, a place to raise their children and put down roots.

"Framingham was just a country town back in 1946," Wood recalls. "There were no malls, and quite a bit of open land; but I expected that development would begin soon."

There were already several insurance agencies in Framingham, but the population and housing boom of the early 1950s increased the demand for fire, casualty, and auto insurance, and the Hayden Wood agency grew steadily from the start.

The firm represented several insurance companies, including Travelers, Kemper, Abington, and Peerless. "We specialize in personal insurance," the founder explains, "although about one-fifth of our business involved commercial interests." The agency is justly proud of the fact that some of its current customers have been clients since the beginning. "We've always liked working with families," says Wood, "and now we're dealing with the children and grandchildren."

The agency owner's father and grandfather were both in the insurance business. And for the past 20 years his son, Hayden Wood, Jr., has been maintaining the four-generation family tradition.

"I didn't want to be in the insurance business at first," he admits, "but Dad was friends with my employer at the time and arranged to get me fired!" Wood had quietly enrolled his son in an insurance training program, which began a few days after he was "fired." "Well, I had four mouths to feed," he adds with mock regret. "I had to get a job somewhere."

Delighted with the reemergence of downtown Framingham, Hayden Wood purchased a run-down building at 134 Franklin Street, and completely renovated it for the firm's office.

The firm recently gave downtown Framingham a tangible vote of confidence. After almost 30 years in rented quarters at 129 Concord Street, it purchased a run-down building at 134 Franklin Street and totally renovated it. "Our first office was in the Kendall Hotel," the founder remembers, "and after all these years we're delighted to see the downtown area getting back on its feet."

The senior Wood has served the community in many capacities, including being chairman of the board of assessors, treasurer of the Rotary Club, and chairman of the board of directors of the Framingham Cooperative Bank.

Hayden Wood, Sr., returned to Framingham after service in World War II to establish Hayden Wood Insurance Agency, which has continued to grow with the community.

Hayden Wood Insurance Agency is looking forward to continued growth during the coming years. "We've just acquired an insurance agency in Saxonville," says Hayden Wood, Jr., "and further acquisitions are likely."

EATON FINANCIAL CORPORATION

Eaton Financial Corporation specializes in leasing "small ticket" equipment costing between $500 and $50,000 to commercial users nationwide. Office copiers comprise nearly 30 percent of its business; other leased items include computers, telephone and telecommunications equipment, office furniture, automotive repair and test equipment, and a wide variety of production and manufacturing machinery.

"We believe we're unique in the small-ticket leasing industry as a decentralized public company with a national network of computer-linked offices," states Eaton Financial's founder and president, Paul Gass, a graduate of Babson College who lives in Framingham. The firm is named for the street where he resided in 1974—when first establishing the enterprise in his home.

After many years' experience in the industry, he had concluded that there

The Beaumont Building, in historic Irving Square in downtown Framingham, houses the corporate headquarters of Eaton Financial Corporation.

Judy and Paul Gass, founders of Eaton Financial Corporation.

was minimum focus on small-ticket leasing. With the help of his wife, Judy, he formed Eaton Financial to fill that niche. The corporation went public three years ago, but is still run to some extent as a "mom and pop" operation. Judy Gass is executive vice-president, and their family retains 30 percent of the company stock.

After several years at a Speen Street location, Eaton Financial needed more space for its corporate headquarters. The historical Beaumont Building on Hollis Street in downtown Framingham was considered to be in the "wrong part of town," remembers Gass, "but it was incredibly cheap and presented an opportunity to initiate the area's rehabilitation." He bought it partly because of the available parking, totally renovating and expanding the original structure, which dates back to the turn of the century. This commitment has been restated with the purchase and renovation of additional

properties in the area including the H.E. Division office on Hollis Street.

"Originally I wanted to be a strictly New England business," the entrepreneur recalls. For the first seven years, 95 percent of Eaton's business came from clients within a 100-mile radius of Framingham. Since then the firm has established seventeen additional offices in nine states—including Florida, Illinois, Colorado, Texas, and California. "In the next few years we expect to add more branch offices," explains Gass, "pos-

sibly in St. Louis, Seattle, and Memphis."

Eaton Financial does not limit itself to any particular type of leasing product. Instead, it tries to keep in touch with thousands of vendors covering a wide array of products, and it can count more than 7,000 of these who actually refer their clients to the organization for financing. Partly as a result of Eaton's growth from a regional to a national business, several large, diversified manufacturers have designated it as the recommended leasing company for all its distributors on a country-wide basis. As Eaton's customer base increases, it is better able to solicit additional business directly—as well as relying on satisfied vendors for leads.

Equipment leasing is a large and highly profitable industry, which has been expanding at a rate of 10 to 15 percent annually. According to Gass, 18 to 20 percent of all products manufactured are leased, more than any other method of finance. Leasing is a $100-billion industry; small-ticket business is approximately $15 billion, of which Eaton has less than one percent. "But we're not in the equipment business," he is quick to explain. "We don't actually handle the items we lease, unless there is a fore-

closure or repossession."

"If you've ever leased anything, you know how helpful it is to have your application approved promptly," says Judy Gass. "In the fall of 1984 we upgraded our data-processing system to support our anticipated growth from a single region to a national level. On March 31, 1986, the cost of the IBM 38 computer system at our main office in Framingham, and the development of unique software we are using reached $2.25 million—an investment exceeding our total 1982 income. The system is linked to all our regional offices, placing essential information at each

Eaton's corporate structure is designed to provide prompt, personal service nationwide through regional offices.

salesman's fingertips. Applications anywhere in the country can usually be approved on the same business day, and we feel this is one of the primary reasons for our success."

Everyone knows that leasing is more expensive than purchasing or financing. So why should a company lease instead of buy small-ticket items?

"Convenience is an important factor," Gass explains. "A firm that needs a computer can get it quickly without a large capital investment. Leasing lets a businessman get needed equipment even if he hasn't got the money to tie up. Essentially, it opens additional lines of credit for the customer."

Eaton Financial emphasizes a decentralized organizational structure, encouraging managerial autonomy at the division, region, and branch levels. "Our people are entrepreneurial, not bureaucratic," Gass relates with obvious pride. "Even at our home office on Hollis Street, we don't have any ego problems." Top executives do not have personal secretaries, and handwritten notes are still the most popular form of interoffice communication. "We've always been an egalitarian company," says the founder, "recognizing that our personnel population is our greatest asset."

Eaton Financial's tangible growth has already earned it a place on *Inc.*'s list of fastest-growing firms. In the five years ending in March 1986, company revenue increased at an average compounded growth rate of 80 percent, with net income swelling at a 60-percent annual rate.

"We have more than 280 people on the payroll," states Gass, "and you don't need that many to support a $150-million leasing company like ours. But lessons learned from historical experience have our organization prepared and able to deal with projected growth over the next five years."

The New England Division, at 112 Hollis Street, was completed in 1986.

Patrons

The following individuals, companies, and organizations have made a valuable commitment to the quality of this publication. Windsor Publications and the MetroWest Chamber of Commerce gratefully acknowledge their participation in *South Middlesex: A New England Heritage.*

Alan's Landscaping & Lawn Care Services*
Annis Corporation*
Bostonia Beverages, Inc.*
Brossi Brothers*
The Cahners Companies, Inc.*
Coan, Inc.*
Cohen & Gaffin*
Comfort Air Systems*
Computer Help
Consolidated Group, Inc.*
CPC Framingham-General Motors Corporation
Tom and Joan Cuddy Real Estate*
Dennison Manufacturing Company*
DeWolfe New England-Five Star Division, Margaret C. Carlson, President
Eaton Financial Corporation*
The Fafard Companies*
Fair & Yeager Insurance Agency Inc.*
Fitts Insurance Agency, Inc.*
Stanton T. Fitts
The Flatley Company*
Framingham Historical Society
Framingham Pest Control, Inc.*
Framingham (MA.) Public Library
Framingham Savings Bank*
Framingham State College*
Framingham Trust Company*
Framingham Union Hospital
G&R Tax and Financial Services
General Motors Corp./Framingham*
Guaranty-First Bank
Hansen Electric Supply, Inc.*
Hargraves, Karb, Wilcox & Galvani*
O.B. Hill Motor Transportation Company, Inc.*
Hopkinton Historical Society, Inc.
Hopkinton Public Library
Ken's Steak House*
Kuhlmann, Inc.
The Albert L. Lemay Family

R.H. Long Motor Sales Company*
Marconi's Restaurant*
George J. Martin, Pub. Acct.
Massachusetts Society of Genealogists-Middlesex Chapter
The Middlesex News*
Mullen Lumber Company*
New England Laminating Company*
Performing Arts Center of MetroWest*
Pyne Sand & Stone Company*
Dr. & Mrs. Vassilios Raptopoulos & Family
William M. Read
Walter B. Robinson
Shawmut Community Bank*
Sherborn Historical Commission
Sherborn Historical Society
Sheridan, Garrahan & Lander*
Shoppers World*
Silton Glass Company, Inc.*
Mr. and Mrs. Frank Lloyd Smith
R.D. Smith, Inc.*
Strehlke Corporation*
Sytron Corporation
Teledex, Ltd.
United Builders Supply Company, Inc.*
Weston Nurseries, Inc.*
White Hardware Company, Inc.*
Paul F. White
W.A. Wilde Company*
WKOX Radio*
Hayden Wood Insurance Agency*
Youth Guidance Center of the Greater Framingham Mental Health Association, Inc.*
Zayre Corporation*

*Partners in Progress of *South Middlesex: A New England Heritage.* The histories of these companies and organizations appear in Chapter 7, beginning on page 177.

In 1840, Shepard's paper mill stood at the border between Framingham and Holliston on the old Central Turnpike. In the background a Boston-Worcester railroad train and the village of Unionville can be seen. A few years later this area was incorporated as the town of Ashland. Courtesy, Ashland Historical Society

APPENDIX A
The Nine Towns of South Middlesex
Population Comparisons 1765-1980

	1765	1776	1800	1820	1840	1860
ASHLAND	——	——	——	——	——	1,554
FRAMINGHAM	1,305	1,574	1,625*	2,037*	3,030*	4,227
HOLLISTON	705	909	783	1,042	1,782	3,339
HOPKINTON	1,027	1,134	1,372	1,655	2,245	4,340
NATICK	477	535	694	849	1,285	5,515*
SHERBORN	670	699	775	811	995	1,129
SOUTHBORO '	731	753	871	1,030	1,145	1,854
SUDBURY	1,773*	2,160*	1,303	1,417	1,422	1,691
WAYLAND	——	——	835	926	998	1,188
TOTAL	6,688	7,764	8,258	9,803	12,902	24,837

*represents most populous town of the period

1880	1900	1920	1940	1960	1980
2,394	1,525	2,287	2,497	7,779	9,165
6,235	11,302*	17,033*	23,214*	44,526*	65,113*
3,098	2,598	2,707	3,000	6,222	12,622
4,601	2,623	2,289	2,697	4,932	7,114
8,479*	9,488	10,904	13,851	28,831	29,461
1,401	1,483	1,558	1,022	1,806	4,049
2,142	1,921	1,838	2,231	3,996	6,193
1,178	1,150	1,211	1,754	7,447	14,027
1,962	2,303	1,935	3,505	10,444	12,170
31,490	34,393	41,762	53,753	115,983	159,914

APPENDIX B
The Nine Towns of South Middlesex
Historical Comparisons

	DATE INC.	SOURCE OF NAME	PREVIOUS NAME(S)	FOUNDER OR EARLY LEADER
ASHLAND	1846	Henry Clay's Kentucky estate	Magunco, Unionville	James Jackson
FRAMINGHAM	1700	Framlingham, England	Danforth's Farms	Thomas Danforth
HOLLISTON	1724	Thomas Hollis	Mucksquit, W. Sherborn	Timothy Leland
HOPKINTON	1715	Edward Hopkins	Magunco	John How
NATICK	(1651) 1781	Local Indians "Place of Hills"	Natick	John Eliot
SHERBORN	1674	Sherborne, England	Boggestow	Thomas Holbrook
SOUTHBORO'	1727	"South of Marlborough"	Cow Commons, Fiddle Neck	Timothy Brigham
SUDBURY	1639	Sudbury, England	Musketaquid	Peter Noyes
WAYLAND	1780	Francis Wayland	Sudbury E. Sudbury	Joseph Curtis

FIRST MINISTER	CHURCH SCHISM CHOICE c.1830	FIRST RAILROAD	SQ. MILES 1980
James McIntire	————	1846	11.9
John Swift	Unitarian	1835	25.65
James Stone	Congregational	1847	18.9
Samuel Barrett	Congregational	1835	26.3
John Eliot	Congregational	1835	14.8
Daniel Gookin	Unitarian	1870	16.1
Nathan Stone	Unitarian (temporarily)	1835	13.7
Edmund Brown	Unitarian	1870	24.5
Josiah Bridge	Unitarian	1880	15.29

Bibliography

Bacon, Oliver N. *A History of Natick from its First Settlement in 1651 to the Present Time.* Boston: Damrell and Moore, 1856

Bailyn, Bernard. *The New England Merchants in the Seventeenth Century.* Cambridge: Harvard University Press, 1979

Barry, the Reverend William. *A History of Framingham, Massachusetts, Including the Plantation, From 1640 to the Present Time.* Boston: James Munroe and Company, 1847

Bigelow, William. *History of Sherburne, Mass. from its Incorporation, 1674, to the End of the Year 1830.* Milford, Massachusetts: Ballou and Stacy, 1830

Crawford, Michael J. *Natick—A History of Natick, Massachusetts 1650-1976.* Natick: Natick Historical Commission, 1976

Cummings, O.R. *Trolleys Along the Turnpike.* Cambridge: Boston Street Railway Association, 1975

Dewar, Martha E., and M. Joan Gilbert, eds. *Framingham Historical Reflections.* Framingham: Town of Framingham, 1974

Emery, Helen Fitch. *The Puritan Village Evolves.* Canaan, New Hampshire: Phoenix Publishing, 1981

Federal Writers' Project of the WPA in Massachusetts. *A Brief History of the Towne of Sudbury in Massachusetts 1639-1939.* Sudbury: Sudbury Historical Society, newly revised and reprinted 1968

Goodstone, Joan. *Love Letters to a Small American Town 1776.* Sudbury: 1975

Gould, Levi S. *Ancient Middlesex.* Boston: Commonwealth of Massachusetts, 1905

Historical Records Survey Division, WPA. *History of the Town of Ashland.* Ashland: Commonwealth of Massachusetts and Town of Ashland, 1942

Hudson, Alfred Sereno. *The History of Sudbury, Massachusetts, 1639-1889.* Sudbury: Town of Sudbury, 1889

-----------------------. *Annals of Sudbury, Wayland, and Maynard, Middlesex County, Massachusetts.* Sudbury: Town of Sudbury, 1891

Hurd, D. Hamilton, ed. *History of Middlesex County, Massachusetts.* Philadelphia: J.W. Lewis Company, 1890

Miller, John C. *The First Frontier: Life in Colonial America.* New York: Dell Publishing Company, 1966

Morrison, Samuel E. *Builders of the Bay Colony.* Boston: Houghton Mifflin Company, 1930

Morse, Abner. *Genealogical Register of the Inhabitants and History of the Towns of Sherborn and Holliston.* Boston: Damrell and Moore, 1856

Myer, Mary Eugenia. *Sudbury Valley Trustees—A Stewardship Report and Property Guide.* Wayland: The Sudbury Valley Trustees, Inc., 1983

Natick Federal Savings and Loan Association. *The Story of Natick.* Natick: Natick Federal Savings and Loan Association, 1948

Osborn, Byrle. *History of Hopkinton, Massachusetts.* Hopkinton: Town of Hopkinton, 1979

Powell, Sumner Chilton. *Puritan Village—The Formation of a New England Town.* Middletown, Connecticut: Wesleyan University Press, 1963

Robinson, William F. *Abandoned New England— Its Hidden Ruins and Where to Find Them.* Boston: New York Graphic Society, 1978

Sewell, Samuel. *Diary of Samuel Sewell.* Boston: Massachusetts Historical Society, 1878

Shaughnessy, Anne Carr. *A Guide to Sherborn.* Sherborn: The 300th Anniversary Committee, Sherborn, 1974

-----------------------. *The History of Sherborn.* Sherborn: The 300th Anniversary Committee, Sherborn, 1974

Sly, John. *Town Government in Massachusetts—1620-1930.* Cambridge: Harvard University Press, 1930

Rees, Dorothy Drinkwater. *Holliston Massachusetts, 1724-1974.* Holliston: The 250th Anniversary Committee, Holliston, 1974

Temple, the Reverend Josiah H. *History of Framingham, Massachusetts, Early Known as Danforth's Farms, 1640-1880.* Framingham: Town of Framingham, 1887

Train, Arthur. *Puritan's Progress.* New York: Charles Scribner and Sons, 1931

Index

246